Bangladesh

DIRECTIONS IN DEVELOPMENT
Countries and Regions

Bangladesh

The Path to Middle-Income Status from an Urban Perspective

Elisa Muzzini and Gabriela Aparicio

THE WORLD BANK
Washington, D.C.

Contents

Foreword   *xiii*
Acknowledgments   *xv*
Abbreviations   *xvii*

Overview   1
    Introduction   1
    Bangladesh's Urban Space Today: Implications for
      the Growth Agenda   2
    Envisioning the Future: A Competitive Urban Space
      for Growth   3
    Economic Growth Drivers in Urban Areas   5
    Drivers of and Obstacles to Urban Competitiveness from
      the Perspective of the Garment Sector   6
    Strategic Directions for Building a Competitive Urban
      Space in a Global Economy   8
    References   9

Chapter 1   **Introduction**   11
    The Path to Middle-Income Status from an Urban
      Perspective   11
    The Importance of a Competitive Urban Space for
      Growth   12
    Organization of the Study   12
    Notes   14
    References   14

Chapter 2   **Bangladesh's Urban Space Today: Implications for**
             the Growth Agenda   15
    Introduction   15
    Rapid Urbanization Accompanied by Strong Economic
      Growth   16
    Exceptionally High Population Density   19
    Primacy of Dhaka   20

Concentrated Economic Production and Low Economic
   Density   22
Specialization in Low-Value-Added, Labor-Intensive
   Garment Production   25
Peri-Urbanization of Garment Employment in
   Metropolitan Dhaka   26
Extremely Poor Infrastructure, Low Level of Services,
   and Lack of Amenities   29
Persistent, Albeit Declining, Regional Disparities in
   Welfare   31
Benchmarking Bangladesh's Urban Features   32
Notes   37
References   38

Chapter 3   Envisioning the Future: A Competitive Urban Space
               for Growth   41
               Introduction   41
               Urbanization, Urban Economic Density, and GDP:
                  The Productivity Advantage of Urban Areas   42
               A Bird's Eye View of a Middle-Income Bangladesh:
                  "Taller Mountains" and "More Hills"   43
               Bangladesh's Journey to Middle-Income Status from an
                  International Perspective   44
               Notes   48
               References   48

Chapter 4   The Economic Growth Drivers of Urban Areas   51
               Introduction   51
               The Economic Base of Urban Areas   53
               The Economic Geography of the Garment Sector   58
               Notes   65
               References   65

Chapter 5   Drivers of and Obstacles to Urban Competitiveness
               from the Perspective of the Garment Sector   67
               Introduction   67
               Dhaka City   69
               Peri-Urban Areas of Metropolitan Dhaka   78
               Chittagong City   81
               Export Processing Zones   84
               Small and Medium-Size Cities   86
               Notes   88
               References   88

Chapter 6	Strategic Directions for Building a Competitive Urban Space in a Global Economy	91
	Introduction	91
	A. Transform Dhaka into a Globally Competitive Metropolitan Area	94
	B. Leverage Chittagong's Natural Comparative Advantage as a Port City	100
	C. Develop Strategically Located Export Processing Zones to Strengthen Competitiveness and Spearhead Urban Reforms	101
	D. Develop an Enabling Environment for Local Economic Development in Small and Medium-Size Cities	101
	Note	103
	References	103
Appendix A	The Location Quotient and Shift-Share Analysis of Urban Areas	105
	Introduction	105
	References	110
Appendix B	Sampling Methodology and Key Findings of the Garment Firm Survey	111
	Introduction	111
	Sampling Methodology	111
	Location Competitiveness	115

Boxes

1.1	Innovation, Connectivity, and Livability as the Drivers of Urban Competitiveness	13
2.1	The Political Economy Advantage of Capital Cities	21
2.2	Deconcentrating Manufacturing in Brazil and Indonesia	29
3.1	Urbanization from an Economic Geographic Perspective	42
4.1	Defining Bangladesh's Urban Space	52
4.2	The Strategically Located Urban Centers of Comilla, Bogra, and Jessore	57
4.3	How Did the Garment Industry Come to Dominate Bangladesh's Economy	59
5.1	Agglomeration Forces and Peri-Urbanization in the Manufacturing Sector	80
5.2	The Competitive Advantages of Coastal Cities	83
5.3	Policy Objectives and Achievements of Bangladesh's Export Processing Zones	86
6.1	One-Tier, Two-Tier, and Voluntary Cooperation Models of Metropolitan Governance	95

6.2   Local Entrepreneurship and Innovation in Urban Areas   98
6.3   Regional Development Policies: What Works and
         What Does Not   102

Figures

O.1   Two Paths to a Lower-Middle-Income Bangladesh   4
2.1   Urbanization and Economic Development in South Asia,
         1960–2009   17
2.2   Urbanization and Annual Growth Rates of Total, Urban, and
         Rural Population in Bangladesh, 1950–2010   17
2.3   Urbanization and per Capita Income, by Region, 2000   18
2.4   Composition of GDP in Bangladesh, 1990–2010   18
2.5   Cross-Country Correlation between Population Density,
         Urbanization, and GDP, 2000   20
2.6   Urban Population in Largest Cities and per Capita GDP in
         Selected Countries   21
2.7   Economic Geography of Bangladesh, 2009   22
2.8   Economic Concentration in Largest Cities and per Capita
         GDP in Selected Countries   23
2.9   Population and Economic Density of Urban
         Agglomerations, 2006   24
2.10   South Asia at Night: Economic Density Proxied by
         Light Emission, 2005   24
2.11   Export Sophistication and per Capita GDP in Selected
         Countries, 2006   25
2.12   Export Concentration in Selected Developing Countries,
         1980–2006   26
2.13   Formal Garment Employment in the Dhaka Metropolitan Area,
         2001–09   27
2.14   International Benchmarking of Infrastructure, Services, and
         Amenities in Dhaka City, 2010   30
2.15   Share of Households with Access to Services and Housing, by
         Urban Location, 2006   31
2.16   Regional Poverty Incidence in Bangladesh, 2000–10   34
2.17   Welfare Gap between Leading and Lagging Areas in Selected
         Countries, 1995–2006   34
2.18   Historical Trends in Regional Inequality in Selected
         High-Income Countries   35
3.1   Cross-Country Correlation between Urbanization, Urban
         Economic Density, and GDP, 2000   43
3.2   Urban-Rural Disparities in Population Density, Productivity,
         and Economic Density in Bangladesh, 2010   44
3.3   Two Paths to a Lower-Middle-Income Bangladesh   45

3.4   Dynamics of Two Paths to Lower-Middle-Income Bangladesh
        by 2021   45
3.5   Rural Nonfarm Employment and Distance from Dhaka City   47
B4.1.1 Overlap between Alternative Urban Perspectives   53
4.1   Economic Base of Urban Areas, 2001–09   55
B4.2.1 Manufacturing Employment in Comilla, Bogra, and
        Jessore by Sector, 2009   58
4.2   Garment Firms' Ranking of Factors Affecting Choice of Location 64
5.1   Garment Firms' Rating of Locations' Performance Factors   68
5.2   Productivity Distribution of Garment Firms in Dhaka City   69
5.3   Reasons Why Garment Firm Managers Go to Dhaka City   70
5.4   Average Number of Hours Spent Traveling by Garment Firm
        Managers to and from Business Meetings, by Location   72
5.5   Share of Visiting Time Spent Traveling by Garment Firm
        Managers, by Location   72
5.6   Impact of Daytime Ban on Commercial Trucks in Dhaka
        City on Garment Firms' Delivery Costs and Time, by Location   73
5.7   Garment Firms' Rent by Location   73
5.8   Land Intensity of Garment Production, by Location   73
5.9   Percentage of Garment Workers with Regular Access to
        Power Supply, by Location   74
5.10   Percentage of Garment Workers with Regular Access to
        Piped Water, by Location   74
5.11   People per Room in Garment Workers' Housing, by Location   75
5.12   Turnover of Manufacturing Workers in Selected Asian
        Countries, 2005   75
5.13   Urban-Related Inefficient Employee Turnover in Garment Firms,
        by Location   76
5.14   Causes of Urban-Related Inefficient Employee Turnover in
        Garment Firms, by Location   76
5.15   International Benchmarking of Living Conditions in Dhaka
        City, 2010   77
5.16   Reasons Why Garment Firms Relocate from Dhaka City to
        Peri-Urban Areas   79
B5.1.1 Life Cycle and Location Choice of High-Tech Firms in Tel
        Aviv-Jaffa   80
5.17   Percentage of Garment Workers with Regular Garbage
        Collection, by Location   81
5.18   Power and Water Outages Reported by Garment Firms,
        by Location   82
5.19   Factors Affecting Order Lead Time in the Garment Industry   84
5.20   Export and Employment Performance of Bangladesh's Export
        Processing Zones, 2011–12   85
5.21   Relocation of Garment Firms   87

A.1   Location Quotient Analysis   106
A.2   Drivers of Local Employment Growth Identified by Shift-
         Share Analysis, by Location, 2001–09   110
B.1   Distribution of Sampled Firms by Location   113
B.2   Distribution of Sampled Firms by Product   113
B.3   Perceptions of Location Performance and Rating of Importance
         of Factors Affecting Firms' Location Decisions, by Location   116
B.4   Comparison of Location Performance in the Factors Affecting
         Firms' Location Decisions   122

Maps
2.1   Population Density of Bangladesh, 2011   19
2.2   Employment Density of Garment Industry in Greater Dhaka
         Metropolitan Area, 2009   28
2.3   Spatial Patterns of Manufacturing Employment in the
         Republic of Korea, 1960–2005   28
2.4   Accessibility to Markets in Bangladesh, 2001   33
2.5   Regional Poverty Incidence in Bangladesh, 2005   33
3.1   Employment Density in Bangladesh's Textile Sector, 2009   47
4.1   Spatial Distribution of Garment Employment in
         Bangladesh, 2009   60
4.2   Clustering of Garment Firms in Dhaka Metropolitan
         Area and Chittagong City   61
B.1   Sampling Areas in the Dhaka Metropolitan Area   112

Tables
2.1   Employment Density in Bangladesh's Main Urban Areas,
         2001–09   23
2.2   International Benchmarking of Features of Bangladesh's
         Urban Space   36
4.1   Values Garment Firms Assign to Factors Affecting Their
         Location Decisions   63
5.1   Garment Firms' Assessment of Disadvantages of Selected
         Small and Medium-Size Cities   87
6.1   Policies and Actions to Improve the Competitiveness of
         Bangladesh's Urban Space   93
A.1   Sector Analysis for Urban Areas of Bangladesh, Based on
         Location Quotient and Employment Growth, 2001–09   106
B.1   Characteristics of Surveyed Firms, by Location   114
B.2   Access to Markets and Labor: Location Performance Relative
         to Dhaka City   125
B.3   Infrastructure: Location Performance Relative to Dhaka City   126
B.4   Accessibility: Location Performance Relative to Dhaka City   126

B.5   Land and Housing: Location Performance Relative to
         Dhaka City   127
B.6   Governance and Regulation: Location Performance Relative
         to Dhaka City   127
B.7   Summary Statistics for Productivity, Wages, and Rent,
         fiscal 2008/09   129
B.8   Estimated Differences in Wage Bill and Rent, by Location   131
B.9   Estimated Total Factor Productivity Premiums, by Location   131

Foreword

To meet its goal of reaching middle-income status by 2021, the 50th anniversary of its independence, Bangladesh needs to accelerate growth from its current rate of 6 percent to more than 8 percent a year. Accelerating growth will inevitably require a significant urban transformation, as urbanization and economic growth occur in tandem. Indeed, no country has ever reached middle-income status without urbanizing.

Strong economic growth has sustained and fueled urbanization in Bangladesh. But the urban transition is not yet yielding all of its potential economic benefits. The economic, social, and environmental costs of unmanaged urban development—slums, traffic, crime—are increasing. Failure to address them could prevent Bangladesh from meeting its goal.

The study presents new and robust empirical evidence on the drivers of and constraints to urban competitiveness through the lens of the garment sector—an industry that has thrived in Bangladesh's urban areas. It does so by presenting the results of a survey of 1,000 garment firms carried out across six locations in Dhaka and Chittagong. The study finds that, to accelerate growth, Bangladesh needs cities that are more capable of innovating, better connected internally and with the global economy, and more livable.

The study strengthens the knowledge base for understanding the economic and spatial dynamics of urbanization in Bangladesh. It helps decision makers think through the costs and benefits of policies intended to spur growth and achieve sustainable development of Bangladesh's cities. I hope it will foster timely dialogue on the urban policy directions that will best support Bangladesh's aspiration to reach middle-income country status by 2021.

Salman Zaheer
Acting Country Director for Bangladesh and Nepal

Acknowledgments

This study was prepared by a team led by Elisa Muzzini, senior economist in the South Asia Urban and Water Unit, and included Gabriela Aparicio, Pedro Amaral, Richard Clifford, Mario Di Filippo, Wietze Lindeboom, Viviana Mora, and Mark Roberts. The study was carried out as part of the preparation of the Bangladesh Growth Report *Bangladesh: Towards Accelerated, Inclusive and Sustainable Growth—Opportunities and Challenges*, led by Lalita Moorty and Zahid Hussain, who provided valuable guidance and inputs to the team. The study was conducted under the overall direction of Ming Zhang (sector manager, South Asia Urban and Water Unit) and Ellen Goldstein (formerly country director for Bangladesh and Nepal). Valuable comments and inputs were received from Shihab Azhar, Songsu Choi, Thomas Farole, Steve Karam, Sanjay Kathuria, Zhaed Khan, Andras Horvai, Bill Kingdom, Bala Menon, Martin Norman, Bernice Van Bronkhorst, Tony Venables, and the participants of the consultative workshops for the Bangladesh Growth Report, in particular Dr. Hossain Zillur Rahman (executive chairman, Power and Participation Research Center, Dhaka); Prof. Nazrul Islam (chair, Centre for Urban Studies, Dhaka); and Prof. Wahiduddin Mahmud (chair, Economic Research Group, Dhaka). The garment firm survey for the study was conducted by NIELSEN (Dhaka), with support from Wietze Lindeboom and Nadeem Rizwan. The Bangladesh Bureau of Statistics (BBS), the Bangladesh Garments Manufacturers and Exporters Associations (BGMEA), the Bangladesh Knitwear Manufactures and Exporters Association (BKMEA), and the Bangladesh Export Processing Zones Authority (BEPZA) provided guidance and support to the survey team. Barbara Karni edited the report. The study was jointly funded by the World Bank, the World Bank–AusAID Policy Facility for Decentralization and Service Delivery, and Cities Alliance.

Abbreviations

BEPZA	Bangladesh Export Processing Zones Authority
BGMEA	Bangladesh Garments Manufacturers and Exporters Association
BKMEA	Bangladesh Knitwear Manufacturers and Exporters Association
EIU	Economic Intelligence Unit
EPZ	export processing zone
GATT	General Agreement on Tariffs and Trade
GDP	gross domestic product
GNI	gross national income
GRUMP	Global Rural-Urban Mapping Project
ICT	information and communications technology
LQ	location quotient
MFA	Multi-Fiber Agreement
NOAA	National Oceanic and Atmospheric Administration
OECD	Organisation for Economic Co-operation and Development
PPP	purchasing power parity
R&D	research and development
SMA	Statistical Metropolitan Area
TFP	total factor productivity
Tk	Bangladesh taka

Overview

Bangladesh needs to build a competitive urban space that is innovative, connected, and livable to reach middle-income status by 2021. Bangladesh cannot reach middle-income status without a competitive Dhaka, the engine of its growth. The results of a survey of 1,000 garment firms—conducted to provide a lens through which to investigate urban competitiveness—reveal that Dhaka City is the most productive location for garment firms in Bangladesh. It is falling behind in accessibility and livability because of high congestion and severe constraints in land and housing markets, however. And it needs to gain a competitive edge in higher-value-added products and services. Peri-urban areas of metropolitan Dhaka are emerging as competitive manufacturing centers, but they suffer from Dhaka City's congestion and have less access to infrastructure. Chittagong City has failed to capitalize on its comparative advantage as the country's largest seaport city. Strategically located export processing zones (EPZs) are partially shielded from the inefficiencies of urban areas. Small and medium-size cities need to foster local entrepreneurship to find their comparative advantages. Strengthening competitiveness across Bangladesh's cities calls for coordinated and multipronged interventions to transform Dhaka into a globally competitive metropolitan area, leverage Chittagong City's natural comparative advantage as a port city, promote strategically located EPZs, and create the enabling environment for local economic development in small and medium-size cities.

Introduction

Bangladesh seeks to attain middle-income status by 2021, the 50th anniversary of its independence. To accelerate growth enough to do so, it will need to undergo a structural transformation that will change the geography of economic production and urbanization. Critical to its transformation will be the creation of a globally competitive urban space—defined here as a space that has the capacity to innovate, is well connected internally and to external markets, and is livable (OECD 2006; World Bank 2010).

This study identifies what is unique about Bangladesh's process of urbanization and examines the implications for economic growth. Through the lens of Bangladesh's most successful industry, the garment sector, it describes the drivers of and constraints to urban competitiveness. Based on the findings, it provides policy directions to strengthen the competitiveness of Bangladesh's urban space in ways that will allow Bangladesh to reach middle-income status by 2021.

Bangladesh's Urban Space Today: Implications for the Growth Agenda

Bangladesh's urban space has exceptionally high population density but relatively low economic density. Excluding city-states and small islands, it has the highest population density in the world (1,015 people per square kilometer); Dhaka City is one of the most densely populated cities in the world. High population density, combined with rapid urbanization, implies a large and rapidly growing urban population. In contrast, the economic density of Bangladesh's urban areas is relatively low from an international perspective. Even in Dhaka, output falls short of what would be expected for a city of comparable population density.

With an estimated population of 15 million, metropolitan Dhaka is a primate city (a city that is at least twice as large as the country's second-largest city) with roughly three times the population of metropolitan Chittagong. For decades researchers have been debating whether Dhaka is too large and what drives the primacy of capital cities. Concern over the size of primate cities is often misplaced: the issue is not whether a primate city is too large but rather how well it is managed. The concentration of the urban population in metropolitan Dhaka (36 percent) is broadly in line with countries at similar levels of economic development. And international experience indicates that population concentration tends to increase as countries develop and urbanize, before it levels off.

Output from Dhaka and Chittagong dominates Bangladesh's economic landscape (figure O.1a). About 10 percent of Bangladesh's population lives in the Dhaka metropolitan area, which generates 36 percent of national gross domestic product (GDP). The Chittagong metropolitan area—home to 3 percent of the population—contributes another 11 percent. The gap between Dhaka and Chittagong on the one hand and small and medium-size cities (including secondary cities and municipalities [pourashava]) on the other is large and widening, as most small and medium-size cities have a narrow economic base and have yet to find their competitive advantages. Economic concentration in Bangladesh, measured as the GDP of the country's densest area as a percentage of total GDP (36 percent), is slightly above the level expected for countries at similar levels of economic development. But international experience shows that economic activities agglomerate as a country develops.

Bangladesh's manufacturing sector specializes in export-oriented, low-value-added garment production. Garments are Bangladesh's biggest economic success story. The industry was born and has thrived in Bangladesh's two largest agglomerations. Specialization of industrial production and exports earning is not uncommon for low-income countries, and Bangladesh's export sophistication is in line with its economic development. As international experience shows, concentration of industrial production in the largest cities is also common at the initial stages of the urban transition.

Although still concentrated in Dhaka City, garment production is sprawling to peri-urban areas. As urbanization intensifies, the cost of producing in core urban areas increases; services usually replace urban factories and workshops, which gradually move to peri-urban areas. Growth of peri-urban areas of metropolitan Dhaka is in line with the experience of rapidly urbanizing countries like Brazil, Indonesia, and the Republic of Korea. Despite the growing economic importance of such areas, however, no institutional mechanism exists for coordination between the Dhaka core and the periphery at the metropolitan level.

Garment production benefits from Bangladesh's labor-abundant urban agglomerations. But urban infrastructure and services have lagged behind. So poor is the quality of infrastructure, services, and amenities that the Economic Intelligence Unit (EIU)'s annual ranking of 140 cities worldwide places Dhaka among the world's 10 worst cities (EIU 2010).

Bangladesh's urban features—exceptionally high population and extremely poor infrastructure and services—have implications that matter for growth. High population density demands high economic density (GDP or value added per square kilometer) if Bangladesh is to reach the per capita income of a lower-middle-income country. Poor infrastructure and services are a constraint for the competitiveness of urban areas, negatively affecting the productivity, connectivity, and livability of the urban space.

Bangladesh's spatial concentration of economic production and specialization in low-value-added garments are broadly in line with international experience, yet they have important implications for the journey to middle-income status. Bangladesh cannot reach middle-income status without a competitive Dhaka, given its economic importance for the country. Specialization in low-value-added garments has served Bangladesh well to date—but it is a constraint for the transition to middle-income status. As international experience shows, countries do not reach middle-income status until they diversify and increase the sophistication of their exports.

Envisioning the Future: A Competitive Urban Space for Growth

Bangladesh needs to accelerate annual economic growth from 6 to 8 percent if it is to become a lower-middle-income country by 2021 (World Bank 2012). A cross-country analysis shows that countries experience an increase in the economic density of urban areas and further urbanize as they transition to middle-income status.

A scenario analysis shows that from an economic geography perspective, Bangladesh needs "taller mountains" (greater economic density in its largest metropolitan areas) and "more hills" (broader urbanization) to reach lower-middle-income country status. First, it needs to make its "economic mountains taller"— that is, increase economic density in its largest metropolitan areas. Doing so requires shifting toward a higher-value-added industrial and service mix in Dhaka and Chittagong. Second, Bangladesh needs to create "more hills," by increasing the percentage of the population engaged in nonfarm employment. Figure O.1b shows two economic geography scenarios for a lower-middle-income Bangladesh. Scenario A emphasizes the path of increased economic density (higher-value-added production in Dhaka and Chittagong). Scenario B emphasizes the path of urbanization (nonfarm diversification outside the two main cities).

Given its exceptionally high population density, Bangladesh has to increase the economic density of its urban areas and urbanize even more forcefully than did countries that have already undergone this transformation. Even if Bangladesh reaches a level of urbanization in line with other lower-middle-income countries (52 percent), it would still require urban economic density four times as high as the average lower-middle-income country.

This finding has important implications for Bangladesh's growth agenda. It suggests that Bangladesh needs a competitive urban space to accelerate growth. Only competitive urban areas can sustain the high economic density that Bangladesh needs to reach lower-middle-income status. The finding also indicates that Bangladesh cannot accelerate growth without "making Dhaka's economic mountain taller." Doing so requires diversifying the area's economic base and moving toward a higher-value-added industrial and service mix.

Figure O.1 Two Paths to a Lower-Middle-Income Bangladesh

a. Bangladesh in 2009   b. Bangladesh as a lower-middle-income country, two scenarios

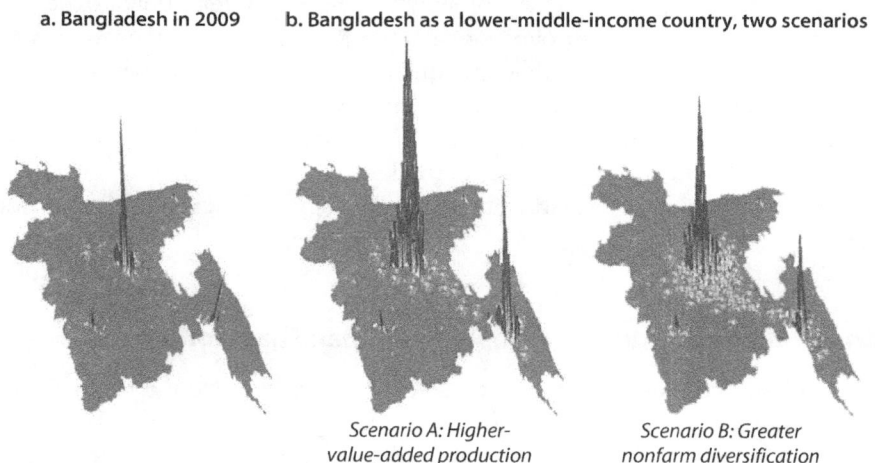

Scenario A: Higher-   Scenario B: Greater
value-added production   nonfarm diversification

Source: Based on data from Bangladesh Bureau of Statistics 2009.

Bangladesh • http://dx.doi.org/10.1596/978-0-8213-9859-3

Economic Growth Drivers in Urban Areas

Dhaka City is an important garment production center, but it is losing competitiveness to peri-urban areas—and as garment production peri-urbanizes, there is limited evidence of replacement industries emerging to ensure continued urban vitality in Dhaka City. The peri-urban areas of metropolitan Dhaka are emerging as competitive garment production centers, and the contribution of peri-urban areas to garment production is increasing rapidly.

Chittagong City has a highly specialized and growing industrial base. About 84 percent of formal employment is in the manufacturing sector. The garment industry is the largest and most important source of employment. Unlike in metropolitan Dhaka, where peri-urban areas play an increasingly important role, garment employment in Chittagong is still concentrated in the city proper; the industry is virtually absent in peri-urban areas. The city's peri-urban areas have a narrow but growing industrial base, with a competitive advantage in the manufacture of cotton textiles.

Secondary cities (that is, the metropolitan areas and city corporations, which are the higher tier of urban local governments, other than Dhaka and Chittagong) have yet to find their competitive advantages. They are service-based economies, with a narrow and declining industrial base. The garment industry is virtually absent in these cities. The largest industrial clusters—jute, fabricated metals, and chemicals—are growing at a slower rate than the national average. Agro-processing is a potential emerging cluster.

Nonmetropolitan municipalities have a small but expanding manufacturing base, with a competitive advantage in cotton textiles. The garment industry is of minor importance. Comilla, which gained city corporation status in 2011, has traditionally had one of the most vibrant urban bases, largely because of its strategic location on the Dhaka-Chittagong corridor. It has a large cluster of footwear manufacturers. Together with Bogra and Jessore (two other strategically located urban centers), it also has clusters of ceramic manufacturers.

The garment sector is the main driver of economic growth in urban areas. It has been highly successful in increasing economic density since the first garment firm was established, in Chittagong in 1977. It is Bangladesh's largest export industry, accounting for 40 percent of formal industrial employment. The industry is predominantly in urban (including peri-urban) areas, which account for 93 percent of formal garment sector jobs. Bangladesh's main garment production centers are Dhaka City, the peri-urban areas of metropolitan Dhaka, and Chittagong City.

The survey of garment firms carried out for this study shows that forces promoting agglomeration of garment production prevail, although traffic congestion and the high cost of land and housing are emerging forces promoting dispersion of garment production. When choosing their location, garment firms value access to skilled labor and access to power supply the most, followed by access to the highway and port, proximity to support businesses, availability of telecommunications, and access to the airport. All of these factors draw firms to cities. Traffic congestion and the high cost of land and housing work against agglomeration forces to promote dispersion of economic activities to lower-cost locations.

Drivers of and Obstacles to Urban Competitiveness from the Perspective of the Garment Sector

The survey of garment firms conducted as part of the study provides a lens through which to investigate urban competitiveness. Concentrated largely in urban areas, Bangladesh's garment sector provides a large enough sample to allow comparison of competitiveness across urban locations. The survey of garment survey is representative of six locations where garment production is concentrated: Dhaka City, urban peri-urban areas of metropolitan Dhaka, rural peri-urban areas of metropolitan Dhaka, the Dhaka EPZ, Chittagong City, and the Chittagong EPZ. The survey of garment firms reveals significant variation in competitiveness across the surveyed locations.

Dhaka City

Dhaka City is the most productive location for garment firms in Bangladesh. It has a total factor productivity premium over both Chittagong City and peri-urban areas of metropolitan Dhaka in garment production. It is the best-performing city location in Bangladesh for access to skilled labor and power supply (the two factors garment firms value the most when selecting their locations) as well as proximity to suppliers, subcontractors, machine repair technicians, and support businesses.

It is falling behind other locations in accessibility, however—and for some firms, the costs of operating in Dhaka City have started to outweigh the benefits. Dhaka City is the worst-performing location for urban mobility and access to the highway. Compared with firms in Chittagong City, firms in Dhaka City also have a disadvantage in accessing the port and the airport. Firms and workers alike in Dhaka suffer from the limited availability and high prices of land and housing.

The high productivity of the garment workforce in Dhaka City has not led to better living conditions for production workers, who live in a deteriorating urban environment characterized by overcrowding and lack of amenities. These workers have significantly less access to housing and services than the average Dhaka urban dweller. The share of urban-related inefficient worker turnover (defined as separations caused by urban inefficiency rather than by more competitive job offers) is higher in Dhaka City than elsewhere in Bangladesh. Workers in Dhaka City cite the housing shortage as the main reason for urban-related separations, followed by the high cost of living. Inadequate access to land and transport infrastructure is the leading cause of firm relocation to peri-urban areas.

Peri-Urban Areas of Metropolitan Dhaka

The birth of new garment firms, rather than the relocation of existing firms, is driving peri-urbanization. Understanding the causes of relocation can nevertheless shed light on the main drivers of peri-urbanization.

About half of the firms that relocated from Dhaka City to peri-urban areas cite a desire to gain better access to transport infrastructure and avoid Dhaka's congestion as the primary reason for relocating. Another 25 percent relocated because of high costs and the limited availability of land, buildings, and housing in Dhaka City.

Peri-urbanization is associated with the growth of a more competitive, vertically integrated business model in the garment sector. Peri-urban garment firms are more land intensive and more likely to be vertically integrated than garment firms in Dhaka City, suggesting that younger firms are opting for a consolidated, vertically integrated business model, which has significant advantages for international competitiveness. Vertically integrated firms have statistically significantly lower lead times than the average garment firm and are therefore better equipped to compete internationally.

Peri-urban areas benefit from proximity to Dhaka City, and they have a comparative advantage in accessibility, land, and housing. But they suffer from Dhaka City's congestion and have less access to infrastructure than the city proper. Peripheral municipalities perform as well as Dhaka City in access to skilled labor, suggesting that they benefit from proximity to Dhaka City. However, peripheral rural areas are less competitive than Dhaka City in access to markets, including buyers, suppliers, subcontractors, competitors, and support businesses.

Chittagong City

Chittagong City is a lower-productivity, lower-cost location for garment firms relative to Dhaka. Chittagong is less competitive than Dhaka in access to markets, in particular access to skilled labor (the factor garment firms value the most), suppliers, and support businesses. But it has a cost advantage in land and housing and accessibility. Garment firms rank Chittagong City the best-performing location for the availability and cost of land, buildings, and housing for workers. They also rate it as the top location for access to the port, airport, and highway and urban mobility.

Despite its accessibility advantage, Chittagong has not been able to capitalize on its comparative advantage as the largest seaport city in Bangladesh, as it is one of the most inefficient ports in Asia. The port handles 80–85 percent of Bangladesh's foreign trade, including the bulk of its main export (garments). Its slow turnaround times hamper exports, in particular garments. The Chittagong port is cited as the main factor negatively affecting lead times in the industry, which are as much as twice as long as competitors (88 days among the surveyed firms against 40–60 days in China and 50–70 days in India) (Haider 2007). Half of the firms surveyed cite the time it takes to unload at port as the main bottleneck, and another 30 percent cite the time required to obtain port clearance.

Export Processing Zones

EPZs in Bangladesh are higher-productivity, higher-cost locations that are partially shielded from the inefficiencies of Dhaka and Chittagong. Wages and building rents are higher in EPZs. The cost differential suggests that the attractiveness of EPZs is interacting with constraints on the supply side to bid up wages and rents.

Among the surveyed locations, the Chittagong EPZ is the best-performing location and the only one with satisfactory performance across all locations factors, including access to power supply. Unlike the very successful EPZs in Dhaka and Chittagong, the EPZs located in locations distant from Dhaka and Chittagong have not succeeded in attracting garment firms.

Small and Medium-Size Cities

Garment firms perceive small and medium-size cities as uncompetitive "distant places." Garment firms cite poor access to markets, in particular skilled labor, as the main disadvantage in these cities.

Small and medium-size cities need to develop a competitive advantage by relying on local entrepreneurship rather than by attempting to attract firms from elsewhere through relocation incentives. A major reason why these cities have not been able to attract garment firms is that only 10 percent of the sampled firms relocated at all—and among firms that did, no firms moved to another city. Rather than attempt to attract firms from elsewhere, small and medium-size cities in Bangladesh need to foster local entrepreneurship to find their comparative advantages.

Strategic Directions for Building a Competitive Urban Space in a Global Economy

Bangladesh needs to build a competitive urban space to accelerate growth if it is to attain middle-income status by 2021. The country's urban areas have to take proactive measures to improve and sustain all three drivers of competitiveness: innovation, connectivity, and livability.

- The Dhaka metropolitan area needs to evolve into a diversified economy with highly skilled human resources and an innovation capacity fueled by the cross-fertilization of ideas that characterizes large metropolitan areas. It also needs to be better connected internally and with its peri-urban areas.
- Both Dhaka and Chittagong have to strengthen their connection to the global economy. Improved connectivity within Bangladesh's system of cities—in particular along the Dhaka-Chittagong corridor—is also important for increasing productivity and export competitiveness.
- The development of an economically dynamic urban space, in particular in the Dhaka metropolitan area, has occurred at the expense of livability. As Bangladesh transitions to a new economic model based on higher-value-added industries and services, requiring a highly skilled and internationally mobile workforce, livability will become increasingly important.

Strengthening competitiveness across the entire spectrum of cities calls for coordinated and multipronged interventions encompassing infrastructure, institutions, and incentives, in line with the following strategic directions:

- *Transform Dhaka into a globally competitive metropolitan area*, by developing appropriate institutional mechanisms for core-periphery coordination in the Dhaka metropolitan area; improving infrastructure to leverage Dhaka's productivity advantage while enhancing accessibility to manage the growing diseconomies of agglomeration; and upgrading peripheral infrastructure in order to transform peri-urban areas into globally competitive manufacturing centers. In parallel, priority should be given to strengthening institutions to create a more efficient and integrated land and housing market; enhance the coordinating role of local authorities to foster a business environment that rewards entrepreneurship and innovation in the metropolitan area; and improve livability and amenities to make urban growth in Dhaka more environmentally and socially sustainable.
- *Leverage Chittagong City's natural comparative advantage as a port city* by expanding the capacity and improving the operational effectiveness of its port. Investments in institutions and infrastructure are also needed to sustain Chittagong City's advantage as a lower-cost location as the city expands.
- *Promote strategically located EPZs*—near markets and in line with locations' comparative advantages—to foster industry competitiveness and spearhead urban reforms. Rather than fighting agglomeration forces by developing zones in "distant" locations, Bangladesh's growth strategy should include the development of a coherent EPZ policy based on a transparent set of criteria for determining locations.
- *Create an enabling environment for local economic development in small and medium-size cities*. The priority is to connect them to markets and create a level playing field in the provision of basic services across locations in order to improve livability and promote local entrepreneurship.

References

Bangladesh Bureau of Statistics. 2009. *Economic Census*. Dhaka.

EIU (Economic Intelligence Unit). 2010. *Liveability Ranking Report*. London.

Haider, Mohammed. 2007. "Competitiveness of the Bangladesh Ready-Made Garment Industry in Major International Markets." *Asia-Pacific Trade and Investment Review* 3 (1): 3–27.

OECD (Organisation for Economic Co-operation and Development). 2006. *Competitive Cities in the Global Economy*. OECD Territorial Review. Paris: OECD.

World Bank. 2010. *Competitiveness and Growth in Brazilian Cities: Local Policies and Actions for Innovation*. Washington, DC: World Bank.

———. 2012. "Bangladesh: Toward Accelerated, Inclusive and Sustainable Growth: An Overview." Poverty Reduction and Economic Management Sector Unit, Washington, DC: World Bank.

CHAPTER 1

Introduction

Bangladesh needs a competitive urban space to accelerate growth and reach middle-income status by 2021. The study focuses on the economic dimension of the urban transition in Bangladesh and its implications for the growth agenda. It assesses the drivers and obstacles of urban competitiveness from a private sector perspective, and discusses policy directions on how urban areas can leverage their comparative advantages and address their competitiveness constraints to accelerate growth.

The Path to Middle-Income Status from an Urban Perspective

This study presents Bangladesh's path to middle-income status from an urban perspective. Countries that have reached middle-income status have done so by shifting from agriculture to manufacturing and services, diversifying their output, increasing their export product sophistication, and urbanizing.[1] Manufacturing and service firms often locate close to urban areas in order to capture the productivity advantages generated by agglomeration economies—such as access to markets, including a large labor market, and knowledge spillovers. The productivity advantages of cities are magnified in developing countries, where transportation and communication costs are highest.

The urban agenda is an essential part of the growth agenda in Bangladesh, where urbanization and economic growth have been strongly correlated since the 1980s. Urban areas produce about 60 percent of the country's gross domestic product (GDP) (UNICEF 2010), with the Dhaka metropolitan area alone—Bangladesh's largest urban center—generating 36 percent of total output. The focus of the study is on the economic dimension of the urban transition and its implications for the growth agenda. The study defines urbanization based on the agglomeration of economic activities, as measured by economic density (GDP or value added per square kilometer) rather than the agglomeration of people, because it is the agglomeration of economic activities that allows for the productivity gains associated with urbanization to materialize.

The study focuses on the linkages between the urban and growth agenda; assessment of the role of rural areas for economic growth is beyond its scope. The study does not discuss the welfare implications associated with high and sustained economic growth in urban areas. A separate study of the assessment of the redistributive policies needed to reduce welfare disparities between leading and lagging regions and between urban and rural areas should complement it.

The Importance of a Competitive Urban Space for Growth

Bangladesh needs a competitive urban space to reach middle-income status. The study defines a competitive urban space as a space that is innovative, connected, and livable. Competitiveness captures a city's comparative advantage in attracting mobile production factors and its ability to leverage these advantages to sustain growth. International empirical evidence suggests that cities that have high innovation levels, are globally connected, and have a livable and high-quality environment are economically successful, because they are attractive locations for firms and workers (box 1.1).

This study assesses the drivers and obstacles of urban competitiveness from a private sector perspective. It presents original evidence on urban competitiveness based on the results of a survey of 1,000 garment firms carried out in 2011. The study is not about the garment sector per se. The sector is the lens through which the competitiveness of urban areas in Bangladesh is viewed. The lessons learned and policy directions emerging from the analysis can shed light on how to create a better urban environment benefiting not only the garment sector but other urban-based sectors as well.

Concentrated largely in urban areas, Bangladesh's garment sector provides a large enough sample to allow comparison of competitiveness across urban locations and to assess the impact of the local environment on firm competitiveness.[2] The sample of firms is therefore stratified by location. The survey is representative of six locations: Dhaka City, urban peri-urban areas of metropolitan Dhaka, rural peri-urban areas of metropolitan Dhaka, the Dhaka export processing zone (EPZ), Chittagong City, and the Chittagong EPZ. The sampling frame was selected in a way that ensured adequate coverage of small, medium, and large-size firms as well producers of both knitwear and woven (or ready-made) garments.

Organization of the Study

This study is structured as follows. Chapter 2 analyzes the main features of Bangladesh's urban space today and compares them with international experience in order to examine what is unique about its process of urbanization and to identify the implications for the growth agenda. Chapter 3 highlights the importance of a competitive urban space for growth by providing a bird's eye view of the geography of economic production of a middle-income Bangladesh based on a scenario analysis. Chapter 4 assesses competitiveness from a city-level perspective by identifying the growth drivers and comparative advantages of the urban areas comprising Bangladesh's urban hierarchy. It then delves into the garment sector—a thriving, urban-based, export-oriented

---

Box 1.1 Innovation, Connectivity, and Livability as the Drivers of Urban Competitiveness

Competitive cities have high innovation levels, are internally and globally connected, and have livable and high-quality environments. Market forces drive economic dynamism and competitiveness, but public policy has to deal with the urban externalities that affect innovation, connectivity, and livability, such as congestion, slum formation, and environmental degradation.

Innovation

Because innovation emerges through market forces, the knowledge spillovers that foster innovation are easier to capture within the urban space. More than 81 percent of patents—an important indicator of innovation activities—are filed by applicants in urban areas in Organisation for Economic Co-operation and Development (OECD) countries. Paris and London alone account for more than 40 percent of their countries' total patent applications (OECD 2006). The economic exploitation of innovative knowledge depends not only on the skill mix of the local workforce but also on knowledge exchanges by universities, research centers, and business communities. Cities have a role to play in identifying educational needs, providing incentives to meet them, and brokering exchanges between universities and the business community to foster innovation. Skill upgrading and knowledge exchanges are important for nurturing the competitiveness of existing specialized clusters and facilitating new business growth and product development (World Bank 2010).

Connectivity

The advantage of proximity fosters competitiveness. Successful cities have better accessibility: they are connected internally through an efficient road network and public transport system, as well as externally, to the global economy. Firms located in well-connected cities find it easier to access networks of resources, including labor and components of the supply chain. Transportation and communication networks multiply interfirm linkages among cities, including flows of goods, people, and ideas, creating an integrated system of cities.

Livability

A livable city is a competitive city, especially in a rapidly changing global economy characterized by increasingly mobile human resources. There is no trade-off between economic dynamism and livability. On the contrary, international evidence indicates a strong association between economically vibrant cities and a high-quality environment. Firms in advanced sectors compete for high-skilled workers, who want to live in an attractive environment with good services and amenities. Livability calls for proactive public policies, as a high-quality city environment is very expensive to restore once problems develop. Slums, for example, are difficult to eradicate without massive disruption to people's lives.

Sources: OECD 2006; World Bank 2010.

---

industry—and its economic geography. Chapter 5 compares the drivers of and obstacles to urban competitiveness across locations through the lens of the garment sector. Chapter 6 discusses policy directions on how urban areas can leverage their comparative advantages and address their competitiveness constraints to accelerate growth. The full results of the analysis are presented in the appendixes. Appendix A presents the results of the diagnostic assessment of the economic base and cluster composition of Bangladesh's urban areas based on location quotient and shift-share analysis techniques. Appendix B presents the quantitative analysis of the 2011 garment survey. It describes the sampling strategy and survey methodology and presents regression results of the location competitiveness and productivity analysis.

Notes

1. Urbanization explains 55 percent of regional variation in GDP per capita, although the relation does not imply causality (Buckley and others 2009).
2. The analysis is not a full competitiveness assessment of the garment sector, as industry-specific factors affecting firms' competitiveness are outside the scope of the study.

References

Buckley, Robert M., Patricia Clarke Annez, and Michael Spence, eds. 2009. *Urbanization and Growth*. Washington, DC: Commission on Growth and Development, World Bank.

OECD (Organisation for Economic Co-operation and Development). 2006. *Competitive Cities in the Global Economy*. OECD Territorial Review. Paris: OECD.

UNICEF (United Nations Children's Fund). 2010. *Understanding Urban Inequalities in Bangladesh: A Pre-requisite for Achieving Vision 2021*. Dhaka: UNICEF.

World Bank. 2010. *Competitiveness and Growth in Brazilian Cities: Local Policies and Actions for Innovation*, edited by Ming Zing. Directions in Development. Washington, DC: World Bank.

CHAPTER 2

Bangladesh's Urban Space Today: Implications for the Growth Agenda

Bangladesh's urban space is characterized by extraordinarily high population density, relatively low economic density, and extremely poor infrastructure and services. If Bangladesh is to grow enough to attain middle-income status, it needs high economic density (gross domestic product [GDP] or value added per square kilometer) to support its high population density. To increase the productivity, connectivity, and livability of urban areas, it also needs better urban infrastructure and services. Given the economic importance of its capital city, Bangladesh cannot reach middle-income status without a competitive Dhaka, the engine of its growth. Specialization in low-value-added garments has served Bangladesh well, but international experience shows that countries do not reach middle-income status until they diversify and increase the sophistication of their exports.

Introduction

Bangladesh's process of urbanization presents distinct features. The chapter reviews the main characteristics of Bangladesh's urban space and benchmarks them against international experience to identify what is unique about the country's process of urbanization. Eight main features characterize Bangladesh's urban space today:

- rapid urbanization accompanied by strong economic growth;
- exceptionally high population density;
- primacy of Dhaka;
- concentrated economic production and low economic density;
- specialization in low-value-added, labor-intensive garment production;
- peri-urbanization of garment employment in metropolitan Dhaka;
- extremely poor infrastructure, low level of services, and lack of amenities;
- persistent, albeit declining, regional disparities in welfare.

Rapid Urbanization Accompanied by Strong Economic Growth

Bangladesh experienced one of the most rapid increases in urbanization in South Asia over the past 50 years, making it the third most urbanized country in the region, after Pakistan and India (figure 2.1). Between 1960 and 2010, Bangladesh's urban population grew at an average annual rate of 5 percent, and the share of the urban population almost doubled, from 15 to 28 percent (figure 2.2). Despite strong urban growth, Bangladesh's urban transition is broadly in line with urbanization of countries at a similar stage of economic development (figure 2.3).

Both metropolitan Dhaka and Chittagong—the largest urban areas in Bangladesh—have sustained population growth rates in the range of 3–4 percent since 1991.[1] Metropolitan Dhaka's population increased at a rate of 3.9 percent over 1991–2001, and estimates indicate that the population in Dhaka City is still growing at more than 3 percent.[2]

Since the 1980s, Bangladesh's urbanization has been sustained and fuelled by strong economic growth and accompanied by structural transformation of the economy. The contribution of agriculture to GDP fell from 30 percent in 1990 to 20 percent in 2010, and the contribution of the urban sector to GDP increased from 37 percent in 1990 to an estimated 60 percent in 2010 (figure 2.4).

Dhaka City, the capital of Bangladesh and the core of the Dhaka metropolitan area, is experiencing rapid population growth.

Figure 2.1 Urbanization and Economic Development in South Asia, 1960–2009

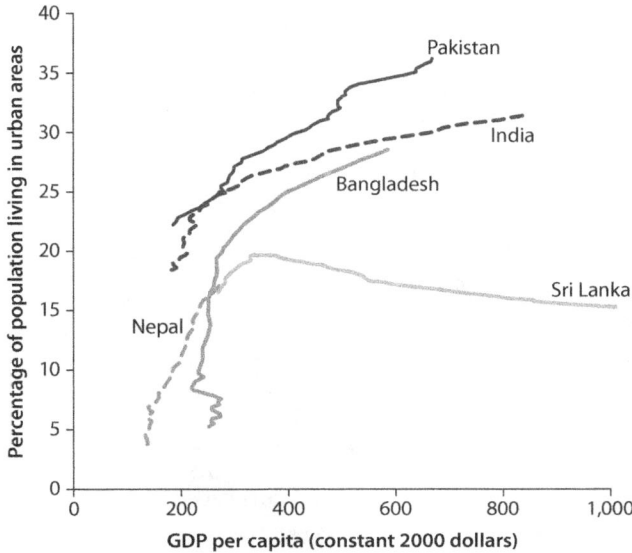

Source: Based on data from UN 2011; World Bank 2011c.
Note: GDP = gross domestic product. Urbanization is defined as the percentage of the population living in urban areas. Analysis excludes Afghanistan (because of lack of historic data) and Bhutan (because of lack of comparability given the country's small population). The decline in Sri Lanka's level of urbanization is associated with a change in that country's definition of urban areas, which led to the reclassification of urban centers as rural areas.

Figure 2.2 Urbanization and Annual Growth Rates of Total, Urban, and Rural Population in Bangladesh, 1950–2010

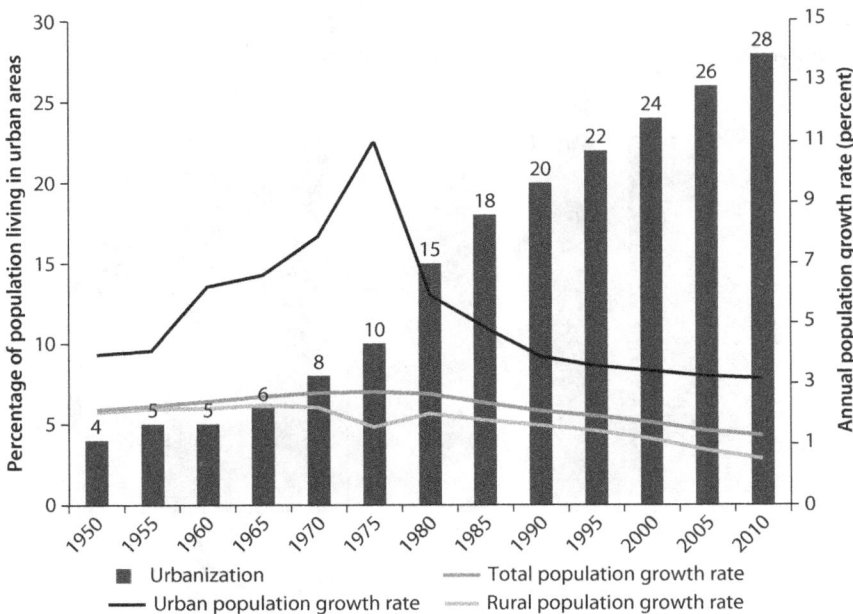

Source: UN 2011.
Note: Urbanization is defined as the percentage of the population living in urban areas.

Figure 2.3 Urbanization and per Capita Income, by Region, 2000

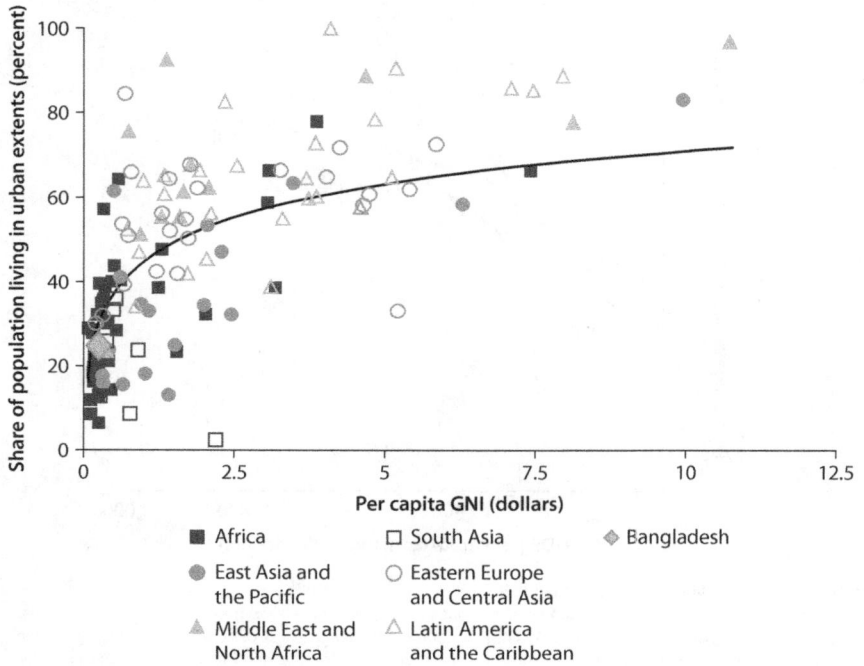

Source: Based on data from Center for International Earth Science Information Network 2004; World Bank 2011c.
Note: GNI = gross national income. GNI was calculated using the Atlas method. Urbanization is proxied by a globally comparable measure, defined as the percentage of the population living in urban extents (places dominated by built environment), as identified from satellite images of night-time lights.

Figure 2.4 Composition of GDP in Bangladesh, 1990–2010

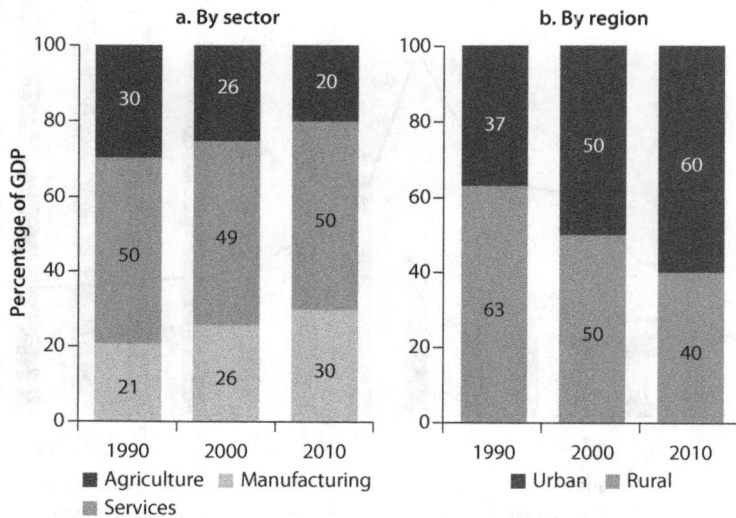

Source: Based on data from World Bank 2011c; UNICEF 2010.
Note: GDP = gross domestic product.

Exceptionally High Population Density

Bangladesh's population density is exceptionally high. According to 2011 census data, the total population density is about 1,015 people per square kilometer; urban population density is about 1,900 people per square kilometer (map 2.1).[3] Bangladesh has the highest population density in the world—three times higher than India—excluding city-states and small islands (figure 2.5).

Bangladesh has one of the top 20 urban populations in the world, with an estimated 42 million urban residents (UN 2011). Dhaka City is one of the most densely populated urban areas in the world, with 25,000 people per square kilometer. At 15,700 people per square kilometer, the density of the Dhaka metropolitan area is higher than the density of the largest megacities in the world, such as Manila (10,550 people per square kilometer) and Jakarta (10,500 people per square kilometer).[4]

Map 2.1 Population Density of Bangladesh, 2011

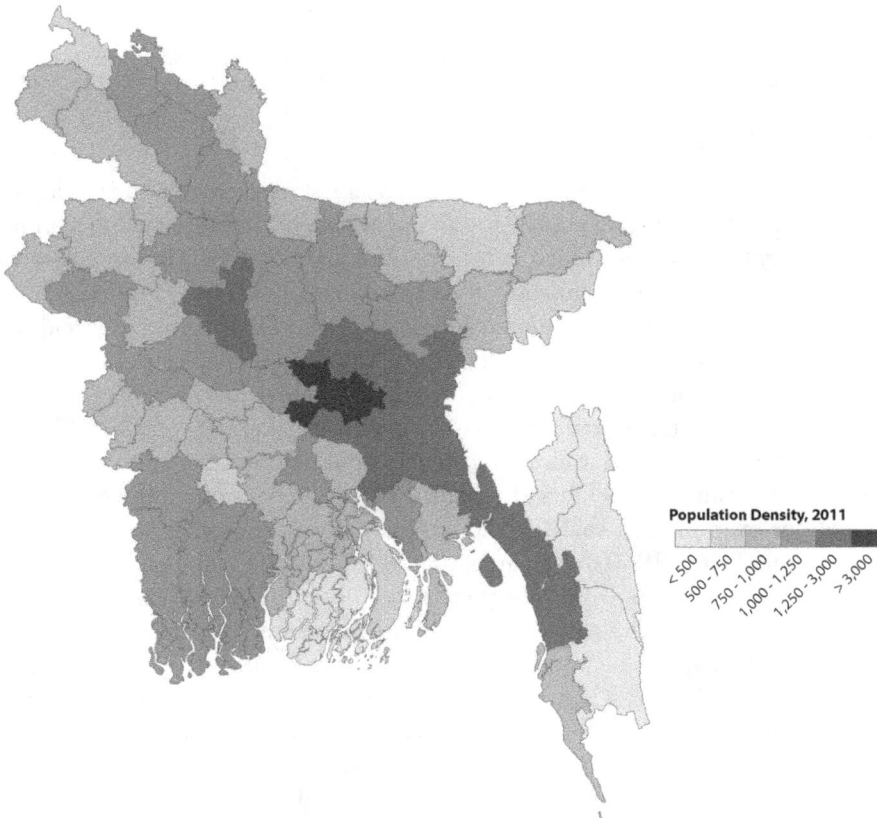

Population Density, 2011

< 500 | 500 - 750 | 750 - 1,000 | 1,000 - 1,250 | 1,250 - 3,000 | > 3,000

Source: Bangladesh Bureau of Statistics 2011a.

Bangladesh • http://dx.doi.org/10.1596/978-0-8213-9859-3

Figure 2.5 Cross-Country Correlation between Population Density, Urbanization, and GDP, 2000

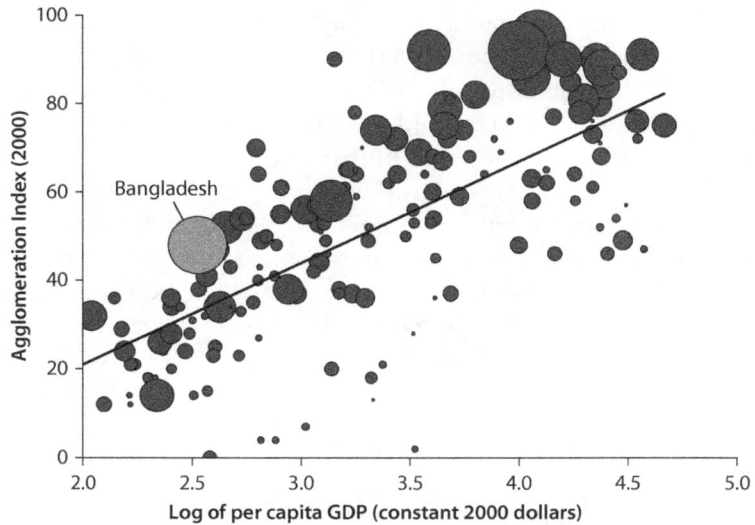

Source: Based on data from Bangladesh Bureau of Statistics 2011a; World Bank 2009.
Note: GDP = gross domestic product. Size of bubble indicates population density. Figure excludes city-states and small islands. Urbanization is proxied by the Agglomeration Index to ensure cross-country comparability. The Agglomeration Index defines urban areas as localities that have a minimum population size of 50,000; a minimum population density of 150 people per square kilometer; and a maximum travel time, by road, to the closest sizable settlement of 60 minutes (World Bank 2009).

Primacy of Dhaka

The Dhaka metropolitan area is among the 10 largest megacities in the world, with an estimated population of about 15 million.[5] Metropolitan Dhaka is also a primate city—a city that is at least twice as large as the country's second-largest city—with roughly three times the population of metropolitan Chittagong (5 million).[6]

For decades, researchers have been debating whether Dhaka is too large and what drives the primacy of capital cities (box 2.1). The evidence indicates that the concentration of the urban population in metropolitan Dhaka (36 percent) is broadly in line with countries at similar levels of economic development (figure 2.6).

International experience also indicates that population concentration tends to increase as countries develop and urbanize, before it levels off. In the Republic of Korea, for example, the share of the population living in urban areas increased from 28 percent in 1960 to 81 percent in 2005. Over the same period, the share of population living in Seoul rose from 8 to 20 percent (World Bank 2011c).

The concern over the size of primate cities is often misplaced: the issue is not whether a primate city is too large but rather how well it is managed. Primate cities pose management and planning challenges, which governments, particularly in low-income countries, are often ill equipped to tackle. But such cities can be successful—as the example of Tokyo, a model for many of Asia's growing megacities, indicates. The relevant question for policy making is therefore not whether a primate city is too large but rather how it can be managed and how policy biases that may indirectly favor the capital city can be avoided.

Box 2.1 The Political Economy Advantage of Capital Cities

Economic fundamentals alone can explain primacy in many cases, but political economy factors play a role in some instances. Global experience suggests that centralized bureaucracies inevitably favor the capital city and the development of metropolis-oriented economies, at the expense of the periphery (World Bank 2010a, 2010c). The more centralized the government, the larger its capital city. Many countries in the Middle East and North Africa inherited highly centralized bureaucracies from their former colonial powers that favored the capital. Historic disadvantages cripple the ability of many peripheral cities to compete with the largest cities. The growth of Tokyo, for example, which rose to prominence as an imperial city, was fostered by a politically centralized government structure.

Empirical evidence suggests that by giving political voice to peripheral cities, accountable democratic governments limit the ability of the capital city to favor itself. Fiscal decentralization also helps level the playing field across cities, by empowering peripheral cities to compete with the primate city. Ades and Glaeser (1995) find that primate cities that are national capitals are 45 percent larger on average than primate cities that are not. Henderson (2004) finds that primate cities in dictatorships are 40–45 percent larger than primate cities in other types of countries.

Bangladesh is one of the most centralized countries in the world. Subnational expenditures are estimated to be about 3–4 percent of total consolidated government expenditures.[8] The comparable figures in two unitary countries that decentralized in the last 15 years are 34 percent for Indonesia and 52 percent for South Africa.[9] On the revenue side, less than 2 percent of total government revenue in Bangladesh is collected at the subnational level, placing it at the low end internationally (World Bank 2010a).

No hard empirical evidence links the primacy of Dhaka to the country's political economy structure. But decentralizing the governance system and, more broadly, creating a more level playing field across cities would help Bangladesh's cities capitalize on their economic advantages and increase productivity. As a byproduct, these measures could also lead to a more balanced pattern of urban growth.

Sources: Ades and Glaeser 1995; Glaeser 2011; Henderson 2004; World Bank 2010a.

Figure 2.6 Urban Population in Largest Cities and per Capita GDP in Selected Countries

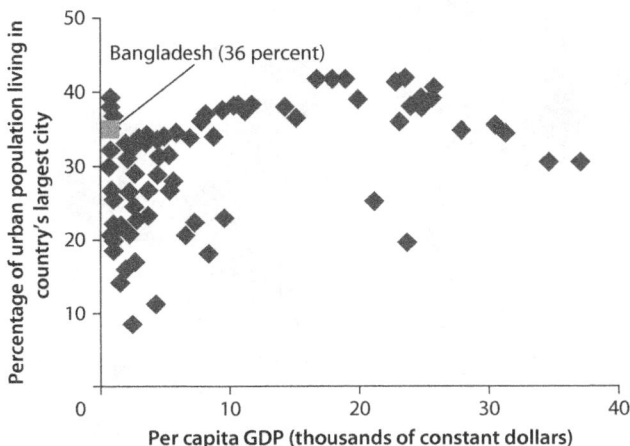

Source: Based on World Bank 2009.
Note: GDP = gross domestic product. Year varies by country, ranging from late 1990s to 2000s.

Bangladesh • http://dx.doi.org/10.1596/978-0-8213-9859-3

Concentrated Economic Production and Low Economic Density

Output from Dhaka and Chittagong dominates Bangladesh's economy (figure 2.7). Agglomeration forces have led to a concentration of economic production in the Dhaka and Chittagong metropolitan areas.

About 10 percent of Bangladesh's population lives in the Dhaka metropolitan area, which contributes 36 percent of the country's GDP. Chittagong metropolitan area, home to 3.4 percent of the population, contributes another 11 percent of GDP.[7] Formal employment density is as high as 4,000 employees per square kilometer in Dhaka City. The gap between Dhaka and Chittagong cities has narrowed slightly over time. Chittagong City, whose employment density was only half that of Dhaka City in 2001, has begun to catch up with Dhaka City, with an average formal employment density of 2,800 employees per square kilometer (Bangladesh Bureau of Statistics 2001, 2009).

At the same time, the gap between Dhaka and Chittagong on the one hand and secondary cities on the other has widened. Secondary cities include metropolitan areas and city corporations (the higher tier of urban local governments) other than Dhaka and Chittagong. Employment density in secondary cities increased only modestly between 2001 and 2009, reaching just one-fourth the density of Chittagong City (table 2.1).

Figure 2.7 Economic Geography of Bangladesh, 2009

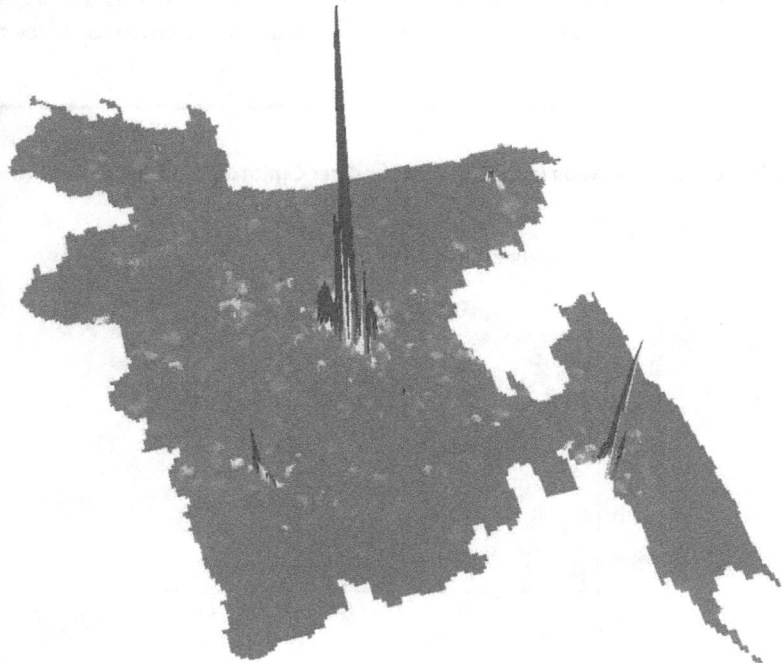

Source: Based on data from Bangladesh Bureau of Statistics 2009.

Table 2.1 Employment Density in Bangladesh's Main Urban Areas, 2001–09

employees per square kilometer

Area	2001	2009
Dhaka metropolitan area	764	940
Dhaka City	3,242	4,241
Chittagong metropolitan area	408	756
Chittagong City	1,649	2,835
Secondary cities	618	712

Sources: Bangladesh Bureau of Statistics 2001, 2009.
Note: Data include formal firms with at least 10 employees. Dhaka City refers to the Dhaka City Corporation. Chittagong City refers to the Chittagong City Corporation. Secondary cities are the Khulna and Rajshahi metropolitan areas and the Sylhet and Barisal City Corporations. Newly established city corporations are excluded from the analysis.

Figure 2.8 Economic Concentration in Largest Cities and per Capita GDP in Selected Countries

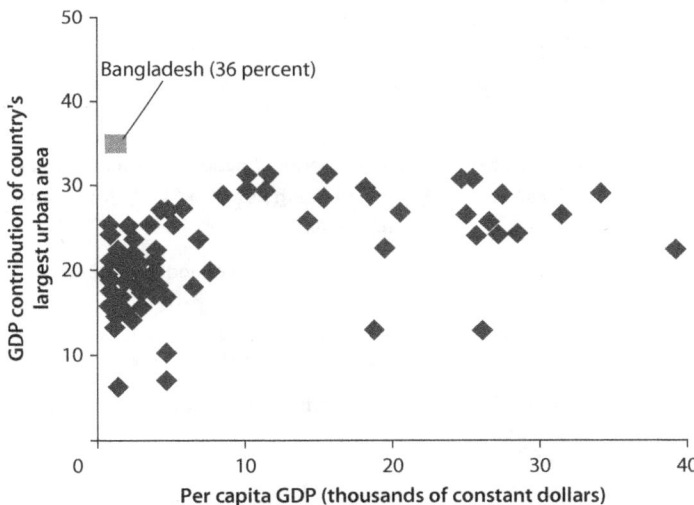

Sources: PricewaterhouseCoopers 2009; World Bank 2009.
Note: GDP = gross domestic product. Year varies by country, ranging from 1990s to 2000s.

Economic concentration in Bangladesh, measured as the GDP of the country's densest area as a percentage of total GDP, is slightly above the level expected for countries at similar levels of economic development. But international experience shows that economic activities agglomerate as a country develops (figure 2.8).

Although economic production is concentrated, economic density in Bangladesh is low from an international perspective. The Dhaka metropolitan area is one of the largest megacities in the world, with an estimated population of about 15 million, surpassed in South Asia only by the metropolitan areas of Mumbai and Delhi (UN 2011). However, annual output in Dhaka falls short of what would be expected for a metropolitan area with its population density (figure 2.9). From a regional perspective, Bangladesh's highest economic peak, with an economic density of $55 million per square kilometer, looks like a hill compared with peaks elsewhere in Asia, such as Singapore ($269 million per square kilometer) and Bangkok ($88 million per square kilometer). The Dhaka metropolitan area barely registers on a view of South Asia at night that shows emission of light (a proxy for energy use and economic output) (figure 2.10).

Figure 2.9 Population and Economic Density of Urban Agglomerations, 2006

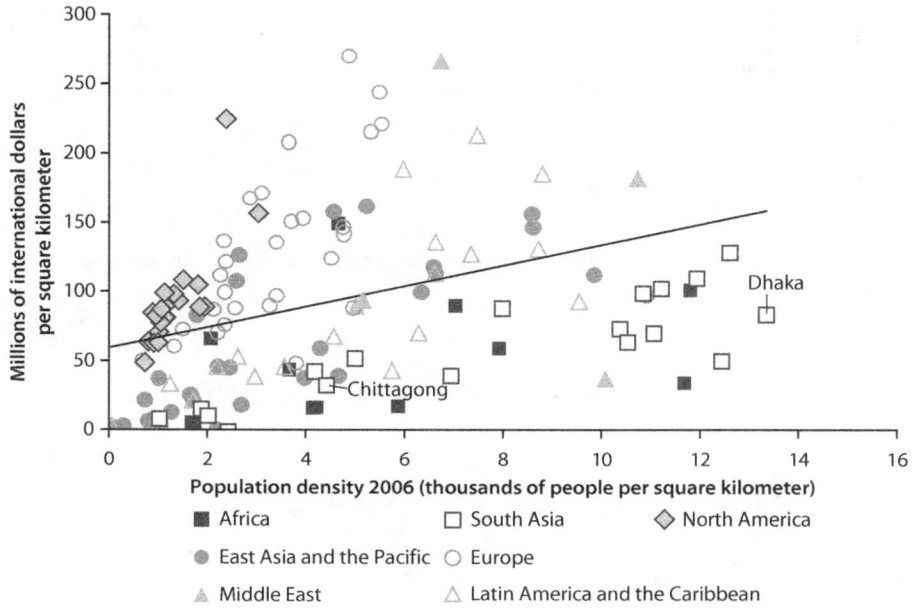

Legend:
- ■ Africa
- □ South Asia
- ◈ North America
- ● East Asia and the Pacific
- ○ Europe
- ▲ Middle East
- △ Latin America and the Caribbean

Sources: PricewaterhouseCoopers 2009; UN 2011.
Note: Output is measured in constant 2008 international dollars using the purchasing power parity method. Economic density is proxied by output (millions of international dollars) per square kilometer. Dhaka and Chittagong refer to the metropolitan areas.

Figure 2.10 South Asia at Night: Economic Density Proxied by Light Emission, 2005

Source: © Atlantic Monthly. Reproduced, with permission, from Florida 2005; further permission required for reuse.

As output and economic density are proxies for productivity and city competitiveness, the regional perspective shows that metropolitan Dhaka still has a long way to go before it fully exploits the benefits of agglomeration economies.

Specialization in Low-Value-Added, Labor-Intensive Garment Production

Bangladesh's manufacturing sector specializes in export-oriented, low-value-added garment production. The garment industry's share of manufacturing employment increased from 44 percent in 2001 to 51 percent in 2009. Garment production accounted for 51 percent of formal manufacturing employment in firms with at least 10 employees in 2009.[10] Woven (or ready-made) garments and knitwear are the two main product lines. The vast majority of formal garment employees (79 percent) work in the woven garment subsector. Garments account for about three-quarter of Bangladesh's export earnings and 18 percent of GDP (International Growth Center 2011).

Concentration of industrial production and exports earning is not unusual for low-income countries. Bangladesh's export sophistication is in line with its economic development (figures 2.11 and 2.12). The Herfindahl-Hirschmann

Figure 2.11 Export Sophistication and per Capita GDP in Selected Countries, 2006

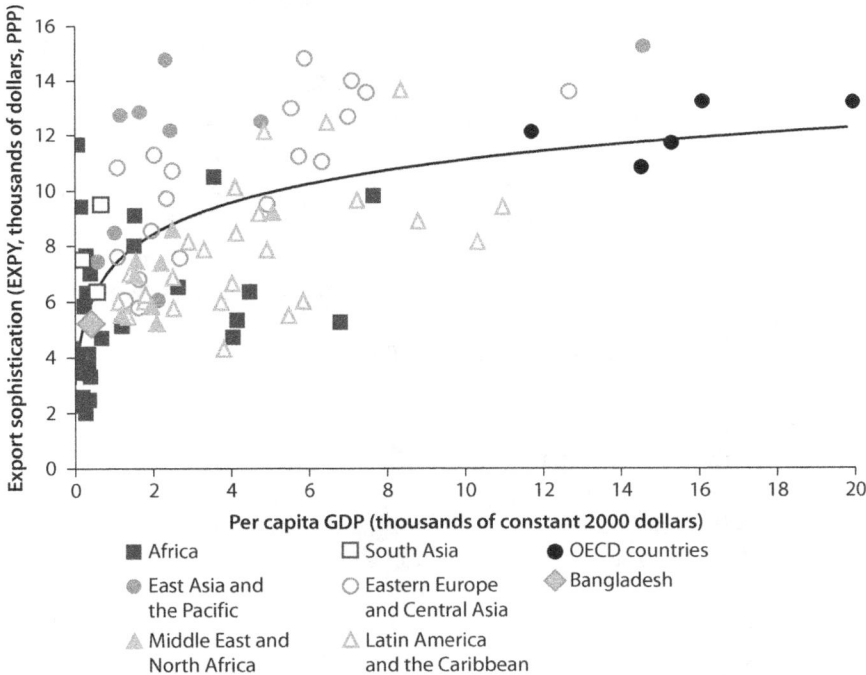

Source: Based on data from Hausmann, Hwang, and Rodrik 2006.
Note: GDP = gross domestic product; OECD = Organisation for Economic Co-operation and Development; PPP = purchasing power parity. EXPY is a measure of the productivity level associated with a country's specialization pattern. It is a weighted PRODY (an index that ranks traded goods by their implied productivity) for that country, where the weights are the value shares of the products in the country's total exports. The PRODY is a weighted average of the per capita GDPs of countries exporting a given product; it thus represents the per capita income level associated with that product.

Figure 2.12 Export Concentration in Selected Developing Countries, 1980–2006

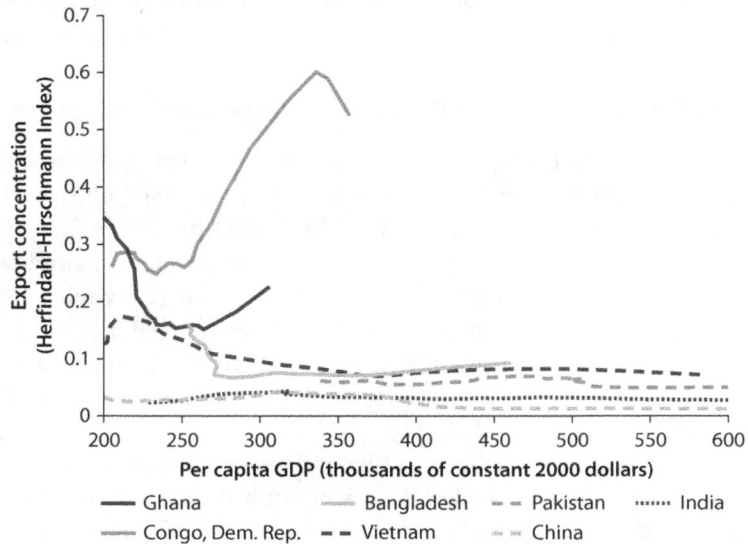

Source: World Bank 2011a.
Note: GDP = gross domestic product. The Herfindahl-Hirschmann Index is the square of the export value shares of all export categories in the market. It gives greater weight to larger export categories, reaching a value of 1.0 when a country exports only one commodity or service.

Index of export concentration for Bangladesh is below 0.1 (the average for low-income countries is 0.3).[11] The value added component of each garment piece is especially low for woven garments, for which most inputs are imported. In 2005, for instance, the unit value of Bangladesh's exports per kilogram to the European Union was €7.8—well below the €11.0 exported by China or the €15.5 exported by Sri Lanka (World Bank 2011b).

The garment sector has thrived in the labor-abundant urban agglomerations of Dhaka and Chittagong, both of which are highly specialized in garment production (Fukunishi 2012). Garments account for half of total formal employment in Dhaka City, 65 percent of formal nonfarm jobs in the peri-urban areas of metropolitan Dhaka, and 67 percent of formal employment in Chittagong City.

Concentration of industrial production in the largest cities is common at the initial stages of the urban transition; as a country's urban structure matures, the largest cities become more diversified. In Brazil, for example, medium-size cities tend to be fairly specialized (in food and beverage production, textiles, shoes, or pulp and paper products); larger cities have a more diverse industrial base and specialize in high-tech and complex business services requiring an educated, highly skilled workforce (Da Mata and others 2005).

Peri-Urbanization of Garment Employment in Metropolitan Dhaka

Although still concentrated in Dhaka City, garment production is sprawling to less densely populated peri-urban areas. By 2009, only 30 percent of garment jobs were located in Dhaka City, down from more than half in 2001. Factories in peri-urban areas of metropolitan Dhaka employed 38 percent of all garment workers, up from 20 percent in 2001.

A garment cluster is emerging about 15 kilometers from Dhaka City's center. This cluster experienced an extraordinary increase in employment per square kilometer, from 175 in 2001 to 356 in 2009 (figure 2.13). Garment employment has also started sprawling outside the boundaries of the Dhaka metropolitan area[12]—in two municipalities (*pourashava*) adjacent to metropolitan Dhaka: Sreepur and to a lesser extent Kaliakair (map 2.2). There is, however, no coordination to ensure integrated planning and management, provision of services, or real estate development at the metropolitan level (Ahmed, Ahmad, and Mahmud 2007).

Dhaka's peri-urban growth is in line with the experience of rapidly urbanizing countries like Brazil and Indonesia (box 2.2). As urbanization advances, the cost of producing in core urban areas increases, because the cost of land and labor rises. At the same time, improvements in connective infrastructure reduce transport costs. As a result, urban factories and workshops are gradually replaced by services and move to peri-urban areas, where they benefit from proximity to markets while taking advantages of lower production costs. International experience shows that peri-urbanization continues after a country reaches middle-income country status. In Korea, for example, manufacturing activities agglomerated between 1960 and 1985 but deconcentrated in 1985–2005, as the country became more developed (map 2.3).

Figure 2.13 Formal Garment Employment in the Dhaka Metropolitan Area, 2001–09

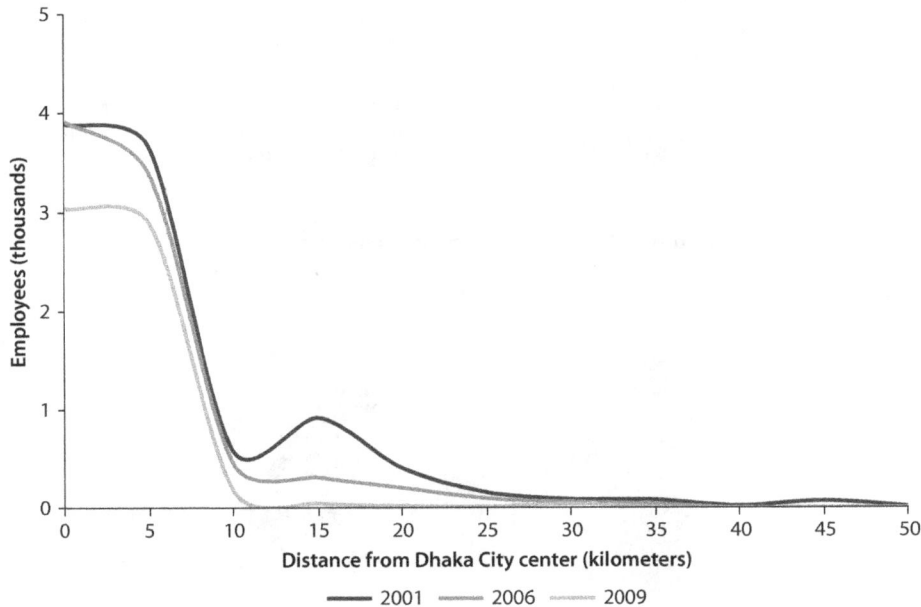

Source: Based on data from Bangladesh Bureau of Statistics 2001, 2009.
Note: Employment figures are for nonfarm employment in enterprises with at least 10 employees. Dhaka City refers to the Dhaka City Corporation.

Map 2.2 Employment Density of Garment Industry in Greater Dhaka Metropolitan Area, 2009

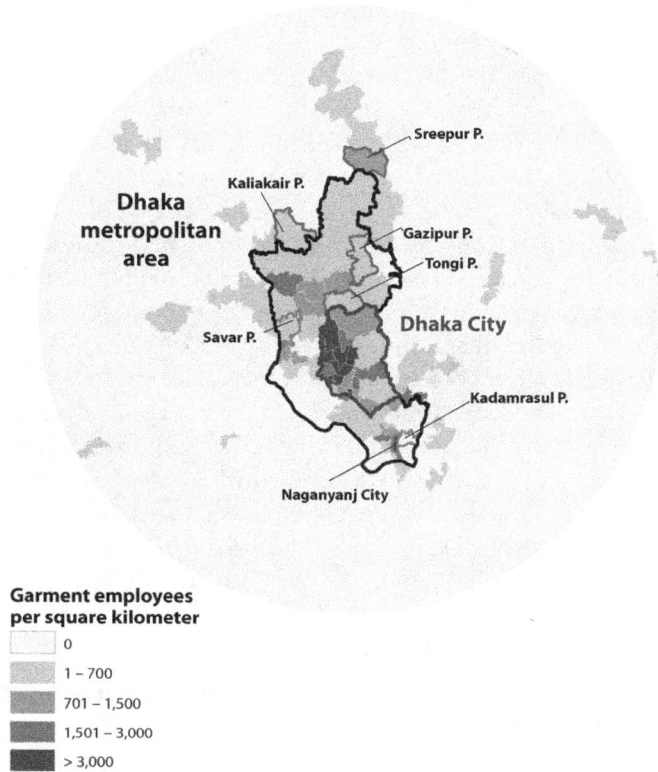

Garment employees per square kilometer

- 0
- 1 – 700
- 701 – 1,500
- 1,501 – 3,000
- > 3,000

Source: Based on data from Bangladesh Bureau of Statistics 2009.
Note: P = *pourashava* (municipality). Employment figures are for garment employment in enterprises with at least 10 employees. All cities refer to city corporations. The boundaries of municipalities are marked in grey. The boundaries of Dhaka City Corporation and Dhaka metropolitan area are marked in blue and black, respectively.

Map 2.3 Spatial Patterns of Manufacturing Employment in the Republic of Korea, 1960–2005

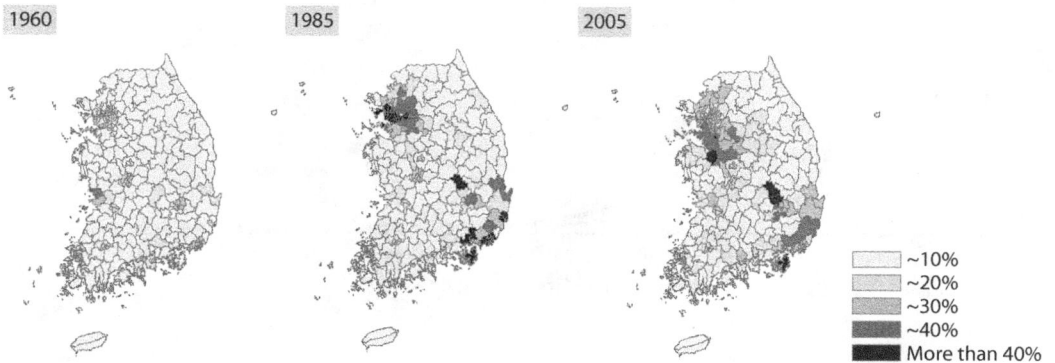

1960   1985   2005

- ~10%
- ~20%
- ~30%
- ~40%
- More than 40%

Source: Park and others 2011.
Note: Maps show the percent of employees in the manufacturing sector.

Box 2.2 Deconcentrating Manufacturing in Brazil and Indonesia

As urbanization increases, manufacturing employment tends to deconcentrate out of core urban centers "first into their suburbs and nearby ex-urban transport corridors and then into smaller cities, with their lower cost of living, lower wages, and lower rents" (De Mata and others 2005, 22). Many developing countries are decentralizing manufacturing from the largest cities to peri-urban areas.

Suburbanization of manufacturing characterized Brazil's industrialization process between 1970 and 2000. During this period, manufacturing moved away from core urban areas toward suburban areas, as cities became larger. Manufacturing employment in core urban areas as a share of total urban manufacturing employment decreased from 64 percent in 1970 to 47 percent in 2000. To a lesser extent, the suburbanization of services shows a similar pattern, although in 2000 the level of concentration of services was higher in core urban areas (66 percent) than in peri-urban areas (55 percent). Suburbanization in Brazil is most evident in the largest cities.

In Indonesia, manufacturing employment deconcentrated from central Jakarta to adjacent districts. Economic census data for 1975–2001, which cover establishments with at least 20 employees, suggest that despite congestion and high factor prices, Jakarta, with more than 13 million people, continues to attract residents and businesses. However, Indonesia experienced deconcentration of manufacturing employment from Jakarta to the districts surrounding it (known as Jabotabek). In the garment sector, central Jakarta lost ground, as the share of the garment establishments in the core city dropped from a high of 25 percent in the 1980s to about 5 percent by 2000. Deconcentration coincided with an increase in the share of establishments in the Jabotabek region and neighboring areas, probably as a result of the establishment of new rather than relocated firms. The largest increase was in districts neighboring cities with at least 1 million residents. Similar patterns are evident in other large industries, such as chemicals, rubber, plastics, machinery, and equipment.

Connective infrastructure facilitated the deconcentration of manufacturing. The construction of toll-ring roads around the city, which allowed firms to retain most of the agglomeration benefits of the region, facilitated the suburbanization of manufacturing production from the core of Jakarta to peri-urban areas. Aggregate transport costs per unit of sales revenue dropped, because a larger market could be accessed by a better road network.

Deconcentration in Brazil and Indonesia did not lead to the relocation of economic activities to secondary cities; firms relocated to districts close to major markets and export or transport hubs in order to continue to benefit from agglomeration economies. Only manufacturing sectors that are closely tied to the natural resource base maintained relatively high establishment shares in districts neighboring small cities far from urban centers. These sectors include tobacco; wood products, including furniture; and, to a lesser extent, food processing.

Sources: Da Mata and others 2005; Deichmann and others 2010; Henderson, Kunkoro, and Nasution 1996.

Extremely Poor Infrastructure, Low Level of Services, and Lack of Amenities

Bangladesh's cities are characterized by extremely poor infrastructure and low level of services. Dhaka ranks among the 10 worst large cities in the world in provision of services (including infrastructure, healthcare,

Figure 2.14 International Benchmarking of Infrastructure, Services, and Amenities in Dhaka City, 2010

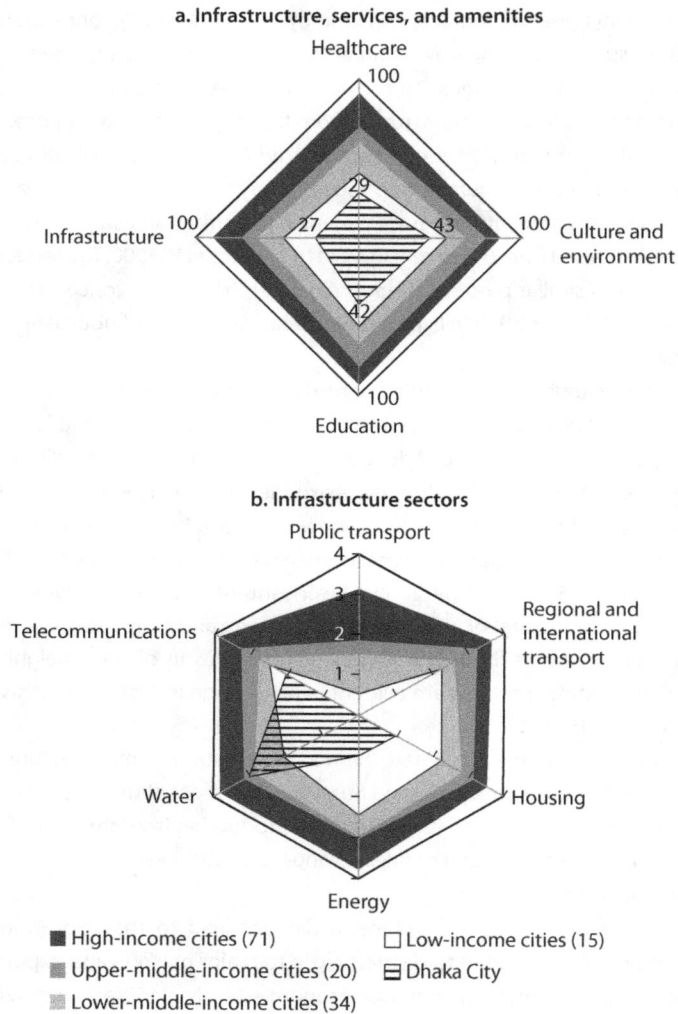

a. Infrastructure, services, and amenities

b. Infrastructure sectors

- High-income cities (71)
- Upper-middle-income cities (20)
- Lower-middle-income cities (34)
- Low-income cities (15)
- Dhaka City

Source: EIU 2010.
Note: In panel a, 1 = lowest; 100 = highest. In panel b, 0 = intolerable; 1= undesirable; 2 = uncomfortable; 3 = tolerable; 4 = acceptable. Figures in parentheses indicate the number of cities. Dhaka City refers to the Dhaka City Corporation.

education, and culture and environment), according to the Economic Intelligence Unit (EIU)'s annual ranking of 140 cities worldwide.[13] Dhaka was rated as the least livable city among the 140 cities surveyed by the EIU in 2012, one position worse than its rank as second least livable city in 2011 (EIU 2012).

Relative to cities in other low-income countries, Dhaka has a significant infrastructure and service delivery gap across all sectors except water supply (figure 2.14). Other cities in Bangladesh fare even worse than Dhaka in the

Figure 2.15 Share of Households with Access to Services and Housing, by Urban Location, 2006

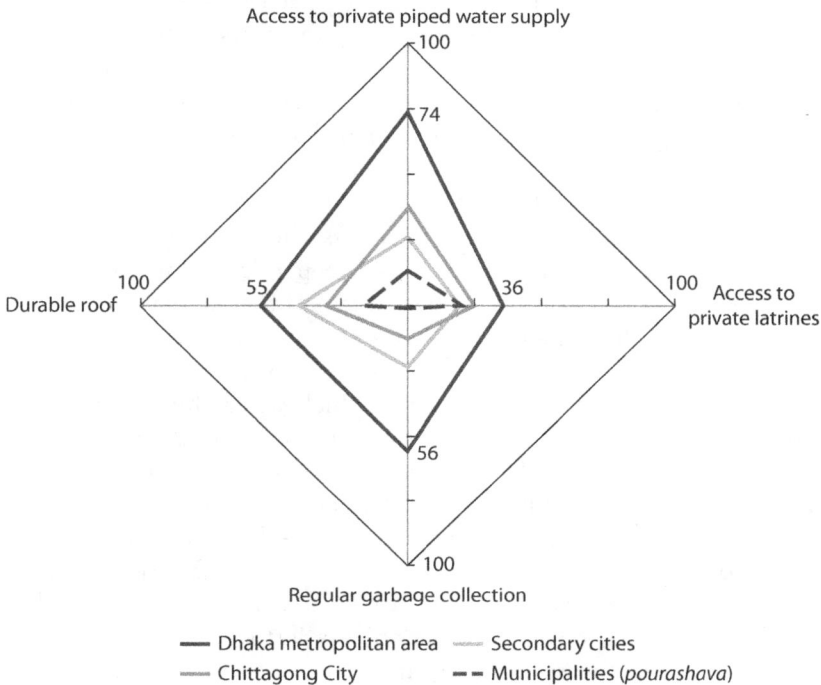

Access to private piped water supply

Durable roof

Access to private latrines

Regular garbage collection

—— Dhaka metropolitan area   Secondary cities
—— Chittagong City   — — Municipalities (*pourashava*)

Source: Based on USAID and others 2008.
Note: Figures show percentage of total households, with the ends of each axis representing 100 percent. Chittagong City refers to the Chittagong City Corporation. Secondary cities are the Khulna and Rajshahi metropolitan areas and the Sylhet and Barisal City Corporations. Newly established city corporations are excluded from the analysis.

provision of infrastructure and services: only 11 percent of solid waste management is collected in Chittagong City, compared with about 56 percent in the Dhaka metropolitan area. Municipalities have relatively good health coverage but virtually no solid waste collection and very low access to piped water supply (14 percent) (USAID and others 2008) (figure 2.15).

Persistent, Albeit Declining, Regional Disparities in Welfare

Although narrowing, the welfare divide between east and west persists in Bangladesh.[14] The country's intricate river system is a barrier to regional integration, although the road network is sufficient to connect major urban centers.

The main transport network within Bangladesh is the Dhaka-Chittagong corridor. The corridor is served by three modes of transportation—road, rail, and inland waterways—which together carry about 20 million tons of freight a year (Asian Development Bank 2004). There are major bridge crossings over the Brahmaputra (or Jamuna) and Ganges rivers. The bridge over the Jamuna River has contributed to open market access in the Rajshahi Division in the north-western region, where better market access has encouraged farmers to diversify into high-value crops. However, parts of Bangladesh are still not integrated with the rest of the country. The Padma River cuts off the south-western region from Dhaka and Chittagong (map 2.4); links across the Padma River still rely on ferries, significantly increasing travel time to Dhaka.

Partially as a result of lack of integration, the benefits of agglomeration economies have not spread equally across the country, leading to large regional differences in living standards. Deep pockets of poverty are also found in economically dense areas: 37 percent of the population of the Dhaka metropolitan area live in slums (USAID and others 2008). Nationwide, real per capita income rose more than 50 percent between 2000 and 2010 (World Bank 2011c). The incidence of poverty, which was as high as 57 percent at the beginning of the 1990s, declined to 49 percent in 2000, 40 percent in 2005, and 31 percent in 2010 (Bangladesh Bureau of Statistics 2011b; World Bank 2008). The differential in living standards between Dhaka and the rest of the country that persisted through the 1990s has evolved into a regional east-west divide (map 2.5). The poverty incidence in the eastern part of the country fell from 46 percent in 2000 to 33 percent in 2005 and 29 percent in 2010. In contrast, poverty reduction was virtually nonexistent between 2000 and 2005 in the south-west, and reductions in the north-west were much smaller than in the east. Poverty estimates for 2010 suggest a decline in poverty in the west from 53 percent in 2005 to 35 percent in 2010 and a significant reduction in the welfare divide (Bangladesh Bureau of Statistics 2011b) (map 2.5 and figure 2.16).

Regional disparities in welfare are common in both low- and middle-income countries (figure 2.17).[15] International evidence indicates that in the early stages of economic development, geographic disparities in welfare (income, poverty, and living standards) are large and widening. In the United States and Europe, for example, spatial inequality rose and remained high before slowly declining as per capita GDP approached $10,000 (figure 2.18).[16] Based on the welfare measures for leading and lagging regions developed for the *World Development Report 2009*, Bangladesh's welfare gap was only slightly above the average for low-income countries over the period 1995–2006. As poverty estimates for 2010 point to a decline in welfare over 2005–10, international comparisons for the period 1995–2006 may overestimate the welfare gap in Bangladesh.

Benchmarking Bangladesh's Urban Features

Table 2.2 describes and benchmarks each of Bangladesh's urban features against international experience, identifying what is unique about Bangladesh's urban space and the implications for the growth agenda.

Map 2.4 Accessibility to Markets in Bangladesh, 2001

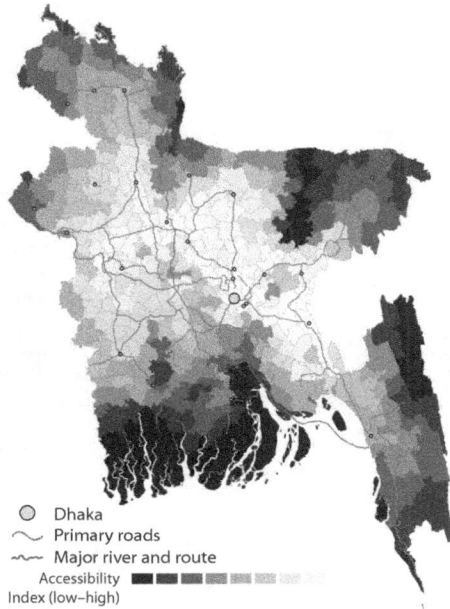

○ Dhaka
⌒ Primary roads
∿∿ Major river and route
Accessibility ▬▬ ▬▬ ▬▬ ▬▬ ▤▤ ▒▒ ░░
Index (low–high)

Source: Blankespoor and Yoshida 2010.
Note: The market accessibility indicator measures how easily people can reach markets. Accessibility is higher the larger the population living in the market areas nearby and the shorter the travel time to those markets.

Map 2.5 Regional Poverty Incidence in Bangladesh, 2005

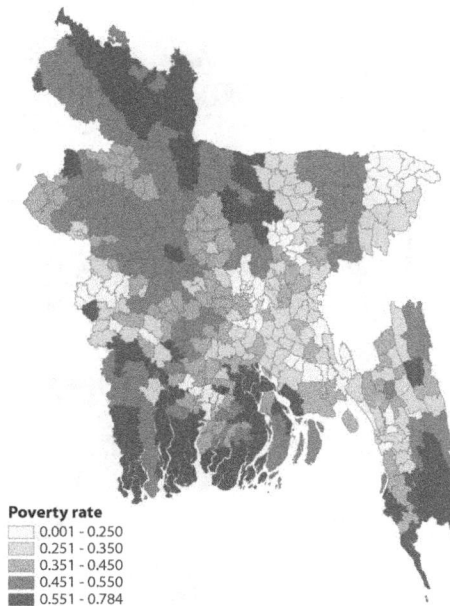

Poverty rate
☐ 0.001 - 0.250
▦ 0.251 - 0.350
▨ 0.351 - 0.450
▥ 0.451 - 0.550
■ 0.551 - 0.784

Source: World Bank 2008.
Note: Each color corresponds to one-fifth of the administrative areas of the mapped country.

Bangladesh • http://dx.doi.org/10.1596/978-0-8213-9859-3

Figure 2.16 Regional Poverty Incidence in Bangladesh, 2000–10

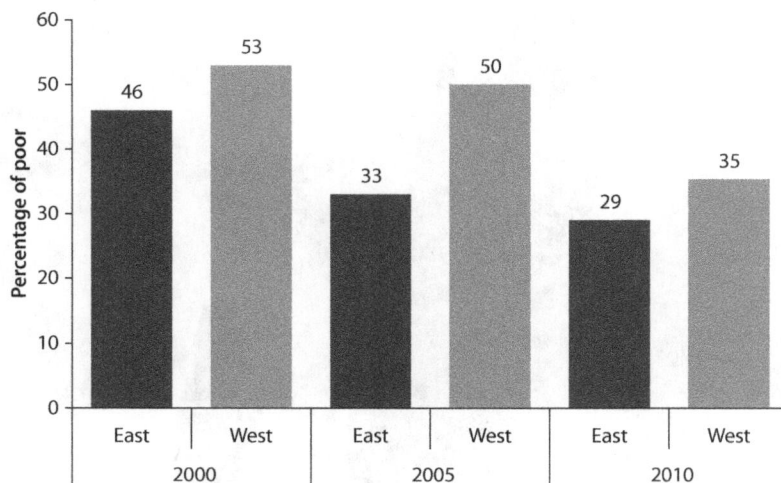

Sources: World Bank 2008, 2011c.
Note: East Bangladesh broadly corresponds to the Dhaka, Chittagong, and Sylhet Divisions. West Bangladesh comprises the Barisal, Khulna, Rangpur, and Rajshahi Divisions.

Figure 2.17 Welfare Gap between Leading and Lagging Areas in Selected Countries, 1995–2006

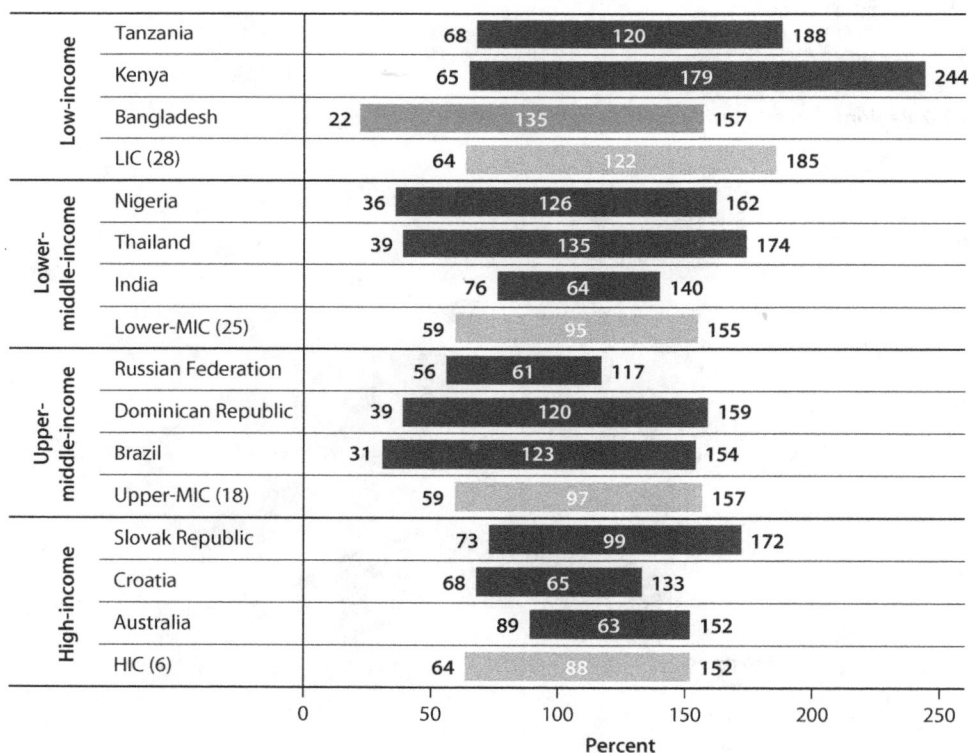

Source: World Bank 2009.
Note: LIC = low-income countries; MIC = middle-income countries; HIC = high-income countries. Number of countries within parentheses.

Figure 2.18 Historical Trends in Regional Inequality in Selected High-Income Countries

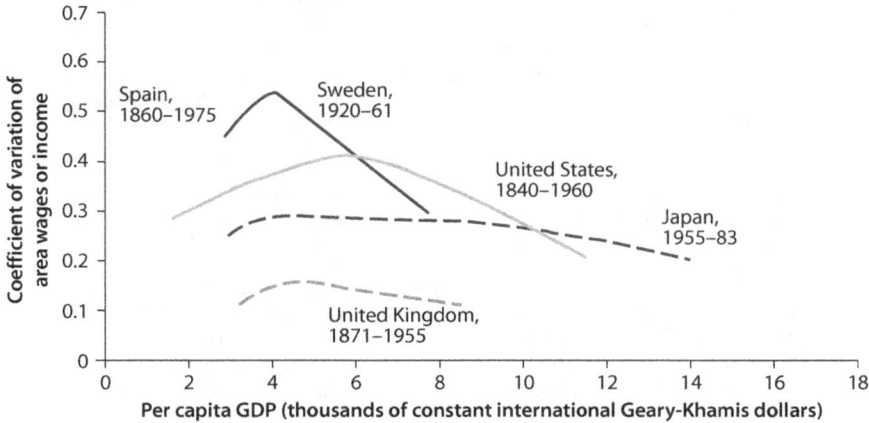

Source: World Bank 2009.
Note: GDP = gross domestic product.

Bangladesh's urban features have implications for the growth agenda. The country's exceptionally high population density and extremely poor urban infrastructure and services are salient features of its urban transition and have important implications for economic growth. Bangladesh's concentration of economic production and economic specialization in low-value-added garments are in line with international experience from comparable countries. But these features have important implications for growth.

Bangladesh's exceptionally high population density, but relatively low economic density, matters for growth. High population density demands equally high economic density (GDP or value added per square kilometer) for economic growth. Increasing economic density requires enhancing the competitiveness of Bangladesh's urban areas: only a competitive urban space can sustain the high economic density Bangladesh needs to reach middle-income status.

The pace of urban growth has stretched infrastructure to its limit. Bangladesh's cities are characterized by extremely poor infrastructure and low level of services from an international perspective. Poor infrastructure is a constraint for urban competitiveness, negatively affecting productivity, connectivity, and livability.

The concentration of economic production in metropolitan Dhaka, and to a lesser extent in Chittagong City, has implication for the growth agenda. Improving the competitiveness of the Dhaka metropolitan area is necessary to accelerate growth given its economic importance for the country. Bangladesh cannot reach middle-income status without a competitive metropolitan Dhaka.

Specialization in low-value-added garments has served Bangladesh well, but it is a constraint for the country's transition to middle-income status. As international experience shows, countries do not reach middle-income status until they diversify and increase the sophistication of their exports. To support the

Table 2.2 International Benchmarking of Features of Bangladesh's Urban Space

Feature	Evidence	International benchmarking
Rapid urbanization accompanied by strong economic growth	Bangladesh experienced one of the most rapid increases in urbanization in South Asia; urbanization has accompanied growth since the 1980s (see figures 2.1 and 2.2).	Typical: Bangladesh's pace of urbanization is in line with its level of economic development (see figure 2.3).
Exceptionally high population density	Bangladesh has exceptionally high population density (1,015 people per square kilometer); urban population density is 1,900 people per square kilometer (see map 2.1).	Outlier: Bangladesh has the highest population density in the world excluding city-states and small islands (see figure 2.5).
Primacy of Dhaka	The Dhaka metropolitan area (15 million) is one the 10 largest megacities in the world. Metropolitan Dhaka is a primate city, with roughly three times the population of metropolitan Chittagong (5 million) (UN 2011).	Typical: As countries urbanize, they experience greater demographic concentration (see figure 2.6). Policy question is how to manage a city of Dhaka's size and primacy.
Concentrated economic production and low economic density	Dhaka and Chittagong's output dominates Bangladesh's economic landscape (see figure 2.7). The Dhaka metropolitan area accounts for 10 percent of Bangladesh's population and 36 percent of gross domestic product (GDP). Chittagong metropolitan area, home to 3 percent of the population, contributes another 11 percent of GDP.	Typical, with implications for growth: Bangladesh's economic concentration is high for low-income countries, but its economic density is low (see figures 2.9 and 2.10). Economic activities agglomerate as a country develops (see figure 2.8).
Specialization in low-value-added, labor-intensive garment production	Metropolitan Dhaka and Chittagong City have specialized industrial and export bases in low-value-added garment production. Garments account for half of total formal employment in Dhaka City, 65 percent of formal nonfarm jobs in peri-urban areas of metropolitan Dhaka, and 67 percent of formal employment in Chittagong City (Bangladesh Bureau of Statistics 2009).	Typical, but a constraint: Countries do not reach middle-income status until they diversify and increase export product sophistication (see figure 2.11).
Peri-urbanization of garment employment in metropolitan Dhaka	A greater Dhaka metropolitan area is emerging as garment employment peri-urbanizes (see figure 2.13 and map 2.2) . There is, however, no institutional coordination mechanism at the metropolitan level.	Typical: As manufacturing activities mature, they sprawl to peri-urban areas, as they have in Brazil, Indonesia, and Korea, Rep. (Da Mata and others 2005; Henderson, Kunkoro, and Nasution 1996). Policy question is how to manage peri-urbanization.
Extremely poor infrastructure, services, and amenities	Bangladesh's main cities are characterized by low level of infrastructure and services and lack of amenities (USAID and others 2008).	Outlier: Dhaka ranks among the worst 10 cities in the world in provision of services and amenities (see figures 2.14 and 2.15).
Persistent, albeit declining, regional disparities in welfare	Although declining, the welfare divide between eastern and western Bangladesh persists. Bangladesh's intricate river system is a barrier to regional integration, and the benefits of agglomeration economies have not spread equally across the country (World Bank 2008; Bangladesh Bureau of Statistics 2011b).	Typical: Regional disparities in welfare widen with income before they start to narrow (see figures 2.17 and 2.18).

transition to middle-income status, Bangladesh needs to gain a competitive edge in higher-value-added products and services. Key to gaining this edge is the Dhaka metropolitan area, the country's capital and growth engine.

Notes

1. Unless otherwise stated, Dhaka refers to the Dhaka metropolitan area, including Dhaka City and the peri-urban areas. Dhaka City refers to the Dhaka City Corporation, the core urban center of the Dhaka metropolitan area. Chittagong refers to the Chittagong metropolitan area, including Chittagong City and the peri-urban areas. Chittagong City refers to the Chittagong City Corporation, the core urban center of the Chittagong metropolitan area. See box 4.1 in chapter 4 for an overview of Bangladesh's urban structure.

2. A population count conducted in 2008 in two wards of Dhaka City (Uttara, a recently established ward, and Dhanmondi, an older and more consolidated ward) indicates that population growth in the core urban center has not slowed since 2001. In Dhanmondi, annual population growth rate over the period 2001–08 exceeded 3.5 percent. Uttara, a new ward with potential for further expansion, grew at an annual rate of more than 12 percent.

3. Population density per square kilometer in Bangladesh increased from 834 in 2001 to 1,015 in 2011. Urban population density was computed based on a census population count of 149 million and an urban population share of 28 percent (Bangladesh Bureau of Statistics 2011a; UN 2011).

4. Population density for Manila and Jakarta are estimates based on City Mayors Foundation (2011).

5. The population of metropolitan Dhaka is 14.9 million and the population of metropolitan Chittagong is 5.1 million, according to the United Nations (2011).

6. Dhaka City (7.3 million) is also a primate city, with more than twice the population of Chittagong City (2.7 million). Population estimates for the cities are based on Bangladesh Bureau of Statistics data, as reported in Brinkhoff (2011).

7. The GDP of the Dhaka metropolitan area for 2008 is estimated at $78 million (purchasing power parity); the GDP of the Chittagong metropolitan area is estimated at $24 million. The projected real annual GDP growth rate for 2008–25 is 6.5 percent for the Dhaka metropolitan area and 6.3 percent for the Chittagong metropolitan area (PricewaterhouseCoopers 2009).

8. Data are based on a randomized but nonrepresentative sample of 30 *upazilas* (subdistricts) and city corporations (the highest tier of urban local governments). Newly established city corporations are excluded from the analysis. See box 4.1 in chapter 4.

9. Analysis is based on 2001 data.

10. The textile sector is the second-largest source of manufacturing employment (24 percent of formal employment), followed by agro-processing (9 percent).

11. The Herfindahl-Hirschmann Index is the square of the export value shares of all export categories in the market. It gives greater weight to larger export categories, reaching a value of 1.0 when a country exports only one commodity or service.

12. In this study, the Dhaka metropolitan area is defined based on the boundaries of the Statistical Metropolitan Area (SMA) set by the Bangladesh Bureau of Statistics. The SMA's peri-urban areas include both urban and rural local governments (see box 4.1

in chapter 4). Evidence based on recent employment patterns suggests that the economic boundaries of the Dhaka metropolitan area are expanding beyond the SMA to form a greater Dhaka metropolitan area.

13. For qualitative indicators, ratings are based on the judgment of in-house analysts and in-city contributors. For quantitative indicators, ratings are calculated based on the relative performance of a number of external data points. The scores are then compiled and weighted to yield a score between 1 (intolerable) and 100 (ideal).

14. East Bangladesh broadly corresponds to the Dhaka, Chittagong, and Sylhet Divisions. West Bangladesh comprises the Barisal, Khulna, Rangpur, and Rajshahi Divisions.

15. Leading and lagging areas are defined as the regions with highest and lowest measures of welfare (income or consumption or GDP). The welfare measures of the poorest and richest region are estimated as a percentage of country's average welfare measure. The welfare gap is the difference in welfare between leading and lagging regions.

16. Trends are studied using the Geary-Khamis dollar, more commonly known as the international dollar, a hypothetical unit of currency that has the same purchasing power parity the U.S. dollar had in the United States at a given point in time.

References

Ades, Alberto, and Edward Glaeser. 1995. "Trade and Circuses: Explaining Urban Giants." *Quarterly Journal of Economics* 110 (1): 195–227.

Ahmed, Sadiq, Junaid Ahmad, and Adeeb Mahmud. 2007. *Making Dhaka Livable*. Dhaka: University Press Limited.

Asian Development Bank. 2004. "Report and Recommendation of the President to the Board of Directors on a Proposed Loan and Technical Assistance Grant to the People's Republic of Bangladesh for the Chittagong Port Trade Facilitation Project." Manila.

Bangladesh Bureau of Statistics. 2001. *Economic Census*. Dhaka.

———. 2009. *Economic Census*. Dhaka.

———. 2011a. *Population and Housing Census 2011: Preliminary Results*. Dhaka.

———. 2011b. *Preliminary Report on Household Income & Expenditure Survey, 2010*. Dhaka.

Blankespoor, Brian, and Nobuo Yoshida. 2010. "Market Accessibility in Bangladesh". Unpublished Background paper to the report.

Brinkhoff, Thomas. 2011. *City Population*. http://www.citypopulation.de.

Center for International Earth Science Information Network. 2004. "Global Rural-Urban Mapping Project (GRUMP) Alpha Version: Urban Extents." Earth Institute, Columbia University, New York. http://sedac.ciesin.columbia.edu/gpw.

———. 2005. "Poverty Mapping Project: Small Area Estimates of Poverty and Inequality." Earth Institute, Columbia University, New York.

City Mayors Foundation. 2011. *Urban Statistics*. http://www.citymayors.com/sections/rankings_content.html.

Da Mata, Daniel, Uwe Deichmann, Vernon Henderson, Somik Lall, and Hyoung Wang. 2005. "Examining the Growth Patterns of Brazilian Cities." IPEA Working Paper 1113, Instituto de Pesquisa Econômica Aplicada, Brasilia. http://www.ipea.gov.br/pub/td/2005/td_1113.pdf.

Deichmann, Uwe, Somik Lall, Stephen Redding, and Anthony Venables. 2010. "Industrial Location in Developing Countries." *World Bank Research Observer* 23 (2): 219–46.

EIU (Economic Intelligence Unit). 2010. *Liveability Ranking Report*. London.

———. 2012. *A Summary of the Liveability Ranking and Overview*. London.

Florida, Richard. 2005. "The World Is Spiky." *Atlantic Monthly*. October.

Fukunishi, Takahiro, ed. 2012. *Dynamics of the Garment Industry in Low-Income Countries: Experience of Asia and Africa*. Wakaba, Mihamaku, Chiba, Japan: Institute of Development Economies/Japan External Trade Organization (IDE-JETRO).

Glaeser, Edward. 2011. *The Triumph of the City*. New York: Penguin Press.

Hausmann, Ricardo, Jason Hwang, and Dani Rodrik. 2006. "What You Export Matters." NBER Working Paper 11905, National Bureau of Economic Research, Cambridge, MA.

Henderson, Vernon. 2004. "Urbanization and Growth." In *Handbook of Economic Growth*, vol. 1, edited by Philippe Aghion and Steven Durlauf, 1543–91. Amsterdam: Elsevier.

Henderson, Vernon, Ari Kunkoro, and Damhuri Nasution. 1996. "The Dynamics of Jabotabek Development." *Bulletin of Indonesian Economic Studies* 32 (1): 71–95.

International Growth Center. 2011. "Export Performance of Bangladesh. Global Recession and After." Working Paper 11/0887, London School of Economics and Political Science, London.

Park, Jaegil, Daejong Kim, Yongseok Ko, Eunnan Kim, Keunhyun Park, and Keuntae Kim. 2011. *Urbanization and Urban Policies in Korea*. Seoul: Korea Research Institute for Human Settlements.

PricewaterhouseCoopers. 2009. *UK Economic Outlook*. London.

UN (United Nations). 2011. "World Urbanization Prospects." Department of Economic and Social Affairs, Population Division, New York.

UNICEF (United Nations Children's Fund). 2010. *Understanding Urban Inequalities in Bangladesh: A Pre-Requisite for Achieving Vision 2021*. Dhaka.

USAID (U.S. Agency for International Development), NIPORT (National Institute of Population Research and Training), MEASURE Evaluation, ICCDR, B (International Centre for Diarrhoeal Disease Research, Bangladesh), and ACPR (Associates for Community and Population Research). 2008. *2006 Bangladesh Urban Health Survey*. Dhaka and Chapel Hill, NC.

World Bank. 2008. "Poverty Assessment for Bangladesh: Creating Opportunities and Bridging the East-West Divide." Bangladesh Development Series Paper 26, Washington, DC.

———. 2009. *World Development Report: Reshaping Economic Geography*. Washington, DC.

———. 2010a. *Bangladesh Public Expenditure and Institutional Review: Toward a Better Quality of Public Expenditure*. South Asia Region, Poverty Reduction and Economic Management Sector Unit, Washington, DC.

———. 2010b. *Poor Places, Thriving People: How the Middle East and North Africa Can Rise above Spatial Disparity*. Middle East and North Africa Region, Washington, DC.

———. 2011a. *Economic Diversification Toolkit*. Washington, DC.

———. 2011b. *Making the Cut? Low-Income Countries and the Global Clothing Value Chain in a Post-Quota and Post-Crisis World*. International Trade Department, Washington, DC.

———. 2011c. *World Development Indicators*. Washington DC: World Bank. http://data .worldbank.org/data-catalog/world-development-indicators.

CHAPTER 3

Envisioning the Future:
A Competitive Urban Space
for Growth

Bangladesh needs to accelerate its annual economic growth from 6 to 8 percent if it is to become a lower-middle-income country by 2021. Increasing growth this rapidly requires a transformation of the geography of economic production. A scenario analysis indicates that to reach lower-middle-income country status, Bangladesh needs "taller mountains" (higher economic density in its largest metropolitan areas) and "more hills" (a larger percentage of its population living in urban areas). It cannot achieve this transformation without a fundamental shift in the economy of the Dhaka metropolitan area toward a more diversified economic base and a higher-value-added industrial and service mix. In fact, because of its very high population density, Bangladesh needs the economic density of an upper-middle-income country if it is to become a lower-middle-income country.

Introduction

Bangladesh needs to accelerate economic growth from 6 to 8 percent a year if it is to become a lower-middle-income country by 2021 (World Bank 2012). This chapter provides a bird's eye view of the economic geography of Bangladesh by simulating its path to middle-income status, taking into account its unique urban features and the experience of countries that have already undergone this transformation. The scenario analysis is based on data from the Socioeconomic Data and Applications Center (SEDAC) at the Center for International Earth Science Information Network.

Economic geography is the study of the location, distribution, and spatial organization of economic activities (box 3.1). Looking at urbanization from an economic geography standpoint means shifting the focus from population density (people per square kilometer) to economic density (gross domestic product [GDP] or value added per square kilometer).[1]

Box 3.1 Urbanization from an Economic Geographic Perspective

A country's economic geography results from the balance between the forces of concentration and dispersion (Fujita, Krugman, and Venables 1999). When concentration forces prevail,
firms have an economic advantage to agglomerate, in order to benefit from proximity to markets, firms, and businesses in the same industry (localization economies) or firms and
businesses in different industries (urbanization economies) (see, for example, Glaeser and
others 1992; Porter 1990). Agglomeration economies drive spatial economic outcomes; if well
managed, they give cities a comparative advantage.

From an economic geography perspective, it is economic density (GDP or value added
per square kilometer) rather than population density (people per square kilometer) that
defines urban areas. The two are conceptually distinct. A large concentration of people is not
enough to create economic density: Bangladesh has the highest population density in the
world, but its economic density is modest compared with other Asian cities. And increasing
economic density does not always imply creating a heavier concentration of people.

Concentration of people and concentration of economic activities go hand to hand in the
early stage of a country's spatial transition. The two processes delink as economies mature. A
shift in the economic structure of a metropolitan area from labor-intensive manufacturing
toward high-tech manufacturing and knowledge-based services, for example, leads to an
increase in economic density (value added per square kilometer)—represented graphically by
"taller mountains"—without necessarily increasing the size of the labor pool. The shift in production processes toward higher-value-added production requires shifts in the workforce's
skill mix, from local and abundant cheap labor to an internationally mobile specialized and
experience workforce.

Urbanization, Urban Economic Density, and GDP: The Productivity Advantage of Urban Areas

The journey to middle-income status implies a major structural transformation
of a country's economy. This transformation involves both an increase in economic density (higher GDP or value added of urban areas) and increased urbanization (a larger percentage of the population living in urban areas). International
experience indicates that economic density and urbanization are positively correlated with a country's GDP: middle-income countries are more urbanized and
their urban areas have higher economic densities than low-income countries.

Figure 3.1 shows the cross-country correlation between urbanization, urban
economic density, and GDP based on a sample of 158 countries. Urbanization
is proxied by a globally comparable measure, defined as the percentage of the
population living in urban extents (places dominated by the built environment), as identified from satellite images of night-time lights (Center for
International Earth Science Information Network 2004).[2] The output of urban
areas is proxied by nonfarm (manufacturing and services) GDP. On average,
68 percent of the population in upper-middle-income countries lives in urban

Figure 3.1 Cross-Country Correlation between Urbanization, Urban Economic Density, and GDP, 2000

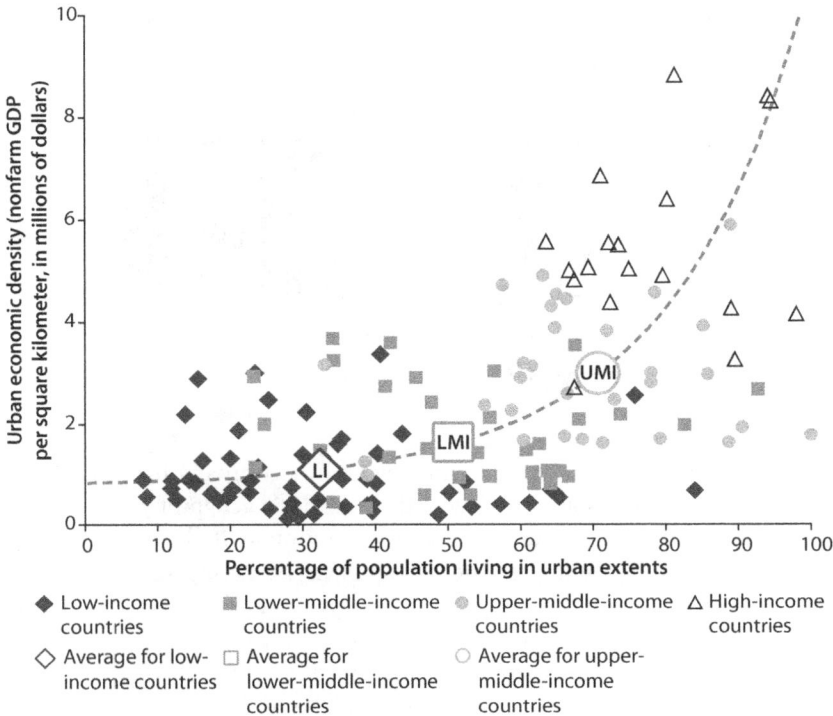

Source: Based on data from Center for International Earth Science Information Network 2004 and World Bank 2011b.
Note: GDP = gross domestic product; LI = low-income countries; LMI = lower-middle-income countries; UMI = upper-middle-income countries.

areas—more than twice the share of low-income countries (32 percent). The correlation between urban economic density and GDP is even stronger: economic density of urban areas is three times higher in upper-middle-income countries than in low-income countries.

The correlation between urbanization, urban economic density, and GDP is indicative of the productivity advantage of urban areas. In Bangladesh, the output and productivity differential between urban and rural areas is larger than the population density differential. Population density in urban areas (1,900 people per square kilometer) is more than twice as high as in rural areas (860 people/square kilometer), but urban economic density is eight times higher ($3.1 million versus $360,000 per square kilometer), and average per capita GDP is almost four times higher ($1,500 versus $400) (figure 3.2).[3]

A Bird's Eye View of a Middle-Income Bangladesh: "Taller Mountains" and "More Hills"

The cross-country analysis shows that both the economic density of urban areas and the extent of urbanization rise as countries transition to middle-income status.

Figure 3.2 Urban-Rural Disparities in Population Density, Productivity, and Economic Density in Bangladesh, 2010

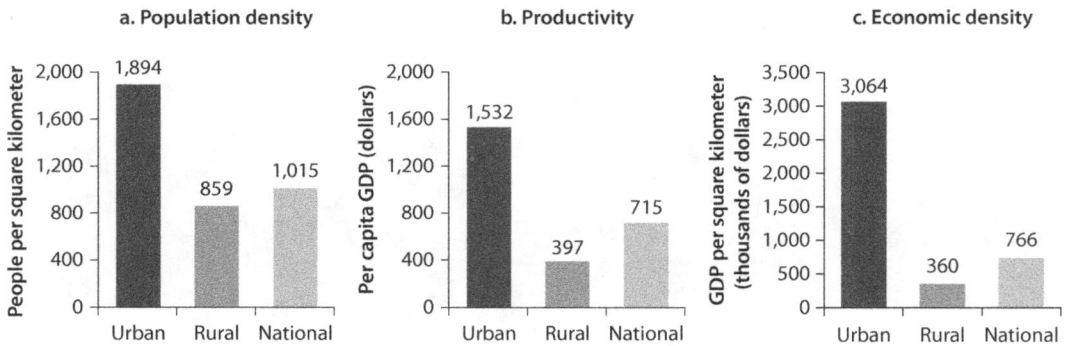

a. Population density   b. Productivity   c. Economic density

Source: Based on data from Bangladesh Bureau of Statistics 2011; UN 2011; World Bank 2011b.
Note: GDP = gross domestic product.

These two spatial economic paths will inevitably accompany Bangladesh's transition to middle-income status, changing the economic geography of the country.

Bangladesh needs to make its "economic mountains taller"—that is, increase economic density in its largest metropolitan areas. Doing so requires shifting toward a higher-value-added industrial and service mix in Dhaka and Chittagong. Bangladesh also needs to create "more hills," by increasing the percentage of the population engaged in nonfarm employment.

Figure 3.3 shows two economic geography scenarios for a lower-middle-income Bangladesh. Scenario A emphasizes the path of increased economic density (higher-value-added production in metropolitan Dhaka and Chittagong). Scenario B emphasizes the path of urbanization (nonfarm diversification outside the two main cities).

Bangladesh's Journey to Middle-Income Status from an International Perspective

The scenario analysis identifies the combinations of urbanization and urban economic density that are compatible with reaching lower-middle-income status by 2021, given Bangladesh's current level of urbanization, urban economic density, and forecasted population based on 2011 population census data.[4] Bangladesh's possible outcomes are then compared with the experience of countries that have already undergone the transition to middle-income country status (figure 3.4).

"Low-income Bangladesh (2010)" in figure 3.4 shows the economic density of existing urban areas and the percentage of the population living in urban areas of Bangladesh in 2010. "Possible lower-middle-income outcomes for Bangladesh in 2021" indicates the combinations of urbanization and urban economic density compatible with reaching lower-middle-income status by 2021. Scenarios A and B in figure 3.3, panel b are two possible outcomes.

Figure 3.3 Two Paths to a Lower-Middle-Income Bangladesh

a. Bangladesh in 2009   **b. Bangladesh as a lower-middle-income country, two scenarios**

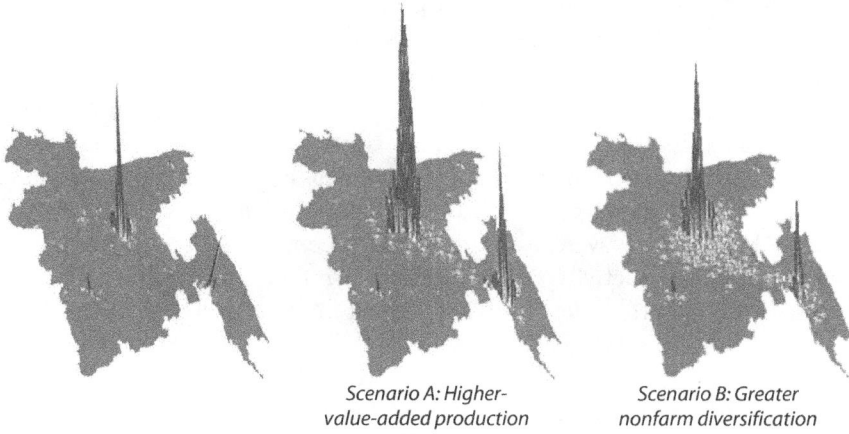

*Scenario A: Higher-
value-added production*

*Scenario B: Greater
nonfarm diversification*

Source: Based on data from Bangladesh Bureau of Statistics 2009.

Figure 3.4 Dynamics of Two Paths to Lower-Middle-Income Bangladesh by 2021

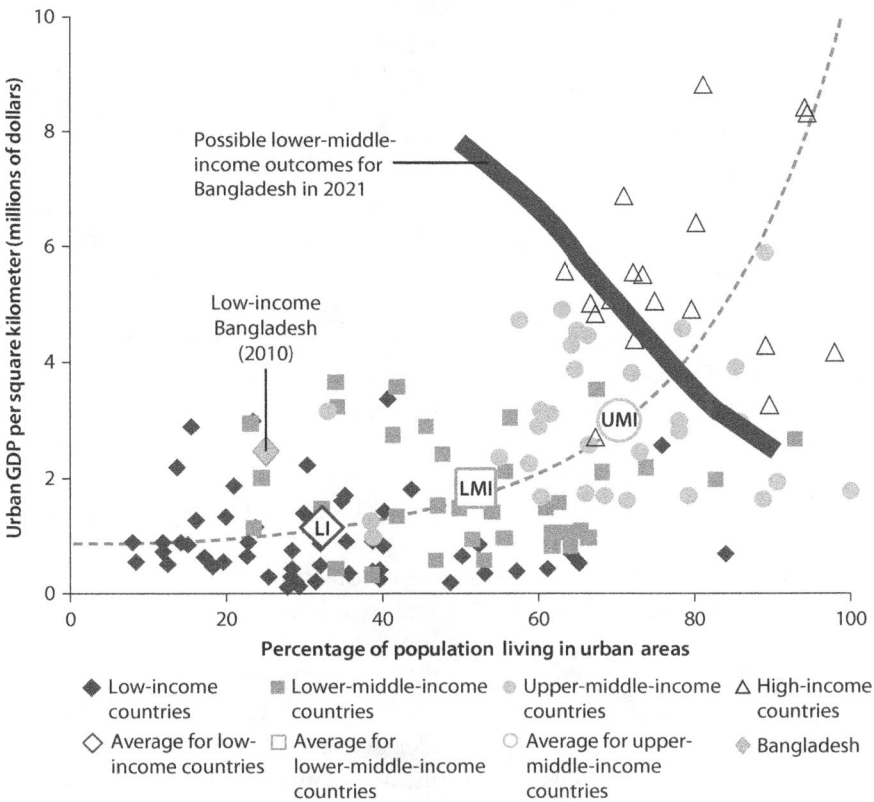

Possible lower-middle-income outcomes for Bangladesh in 2021

Low-income Bangladesh (2010)

- ◆ Low-income countries
- ◇ Average for low-income countries
- ▨ Lower-middle-income countries
- ☐ Average for lower-middle-income countries
- ◉ Upper-middle-income countries
- ○ Average for upper-middle-income countries
- △ High-income countries
- ◈ Bangladesh

Source: Based on data from Center for International Earth Science Information Network 2004; World Bank 2011a.
Note: GDP = gross domestic product; LI = low-income countries; LMI = lower-middle-income countries; UMI = upper-middle-income countries.

Scenario A is reached by increasing the value added of production (higher urban economic density). Scenario B is reached by diversifying into nonfarm economic activities (greater urbanization).

The scenario analysis shows that to reach lower-middle-income country status, Bangladesh needs to increase its economic density and urbanize even more force-fully than historical trends suggest. In fact, to become a lower-middle-income country, Bangladesh needs the economic density of an upper-middle-income country. Even if it reaches a level of urbanization in line with other lower-middle-income countries (52 percent), it will still require urban economic density four times as high as the average lower-middle-income country (see figure 3.4). Doubling rural productivity would reduce the minimum urban economic density associated with the level of urbanization of the average lower-middle-income country by only 15 percent.

Bangladesh's spatial economic paths to lower-middle-income country status are unique because of the country's exceptionally high population density (the highest in the world). High population density (population per square kilometer) needs to be supported by high economic density (GDP or value added per square kilometer) if Bangladesh is to reach lower-middle-income status.

This finding has important implications for Bangladesh's growth agenda. It provides supportive evidence that Bangladesh needs a competitive urban space to accelerate growth, as only competitive urban areas can achieve the high economic density Bangladesh needs to become a middle-income country. It also shows that Bangladesh needs to simultaneously pursue both types of spatial transformation.

Bangladesh cannot reach middle-income country status without "making Dhaka's mountains taller." Creating a "taller" Dhaka requires a fundamental shift in the economy of the metropolitan area toward a more diversified economic base and a higher-value-added industrial and service mix in order to increase its competitiveness. Empirical evidence suggests that urban diversity and knowledge spillovers across rather than within industries matter for long-term growth (Glaeser and others 1992; Jacobs 1969). International evidence indicates that city diversity promotes innovation into higher-value-added products as knowledge spills over industries. Specialized industrial cities such as Manchester and Detroit eventually declined, whereas broadly diversified cities such as New York flourished (see box 6.2 in chapter 6).

Bangladesh needs to accelerate the process diversification of its rural economy to create "more hills." Agro-processing and textiles are significantly contributing to the growth of nonfarm activities in rural areas. The share of agro-processing jobs located in rural areas has increased steadily from 42 percent in 2001 to 55 percent in 2009; the share of textiles jobs rose from 38 percent to 50 percent over the same period (map 3.1). The density of nonfarm employment reveals that proximity to Dhaka favors diversification out of agriculture in rural areas (figure 3.5).

Creating "taller mountains" and "more hills" may lead to further concentration of economic activities. But it does not necessarily imply a widening of regional

Map 3.1 Employment Density in Bangladesh's Textile Sector, 2009

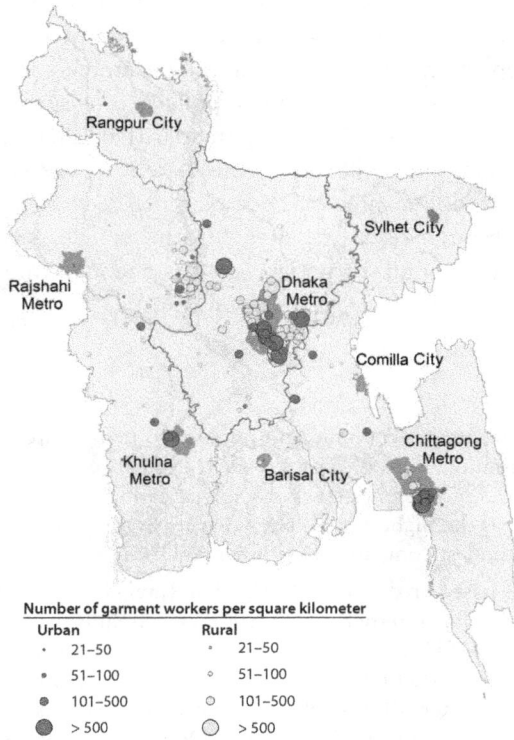

Source: Based on data from Bangladesh Bureau of Statistics 2009.
Note: All cities refer to city corporations. Metro refers to the metropolitan area.

Figure 3.5 Rural Nonfarm Employment and Distance from Dhaka City

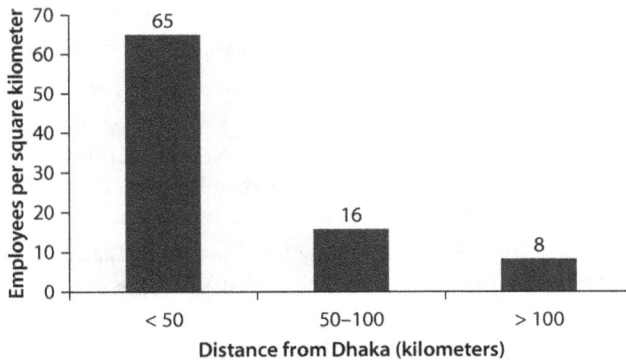

Source: Based on data from Bangladesh Bureau of Statistics 2009.
Note: Data include formal firms with more than 10 employees.

Bangladesh • http://dx.doi.org/10.1596/978-0-8213-9859-3

disparities in welfare as Bangladesh transitions to lower-middle-income country status. The benefits of growth can be equitable if supported by redistributive policies. Although the equity implications of the growth agenda are beyond the scope of this report, they need to be carefully examined. Reconciling growth and equity objectives calls for redistributive policies to ensure that agglomeration of economic activities brings higher living standards for all. It also requires a strategy that captures economic spillovers to the benefit of the entire country. A large competitive metropolitan area may, for example, generate positive spillovers into other regions through fiscal transfers, foreign exchange earnings, and exports, which can help pay for infrastructure, services, and investments in portable assets, such as health and education, across the country.

Notes

1. The two concepts of economic and population density are conceptually distinct. A large concentration of people is not enough to create economic density, and increasing economic density does not always imply creating larger concentration of people: Bangladesh has the highest population density in the world, but its economic density is relatively modest compared with other Asian cities.

2. Estimates are based on data from the Global Rural Urban Mapping Project (GRUMP) at the Center for International Earth Science Information Network, Columbia University. The GRUMP human settlements database is a global database of cities and towns of at least 1,000 people. GRUMP provides a common geo-referenced framework of urban extents by combining census data with satellite images based on night-time lights data from the National Oceanic and Atmospheric Administration (NOAA).

3. The rural dimension of growth is outside the scope of this study. Improving rural productivity by modernizing agriculture and diversifying nonfarm activities, in order to free up manpower for use in more productive activities, is also essential for growth.

4. The baseline scenario assumes constant rural productivity.

References

Bangladesh Bureau of Statistics. 2009. *Economic Census 2009*. Dhaka.

———. 2011. *Preliminary Report on Household Income and Expenditure Survey: 2010*. Dhaka.

Center for International Earth Science Information Network. 2004. "Global Rural-Urban Mapping Project (GRUMP) Alpha Version: Urban Extents." Earth Institute, Columbia University, New York. http://sedac.ciesin.columbia.edu/gpw.

Fujita, Masahisa, Paul Krugman, and Anthony Venables. 1999. *The Spatial Economy: Cities, Regions and International Trade*. Cambridge, MA: MIT Press.

Glaeser, Edward, Hedi D. Kallal, Jose A. Scheinkma, and Andrei Shleifer. 1992. "Growth in Cities." *Journal of Political Economy* 100 (6): 1126–52.

Jacobs, Jane. 1969. *The Economy of Cities*. New York: Vintage.

Porter, Michael. 1990. *The Competitive Advantage of Nations*. New York: Free Press.

UN (United Nations). 2011. "World Urbanization Prospect." Department of Economic and Social Affairs, Population Division, New York.

World Bank. 2011a. *Making the Cut? Low-Income Countries and the Global Clothing Value Chain in a Post-Quota and Post-Crisis World.* International Trade Department, Washington DC.

———. 2011b. *World Development Indicators.* Washington, DC: World Bank. http://data. worldbank.org/data-catalog/world-development-indicators.

———. 2012. *Bangladesh: Toward Accelerated, Inclusive and Sustainable Growth: An Overview.* Poverty Reduction and Economic Management Sector Unit, Washington, DC.

CHAPTER 4

The Economic Growth Drivers of Urban Areas

Dhaka City is an important garment production center, but it is losing competitiveness to peri-urban areas. Chittagong City is a highly specialized and growing industrial center. Its peri-urban areas have a narrow but growing industrial base. Secondary cities are service-based economies with declining industrial bases. Nonmetropolitan municipalities (pourashava) *have a small but expanding manufacturing base. The garment sector—the lens through which urban competitiveness is investigated in chapter 5—is a thriving, export-oriented, urban-based industry. Forces promoting agglomeration of garment production prevail, although traffic congestion and the high cost of land and housing are emerging forces promoting dispersion of garment production.*

Introduction

Bangladesh's urban geography comprises a system of cities of different sizes, economic structure, and sociodemographic characteristics. At the head is the country's largest urban agglomeration, the Dhaka metropolitan area (population 15 million), followed by metropolitan Chittagong (population 5 million). Together, the two metropolitan areas account for 48 percent of the country's urban population (36 percent in Dhaka and 12 percent in Chittagong).[1]

Below the two largest metropolitan areas are six secondary cities—the Khulna and Rajshahi metropolitan areas; the Barisal and Sylhet cities; and the new Comilla and Rangpur cities—in which 10 percent of the urban population lives.[2] The rest of the country's urban population lives in nonmetropolitan municipalities. The number of municipalities has tripled since 1991, rising from 104 in 1991 to 217 in 2001 and 309 in 2011. The study considers peri-urban areas as part of the urban space, even if they are rural areas from a political-administrative perspective (box 4.1). For the purpose of the analysis, small and medium-size cities include secondary cities and nonmetropolitan municipalities.[3]

Box 4.1 Defining Bangladesh's Urban Space

Bangladesh's urban space can be defined in at least four ways:

- *Political-administrative.* Bangladesh's urban focal bodies comprise city corporations and municipalities. An area can be declared an urban local body upon fulfillment of the following conditions: three-fourths of the adult male population of the area is engaged in nonfarm activities, the area has at least 15,000 inhabitants, and the average density is at least 2,000 inhabitants per square mile. City corporations—the highest tier of urban local governments—have more administrative independence and better technical capabilities than municipalities. Until recently, Bangladesh had six urban local governments with city corporation status: Dhaka, Chittagong, Khulna, Rajshahi, Barisal, and Sylhet. Three new city corporations were created since 2011: Comilla (2011); Narayanganj (2011), located within metropolitan Dhaka; and Rangpur (2012). Gazipur City Corporation is being created as a satellite city on the northern edge of Dhaka City by merging Gazipur and Tongi municipalities (Asian Development Bank 2012). In 2011, Dhaka City was split for administrative purposes into two city corporations (Dhaka North and Dhaka South). From a political-administrative perspective, Bangladesh's urban population was 19 million in 2001 (about 15 percent of the population).

- *Metropolitan.* Bangladesh's urban space is formed by metropolitan areas (also known as Statistical Metropolitan Areas [SMAs]), city corporations, and municipalities. Although metropolitan areas do not have political-administrative powers, they are important economic centers. The rationale for classifying the entire agglomeration as an urban area is that urban characteristics spill over into the peri-urban areas surrounding city corporations. There are four metropolitan areas in Bangladesh: Dhaka, Chittagong, Khulna, and Rajshahi. The other city corporations are not part of a metropolitan area. Generally, peri-urban areas include a mix of urban and rural areas from a political-administrative perspective. The peri-urban areas of metropolitan Dhaka encompass five urban local bodies with municipality or city corporation status (Gazipur, Kadamrasul, Narayanganj, Savar, and Tongi) as well as the surrounding rural space. In the Chittagong metropolitan area, there is one municipality (Sitakunda). From a metropolitan perspective, the urban population of Bangladesh was 25.5 million in 2001 (about 20 percent of the population).

- *Statistical.* In its 2001 population census, the Bangladesh Bureau of Statistics considered the following localities as urban: metropolitan areas, city corporations, municipalities, and subdistrict (*upazila* or *thana*) headquarters. From a statistical perspective, the urban population of Bangladesh was 29.4 million in 2001 (about 24 percent of the population).

- *Economic.* The percentage of households whose main source of income comes from nonagricultural activities can be considered a proxy for economic urbanization. Peri-urban areas closer to city cores have high levels of nonagricultural activities; nonfarm activities gradually decline as one moves away from the city center. For the purpose of estimating economic urbanization, a subdistrict is considered urban if at least two-thirds of its households rely on nonfarm employment as their main source of income. Based on this definition, the urban population of Bangladesh was 19 million in 2001 (about 15 percent of the population).

box continues next page

Box 4.1 Defining Bangladesh's Urban Space *(continued)*

The four urban perspectives have significant overlap: the political-administrative perspective is a subset of the metropolitan perspective, which is itself a subset of the statistical perspective. There is a strong positive correlation between the economic and other perspectives, suggesting that households relying on nonfarm employment as the main source of income tend to be located in urban areas (figure B4.1.1). The study defines the urban space based on a metropolitan perspective: peri-urban areas that form part of the four SMAs are considered part of the urban space.

Figure B4.1.1   Overlap between Alternative Urban Perspectives

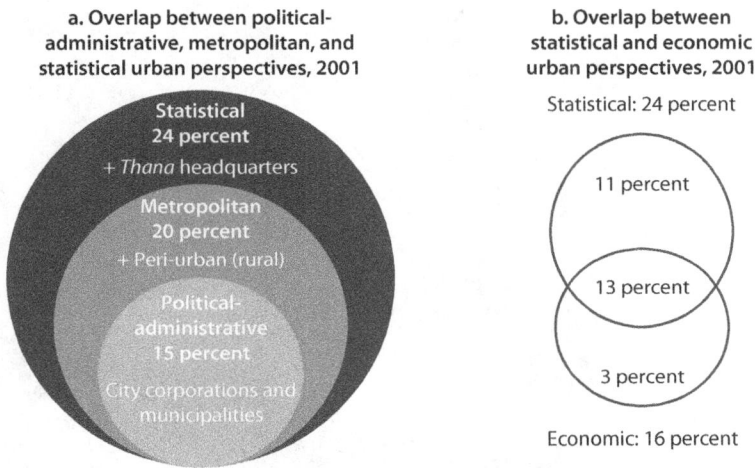

a. Overlap between political-administrative, metropolitan, and statistical urban perspectives, 2001

b. Overlap between statistical and economic urban perspectives, 2001

Source: Based on 2001 population census data from Bangladesh Bureau of Statistics 2001b.
Note: Percentage of urban population based on alternative urban perspectives are 15 (political-administrative), 16 (economic), 20 (metropolitan), and 24 (statistical).

This chapter outlines the economic base and growth drivers of Bangladesh's urban areas, drawing on the results of the location quotient and shift-share analysis carried out for the period 2001–09 based on economic census data (Bangladesh Bureau of Statistics 2001a, 2009). The analysis includes formal employment in firms with more than 10 employees. The chapter then presents the key features of the economic geography of the garment sector and the forces driving garment firms' location choices, based on the results of the garment firm survey conducted as part of the study. The full results of the location quotient and shift-share analysis are presented in appendix A. Appendix B presents the full results of the garment firm survey.

The Economic Base of Urban Areas

Dhaka City is an important garment production center, but it is losing competitiveness to peri-urban areas. In Dhaka City, 49 percent of formal jobs are

A bird's eye view of Dhaka's peri-urban areas shows clusters of urban growth interspersed with farmland.

in the garment sector. Woven (or ready-made) garments continue to be by far the largest contributor to formal employment creation in the city. However, employment growth in the sector is declining. And as garment production peri-urbanizes, there is limited evidence of replacement industries emerging to ensure continued urban vitality in Dhaka City. Annual formal employment in information and communications technology (ICT) grew almost 11 percent over 2001–09, the highest rate of any sector. The telecommunications industry has had a transformative impact on the economy as the largest contributor to foreign direct investment and tax revenues in the country, but ICT still accounts for a relatively small share of service-led employment in Dhaka City (6 percent in 2009). And industry growth, rather than local competitiveness, is

Figure 4.1 Economic Base of Urban Areas, 2001–09

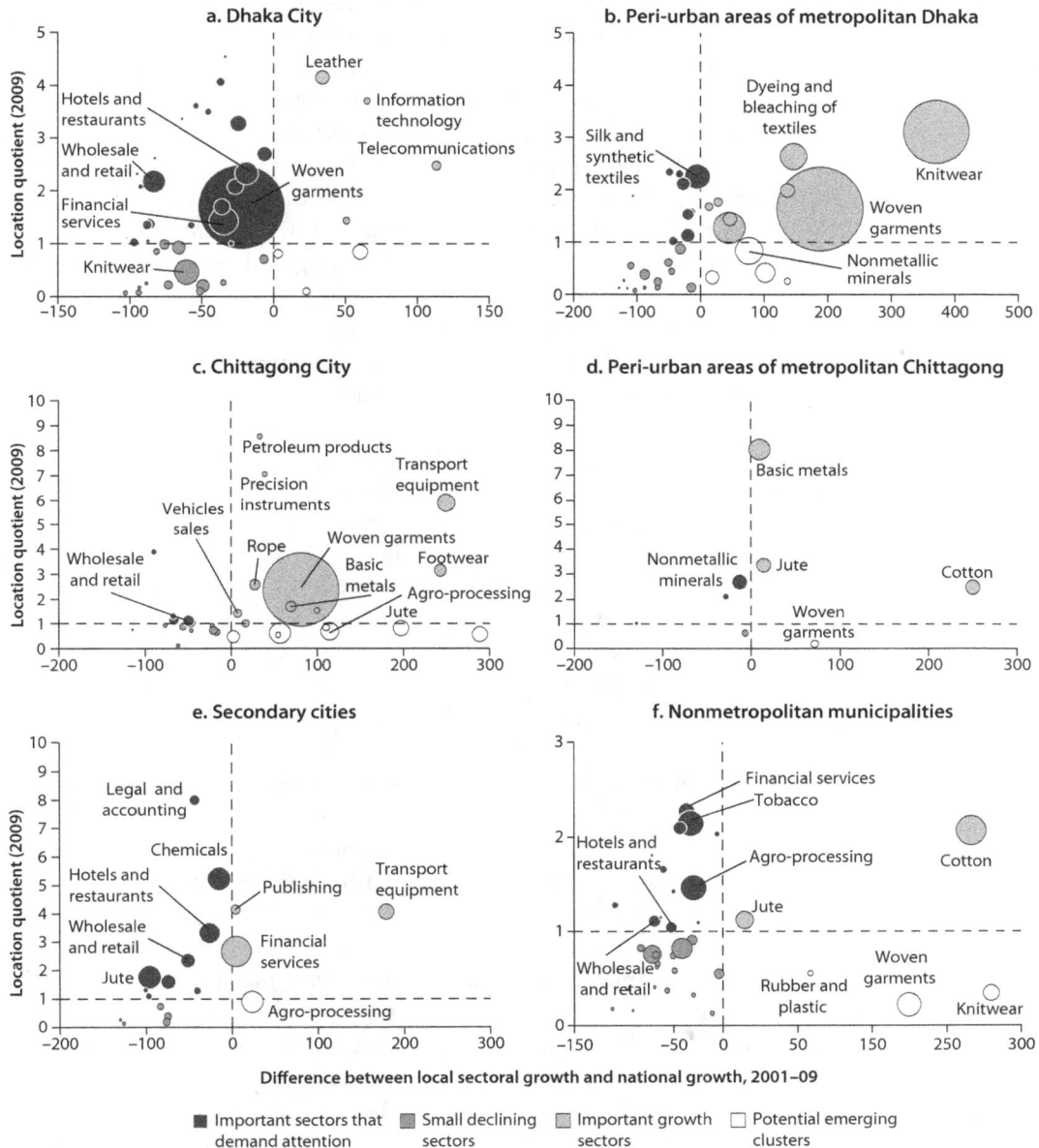

a. Dhaka City

Leather
Hotels and restaurants
Information technology
Telecommunications
Wholesale and retail
Woven garments
Financial services
Knitwear

b. Peri-urban areas of metropolitan Dhaka

Dyeing and bleaching of textiles
Silk and synthetic textiles
Knitwear
Woven garments
Nonmetallic minerals

c. Chittagong City

Petroleum products
Transport equipment
Precision instruments
Vehicles sales
Rope
Woven garments
Wholesale and retail
Basic metals
Footwear
Agro-processing
Jute

d. Peri-urban areas of metropolitan Chittagong

Basic metals
Nonmetallic minerals
Jute
Cotton
Woven garments

e. Secondary cities

Legal and accounting
Chemicals
Hotels and restaurants
Publishing
Transport equipment
Wholesale and retail
Financial services
Jute
Agro-processing

f. Nonmetropolitan municipalities

Financial services
Tobacco
Hotels and restaurants
Agro-processing
Cotton
Jute
Wholesale and retail
Woven garments
Rubber and plastic
Knitwear

Location quotient (2009)

Difference between local sectoral growth and national growth, 2001–09

■ Important sectors that demand attention ▨ Small declining sectors ▨ Important growth sectors □ Potential emerging clusters

Source: Based on data from Bangladesh Bureau of Statistics 2001a, 2009.
Note: Analysis is based on a 2001 classification of secondary cities and nonmetropolitan municipalities to ensure comparability over the 2001–09 period. Dhaka City refers to the Dhaka City Corporation. Chittagong City refers to the Chittagong City Corporation. Secondary cities in 2001 include the Khulna and Rajshahi metropolitan areas and the Sylhet and Barisal City Corporations.

the main driver of employment growth in telecommunications and other emerging clusters (figure 4.1, panel a; see figure A.2 in appendix A).

The peri-urban areas of metropolitan Dhaka are emerging as competitive garment production centers. Garment production accounts for 65 percent of total nonfarm formal jobs, and the contribution of peri-urban areas to garment production is increasing rapidly: in 2009 about half of formal garment jobs in the Dhaka metropolitan area were located in peri-urban areas, up from 18 percent in 2001.[4] The most important and fastest-growing clusters are knitwear and woven garments: between 2001 and 2009, employment rose 20 percent in the knitwear subsector and 15 percent in the woven garment subsector (see figure 4.1, panel b). The shift-share analysis indicates that local competitiveness is an important driver of employment growth in these subsectors, accounting for 60 percent of growth in woven garments and 37 percent in knitwear (see figure A.2 in appendix A). Cotton manufacturing and dyeing and bleaching also represent important growth sectors. Although still small, the telecommunications industry is a potential emerging cluster in the peri-urban areas of metropolitan Dhaka. Employment grew at an annual rate of 24 percent between 2001 and 2009, albeit from a very low base, with 80 percent of the growth driven by local competitiveness.

Chittagong City has a highly specialized and growing industrial base. About 84 percent of formal employment is in the manufacturing sector. Garments are the largest and most important source of employment. Woven garments—the city's most important growth sector—added more than 20,000 new jobs and grew by 10 percent a year over 2001–09. Chittagong City also has an advantage in the manufacturing of basic metals, petroleum products, and precision and medical instruments; local competitiveness accounts for 15–60 percent of job creation in these industries (see figure A.2 in appendix A). Other sectors—including agro-processing, textiles, and knitwear—have potential as emerging clusters (see figure 4.1, panel c).

In contrast to metropolitan Dhaka, where peri-urban areas play an increasingly important role, garment employment in Chittagong is still concentrated in the city proper; it is virtually absent in peri-urban areas. The city's peri-urban areas have a narrow but growing industrial base, with a competitive advantage in the manufacture of cotton textiles (see figure 4.1, panel d).

Secondary cities have yet to find their competitive advantages. They are service-based economies, with a narrow and declining industrial base.[5] The service sector, in particular public administration and social services, generates about 65 percent of formal jobs. The garment industry is virtually absent (see figure 4.1, panel e). The largest industrial clusters—jute, fabricated metals, and chemicals—are growing at a slower rate than the national average. A potential emerging cluster is agro-processing, which grew at an average annual rate of 6 percent between 2001 and 2009, with 20 percent of that driven by local competitiveness (see figure A.2 in appendix A). The jute industry, which was believed to have died in the 1970s, when synthetics crowded out demand for jute in international markets, has the potential to resurge, as demand for jute resurfaces as a result of its environment-friendly nature (World Bank 2007).

Nonmetropolitan municipalities have a small but expanding manufacturing base, with a competitive advantage in textiles. Textiles, particularly cotton and jute, are among the largest and fastest-growing industrial clusters (see figure 4.1, panel f). The growth in jute employment is consistent with the evidence of a resurgence of the global jute market. The garment industry is of minor importance in nonmetropolitan municipalities, although it is a potential emerging growth sector in the eastern region. Two municipalities adjacent to metropolitan Dhaka (Sreepur and Kaliakair) account for 70 percent of garment employment in nonmetropolitan municipalities.

Comilla, which gained city corporation status in 2011, has traditionally had one of the most vibrant urban bases, largely because of its strategic location on the Dhaka-Chittagong corridor. It has a large cluster of footwear manufacturers, although the sector's contribution to local job creation has recently declined. Comilla, as well as Bogra and Jessore (two other strategically located urban centers) also have clusters of ceramic manufacturers (box 4.2).

With the exception of Comilla City and Narayanganj City, areas along the Dhaka-Chittagong corridor have weak industrial bases. The Dhaka-Chittagong corridor carries about 20 million tons of freight annually (Asian Development Bank 2004), but the areas along the corridor (outside metropolitan Dhaka and Chittagong) have a relative narrow industrial base. The garment industry accounts for 30 percent of formal employment in locations along the corridor, but 98 percent of garment employment is concentrated in Comilla City and Narayanganj City. The high concentration of garment employment in Narayanganj City is explained by its proximity to Dhaka and is a manifestation of the peri-urbanization of garment production. Between 2001 and 2009, garment employment in Narayanganj increased from 32 to 48 percent of formal employment; in Comilla, the share of garment employment increased from 7 to 11 percent. Outside these two clusters, the industrial base of the corridor is virtually nonexistent: the economic base along the corridor is not different from the economic base of comparable areas away from the corridor, in the eastern region. The results suggest that connectivity and accessibility may be bottlenecks preventing industrial development along the corridor.

Box 4.2 The Strategically Located Urban Centers of Comilla, Bogra, and Jessore

Comilla, Bogra, and Jessore are strategically located urban centers outside the Dhaka and Chittagong metropolitan areas. Comilla City, with a population of about 320,000, is located in the east, the most industrialized region of Bangladesh, on the Dhaka-Chittagong corridor, which provides access to markets and major urban centers.[a] It is the most industrial of the three urban centers, with 53 percent of jobs in manufacturing. Garment production accounts for the largest share of manufacturing jobs. It generated about 23 percent of total formal jobs in the city in 2009, up from 10 percent in 2001. The important and increasing contribution of the garment sector to jobs is explained largely by the city's strategic location on the Dhaka-Chittagong corridor. Comilla City also has a relatively high concentration of employment in textiles; manufacturing of food products and beverages; ceramics; and manufacture of chemicals, rubber, and plastic (figure B4.2.1).

box continues next page

Box 4.2 The Strategically Located Urban Centers of Comilla, Bogra, and Jessore *(continued)*

Figure B4.2.1 Manufacturing Employment in Comilla, Bogra, and Jessore by Sector, 2009

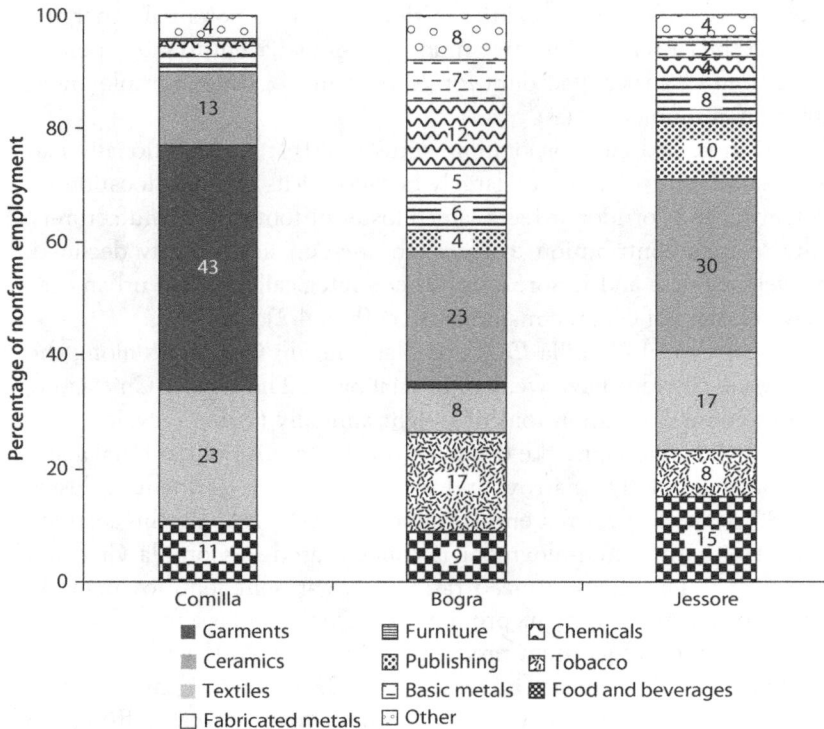

Source: Based on data from Bangladesh Bureau of Statistics 2009.
Note: Comilla is a City Corporation. Bogra and Jessore are municipalities (*pourashava*).

Bogra, with a population of about 350,000, is a municipality located in the center of the north-western region. It is the gateway to North Bengal. About 35 percent of jobs in Bogra are in manufacturing. A high concentration of manufacturing employment is in ceramics (23 percent), followed by agro-processing (mostly tobacco), chemicals, textiles, basic metals, and furniture.

Jessore, with a population of about 202,000, is a municipality located in the south-west, the least industrialized region, but it benefits from proximity to an important transit route to India. About 34 percent of jobs in Jessore are in manufacturing. Ceramics account for the largest share of manufacturing jobs (30 percent), followed by textiles, agro-processing (mostly food and beverages), publishing, furniture manufacturing, tobacco, and fabricated metal products.

a. Population estimates are based on 2011 data from Bangladesh Bureau of Statistics as reported in Brinkhoff 2011.

The Economic Geography of the Garment Sector

The garment sector is a thriving, export-oriented, urban-based industry (Uddin and Jahed 2007). It is Bangladesh's largest export industry, accounting for 40 percent of formal industrial employment. The sector has been highly successful in increasing economic density since the first garment firm was established, in Chittagong in 1977 (box 4.3). The sector's contribution to manufacturing employment has increased, rising from 44 percent of total manufacturing jobs in 2001 to 51 percent in 2009. The industry is predominantly in urban (including peri-urban) areas, which account for 93 percent of formal garment sector jobs.

Bangladesh's main garment production centers are Dhaka City, the peri-urban areas of metropolitan Dhaka, and Chittagong City (map 4.1).

Box 4.3 How Did the Garment Industry Come to Dominate Bangladesh's Economy

When Bangladesh came into being as a nation, jute and tea were its most export-oriented industries. Jute was Bangladesh's main export for decades: during the 1950s and 1960s, Bangladesh produced almost 80 percent of the world's jute. Beginning in the 1970s, the global jute industry faced a long period of decline, as a result of the development of synthetic substitutes.

With the loss of many jobs in the jute sector, the government of Bangladesh took steps to establish a more liberalized environment for trade and investment. The garment sector offered an opportunity for large-scale job creation.

Bangladesh's global competitive presence in the garment industry was facilitated by a set of fortuitous events that followed the creation by the General Agreement on Tariffs and Trade (GATT) of the Multi-Fiber Agreement (MFA) in 1973. The MFA set bilaterally negotiated quotas on developing countries for textiles and clothing exports. As a concession, it set no quotas for least-developed countries that had no garment employment at the time, including Bangladesh. In essence, the MFA created quota rents for quota-free countries, allowing them to export even though their costs of production were initially higher than their competitors. As suppliers started relocating to quota-free countries, the first garment firm was established in Bangladesh.

By the mid-1970s, quotas were severely constraining the established suppliers of garments (Hong Kong SAR, China; India; Indonesia; the Republic of Korea; Malaysia; Singapore; Sri Lanka; Taiwan, China; and Thailand). To maintain their competitiveness in the world market, they relocated garment factories to quota-free countries.

Bangladesh was one of the most suitable countries. Desh Garments, located in Chittagong, was the first large garment factory established in Bangladesh, in 1977, as a joint venture with the Korean multinational Daewoo. This humble beginning led to a global success story. The "learning by doing" that the quota rents allowed, combined with the abundance of low-cost labor, the emergence of a potential investor class in Bangladesh, and a number of investor-friendly government interventions, were the main agents of changes that allowed the garment sector to gain a quick foothold in international markets and to stand its ground after the quota system was removed.

The garment sector is now the prime mover of Bangladesh's socioeconomic development—and a symbol of Bangladesh's dynamism in the world economy. The sector continued to grow after the end of the MFA, in 2005. As of 2010, it accounted for almost four-fifths of Bangladesh's export earnings (McKinsey 2011). Almost 2.5 million people, 90 percent of them women, work in the woven garment subsector. In addition, a large number of workers provide various ancillary and support services to the garment sector.

Sources: Khan 2012; McKinsey 2011; Uddin and Jahed 2007.

Map 4.1 Spatial Distribution of Garment Employment in Bangladesh, 2009

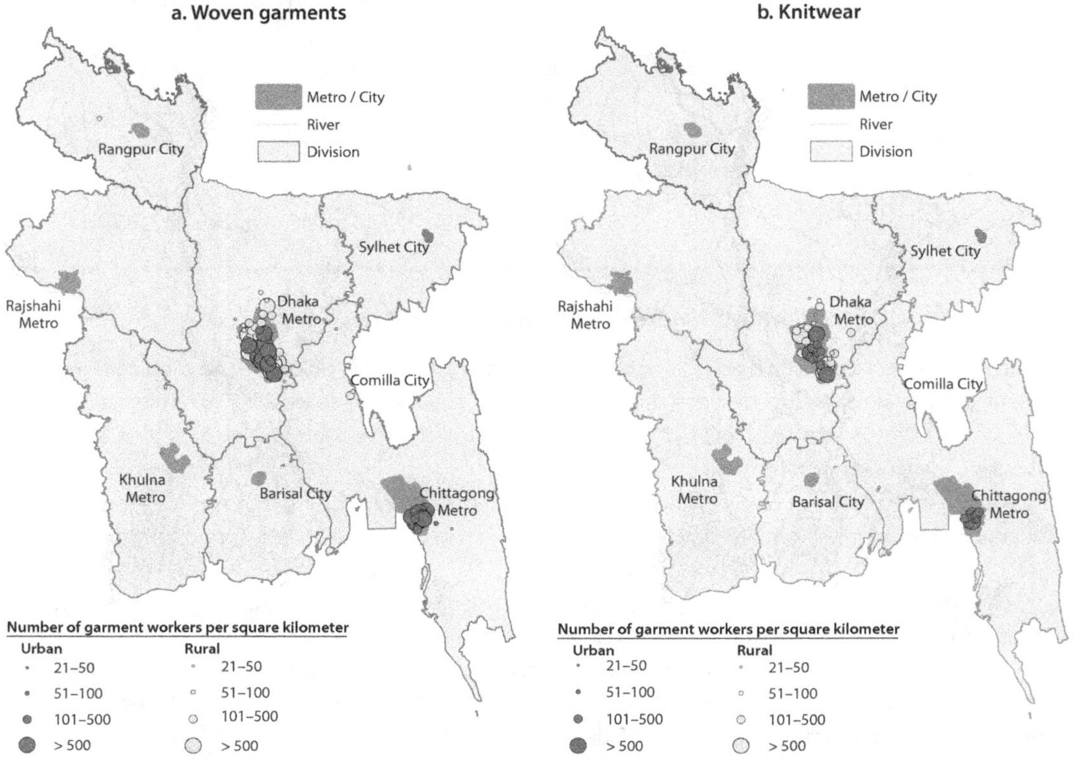

a. Woven garments

Metro / City
River
Division

Rangpur City

Sylhet City

Rajshahi
Metro

Dhaka
Metro

Comilla City

Khulna
Metro

Barisal City

Chittagong
Metro

Number of garment workers per square kilometer

Urban		Rural	
21–50		21–50	
51–100		51–100	
101–500		101–500	
> 500		> 500	

b. Knitwear

Metro / City
River
Division

Rangpur City

Sylhet City

Rajshahi
Metro

Dhaka
Metro

Comilla City

Khulna
Metro

Barisal City

Chittagong
Metro

Number of garment workers per square kilometer

Urban		Rural	
21–50		21–50	
51–100		51–100	
101–500		101–500	
> 500		> 500	

Source: Based on data from Bangladesh Bureau of Statistics 2009.
Note: All cities refer to city corporations. Metro refers to the metropolitan area.

The rest of the chapter examines the economic geography of the garment sector—the lens through which urban competitiveness will be investigated in chapter 5.

Garment firms tend to be highly specialized in one of four product lines: t-shirts, pants, shirts, and sweaters. On average, a firm's main piece of clothing accounts for 74 percent of its sales. Eleven major clothing items represent the main product for 98 percent of firms; 75 percent of surveyed firms produced t-shirts, pants, shirts, or sweaters as their main piece of clothing in fiscal 2008/09. For another 13 percent of firms, the main piece produced was trousers, jackets, undergarments, suits, shorts, pajamas, or skirts (analysis based on Garment Firm Survey 2011).

The garment sector is characterized by regional specialization, clustering, and market segmentation based on product lines (map 4.2). The mapping of the sampled firms indicates a clustering of firms by product lines. This

Map 4.2 Clustering of Garment Firms in Dhaka Metropolitan Area and Chittagong City

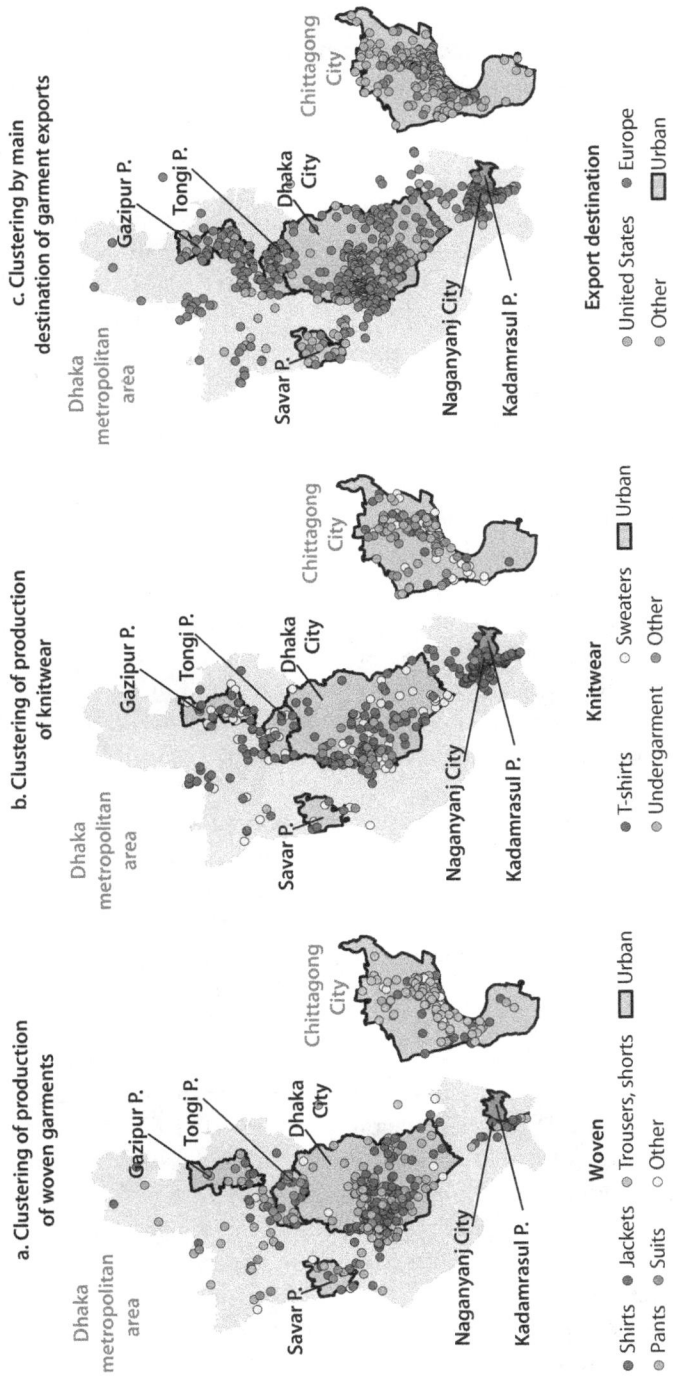

a. Clustering of production
of woven garments

b. Clustering of production
of knitwear

c. Clustering by main
destination of garment exports

Source: Garment Firm Survey 2011.

Note: P = *pourashava* (municipality). All cities refer to city corporations.

clustering can also be seen by examining firm location quotients.[6] In Dhaka City, 4 of the 11 major clothing lines (suits, t-shirts, pants, and shirts) have location quotients greater than 1.0. Dhaka's specialization is most pronounced in the production of suits: 94 percent of surveyed firms that identify suits as their main piece are located in Dhaka City. Chittagong City is highly specialized in the production of undergarments, followed by trousers, shorts, skirts, jackets, sweaters, and pajamas.

There is also strong evidence of clustering of firms by export market (see map 4.2, panel c). Products from Dhaka are more likely to be exported to Europe, and products from Chittagong are more likely to be exported to the United States. About 60 percent of products in Dhaka City are sold in Europe and 30 percent in the United States. The percentage of sales to Europe is even higher—at 70 percent—in the peri-urban areas of metropolitan Dhaka. In contrast, two-thirds of sales from firms in Chittagong are shipped to the United States (see table B.1 in appendix B).

The interplay between agglomeration and dispersion forces governs location decisions and shapes the economic geography of the garment sector. Firms choose their location after weighing the opposing forces promoting agglomeration and dispersion. Agglomeration (centripetal) forces—localized positive externalities, such as pooled labor markets, knowledge spillovers, and provision of infrastructure—attract firms to urban areas. Dispersion (centrifugal) forces—diseconomies associated with rising factor costs and negative externalities, such as road congestion and pollution—push firms out of urban areas (Lall, Shalizi, and Deichmann 2001). The survey of garment firms carried out for the study sheds light on the forces driving garment firms' location decisions.[7]

Forces promoting agglomeration prevail in the garment sector. The survey results indicate that when choosing their location, the factors garment firms value the most are access to skilled labor and access to power supply, followed by access to the highway and port, proximity to support businesses, access to the airport, and telecommunications (table 4.1 and figure 4.2). All of these factors draw firms to cities.

The ranking of location factors by garment firms is broadly consistent across the six surveyed locations (Dhaka City, urban peri-urban areas of metropolitan Dhaka, rural peri-urban areas of metropolitan Dhaka, the Dhaka export processing zone [EPZ], Chittagong City, and the Chittagong EPZ).[8] The survey results are consistent with international findings that the price of the final garment product and the lead time (the time it takes to deliver the order to the client), which depend on access to labor and connectivity, are the most important drivers of the international competitiveness of the garment sector (UNESCAP 2007).

Traffic congestion and the high cost of land and housing are emerging forces promoting dispersion of garment production. Garment firms rank low

Table 4.1   Values Garment Firms Assign to Factors Affecting Their Location Decisions

Factor	Percentage of firms rating the factor as important or very important
Access to markets and labor	
Access to skilled labor	96
Proximity to support businesses	82
Proximity to suppliers	73
Proximity to machine repair technicians	62
Proximity to buyers	61
Access to unskilled labor	46
Proximity to competitors	37
Proximity to subcontractors	31
Infrastructure	
Reliability of public power supply	96
Access to and quality of telecommunication services	74
Availability and quality of public water and sewerage	58
Access to and quality of social services	46
Accessibility	
Low traffic congestion	88
Access to the highway	87
Access to the port	84
Access to the airport	77
Land and housing	
Safety/low crime in the vicinity of the factory	66
Availability of adequate and affordable housing/low commuting for workers	62
Availability and price of buildings	58
Availability and cost of land	57
Governance and regulation	
Proximity to government offices	48
Time to obtain permits	38
Ease of access to government	32
Ability to operate at night	31

Source: Garment Firm Survey 2011.

traffic congestion as the third most important factor affecting location choices, after access to skilled labor and power supply. Garment firms also highly value the availability and cost of land and the price of buildings. These location factors work against agglomeration forces to promote dispersion of economic activities to lower-cost locations. They are particularly important for urban policy formulation, because cities can control their costs, through effective city management.

Bangladesh • http://dx.doi.org/10.1596/978-0-8213-9859-3

Figure 4.2 Garment Firms' Ranking of Factors Affecting Choice of Location

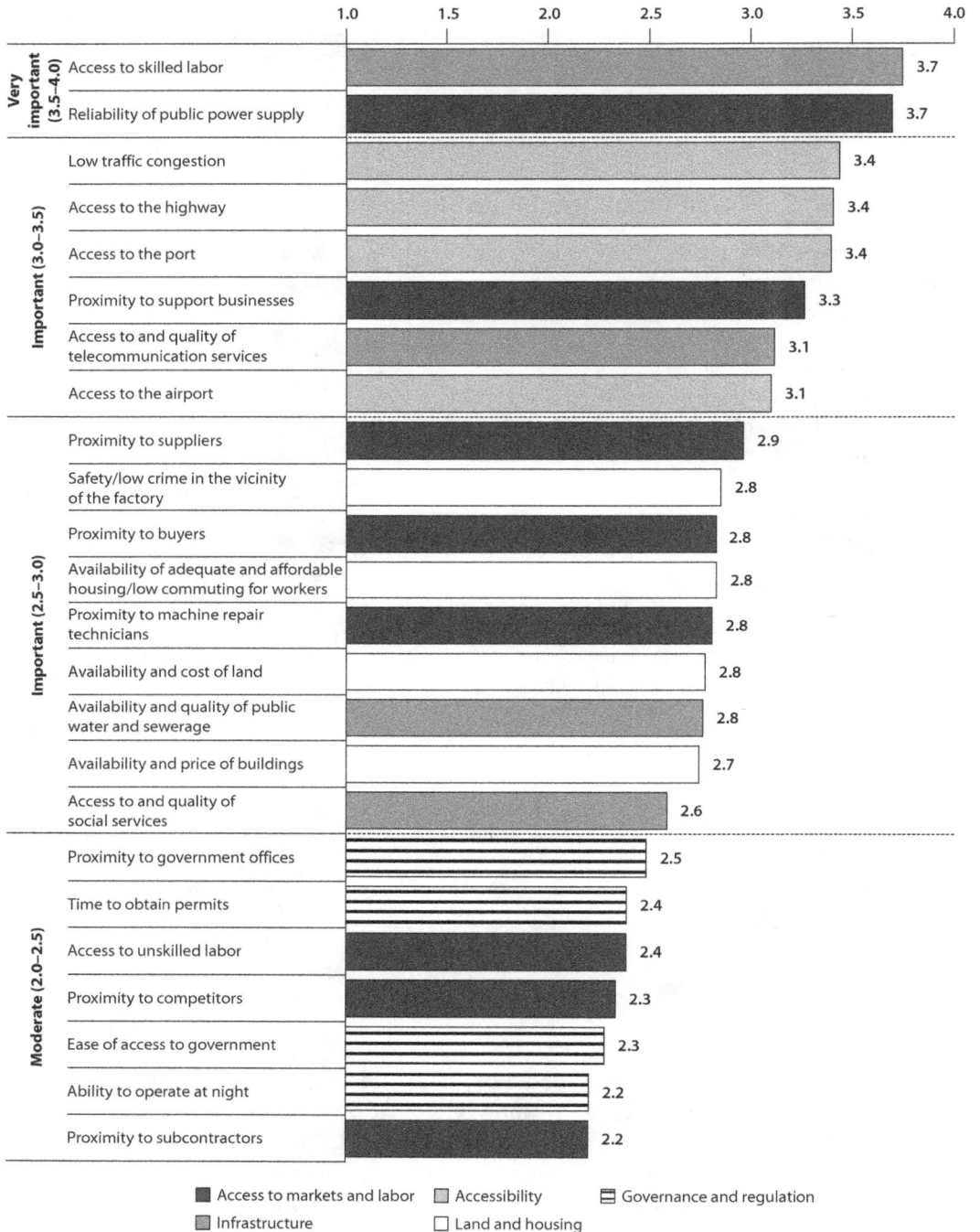

Very important (3.5–4.0)	
Access to skilled labor	3.7
Reliability of public power supply	3.7
Important (3.0–3.5)	
Low traffic congestion	3.4
Access to the highway	3.4
Access to the port	3.4
Proximity to support businesses	3.3
Access to and quality of telecommunication services	3.1
Access to the airport	3.1
Important (2.5–3.0)	
Proximity to suppliers	2.9
Safety/low crime in the vicinity of the factory	2.8
Proximity to buyers	2.8
Availability of adequate and affordable housing/low commuting for workers	2.8
Proximity to machine repair technicians	2.8
Availability and cost of land	2.8
Availability and quality of public water and sewerage	2.8
Availability and price of buildings	2.7
Access to and quality of social services	2.6
Moderate (2.0–2.5)	
Proximity to government offices	2.5
Time to obtain permits	2.4
Access to unskilled labor	2.4
Proximity to competitors	2.3
Ease of access to government	2.3
Ability to operate at night	2.2
Proximity to subcontractors	2.2

Legend: Access to markets and labor; Accessibility; Governance and regulation; Infrastructure; Land and housing

Source: Garment Firm Survey 2011.
Note: 1 = not important; 2 = moderately important; 3 = important; 4 = very important.

Notes

1. Population estimates are based on UN (2011). Metropolitan Dhaka, or Dhaka, refers to the Dhaka metropolitan area, including Dhaka City and the peri-urban areas. Dhaka City refers to the Dhaka City Corporation, the core urban center of the Dhaka metropolitan area. Metropolitan Chittagong, or Chittagong, refers to the Chittagong metropolitan area, including Chittagong City and the peri-urban areas. Chittagong City refers to the Chittagong City Corporation, the core urban center of the Chittagong metropolitan area.

2. Population estimates for secondary cities are based on UN (2011) and Bangladesh Bureau of Statistics data reported in Brinkhoff (2011). All cities refer to city corporations.

3. Nonmetropolitan municipalities are *pourashava* located outside metropolitan Dhaka and Chittagong. There are only rural local bodies in the peri-urban areas of metropolitan Khulna and Rajshahi.

4. Analysis based on economic census data from Bangladesh Bureau of Statistics 2001a and 2009.

5. Analysis includes urban areas (other than Dhaka and Chittagong) with the status of metropolitan area or city corporation in 2001, the base year of the analysis.

6. A firm's location quotient measures a location's share of the number of sampled firms that produce a particular product as their first main piece relative to its share of the overall number of sampled firms. A locality's location quotient for a particular product is greater than 1 if it has a greater concentration of firms producing that product than the overall pattern of spatial agglomeration would predict. A location quotient greater than 1 indicates specialization.

7. For the full results of the garment firm survey and a description of the methodology used to conduct it, see appendix B.

8. Full results of the ranking of location factors are presented in figure B.3 in appendix B.

References

Asian Development Bank. 2004. "Report and Recommendation of the President to the Board of Directors on a Proposed Loan and Technical Assistance Grant to the People's Republic of Bangladesh for the Chittagong Port Trade Facilitation Project." Manila.

———. 2012. *Technical Assistance: Transit-Oriented Development and Improved Traffic Management in Gazipur City Corporation.* Manila.

Bangladesh Bureau of Statistics. 2001a. *Economic Census 2001.* Dhaka.

———. 2001b. *Population Census 2001.* Dhaka.

———. 2009. *Economic Census 2009.* Dhaka.

Brinkhoff, Thomas. 2011. *City Population.* http://www.citypopulation.de.

Khan, Mushtaq. 2012. "Bangladesh: Economic Growth in a Vulnerable Limited Access Order." In *In the Shadow of Violence: The Problem of Development in Limited Access Societies,* edited by. Douglass North, John Wallis, Steven Webb, and Barry Weingast. Cambridge: Cambridge University Press.

Lall, Somik, Zmarak Shalizi, and Uwe Deichmann. 2001. "Agglomeration Economies and Productivity in Indian Industry." Policy Research Working Paper 2663, World Bank, Washington, DC.

McKinsey. 2011. "Bangladesh's Ready Made Garments Landscape: The Challenge of Growth." Apparel, Fashion and Luxury Practice, Frankfurt, Germany.

Uddin, Salim, and Mohammed Abu Jahed. 2007. "Garments Industry: A Prime Mover of the Socio-Economic Development of Bangladesh." *Cost and Management* 35 (1): 59–70.

UN (United Nations). 2011. "World Urbanization Prospects." Department of Economic and Social Affairs, Population Division, New York.

UNESCAP (Economic and Social Commission for Asia and the Pacific). 2007. "Competitiveness of the Bangladesh Ready-Made Garment Industry in Major International Markets." *Asia-Pacific Trade and Investment Review* 3 (1): 3–27.

World Bank. 2007. "Bangladesh Jute Industry: Time to Rise to the Occasion." Op-ed by Xian Zhu, Country Director, Word Bank Office, Dhaka, September 24.

CHAPTER 5

Drivers of and Obstacles to Urban Competitiveness from the Perspective of the Garment Sector

The results of a survey of garment firms—conducted to provide a lens through which to investigate urban competitiveness—reveal that Dhaka City is the most productive location for garment firms in Bangladesh. It is falling behind in accessibility and livability because of high congestion and severe constraints in land and housing markets, however, and it needs to gain a competitive edge in higher-value-added products and services. Peri-urban areas of metropolitan Dhaka are emerging as competitive manufacturing centers, but they suffer from Dhaka City's congestion and have less access to infrastructure. Chittagong City has failed to capitalize on its comparative advantage as the country's largest seaport city. Strategically located export processing zones (EPZs) are higher-productivity, higher-cost locations that are partially shielded from the inefficiencies of urban areas. Small and medium-size cities are uncompetitive "distant places," which need to foster local entrepreneurship to find their comparative advantages.

Introduction

This chapter presents original evidence on urban competitiveness based on the results of a survey of garment firms carried out in 2011. The study is not about the garment sector per se. The sector is the lens through which to investigate the competitiveness of urban areas in Bangladesh and the impact of the local environment on firm productivity. Concentrated largely in urban areas, Bangladesh's garment sector provides a large enough sample to allow comparison of competitiveness across urban locations.[1] The lessons learned and policy directions emerging from the analysis can shed light on how to create a better urban environment benefitting not only the garment sector but other urban-based sectors as well.

The survey of garment firms is representative of six locations where garment production is concentrated: Dhaka City, urban peri-urban areas of metropolitan Dhaka, rural peri-urban areas of metropolitan Dhaka, the Dhaka EPZ,

Chittagong City, and the Chittagong EPZ.[2] The sampling frame was drawn to ensure adequate coverage of small, medium, and large-size firms as well as producers of both knitwear and woven (or ready-made) garments. Garment managers and accountants were interviewed at the sampled firms. Two hundred workers, in a subsample of randomly selected garment firms, were also surveyed. The stratification led to a required total sample of 1,000 firms. (See appendix B for details on the survey methodology; figure B.1 and table B.1 in appendix B describe the characteristics of the sample.)

The survey of garment firms reveals significant variation in competitiveness across the surveyed locations (figure 5.1). Access to markets/labor and power supply—the two factors' garment firms value the most—are Dhaka City's main comparative advantages. Dhaka City is falling behind in accessibility and livability, because of heavy traffic congestion and severe constraints in land and housing markets. Peri-urban areas of metropolitan Dhaka benefit from access to markets, given the proximity to Dhaka, but they suffer from Dhaka City's congestion and have less access to infrastructure. Chittagong City has advantages in accessibility, land, and housing relative to Dhaka but is at a disadvantage in access to markets. The Dhaka and Chittagong EPZs are partially shielded from the inefficiencies of urban areas.

Figure 5.1 Garment Firms' Rating of Locations' Performance Factors

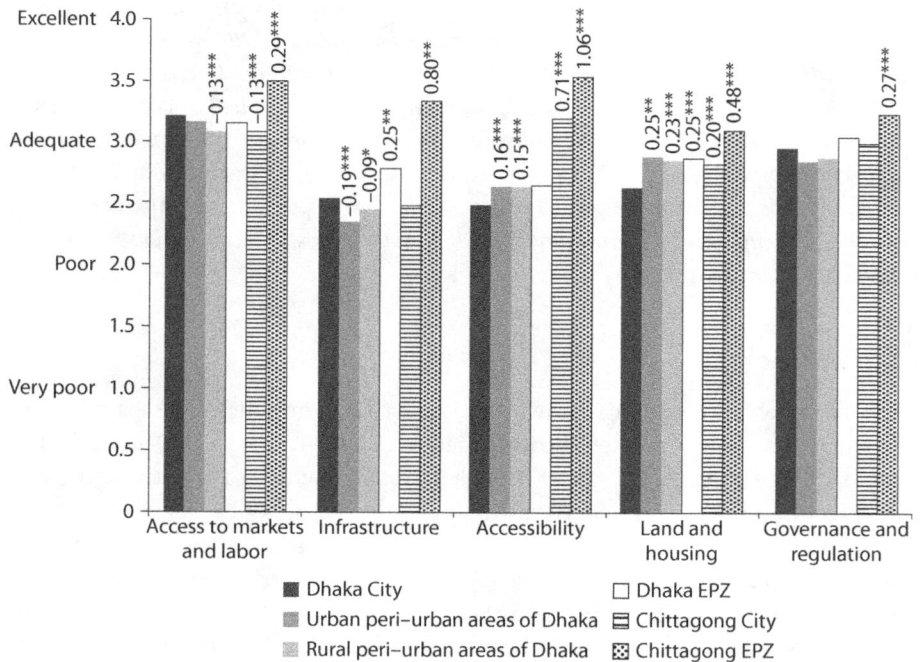

Source: Garment Firm Survey 2011.
Note: EPZ = export processing zone. Dhaka City refers to the Dhaka City Corporation. Chittagong City refers to the Chittagong City Corporation. Dhaka refers to the Dhaka metropolitan area. Statistically significant differences relative to Dhaka City are reported.
Significance level: *** = 1 percent; ** = 5 percent; * = 10 percent.

Dhaka City

Dhaka City is the most productive urban location for garment firms in Bangladesh, excluding EPZs, but it is losing competitiveness as a manufacturing growth center, as dispersion forces begin to outweigh agglomeration forces. Total factor productivity and labor productivity in garment production are higher in Dhaka City than in Chittagong City or peri-urban areas of metropolitan Dhaka (but lower than in the Dhaka EPZ, as discussed later in the chapter).[3] The productivity premium persists when controlling for firm characteristics, indicating that most of the premium is location specific. The average firm in Dhaka City is 7.9 percent more productive than the average firm in Chittagong City and 5.6 percent more productive than the average firm in peri-urban areas of metropolitan Dhaka (figure 5.2; for full results, see tables B.7–B. 9 in appendix B). Dhaka City retains its productivity premium over Chittagong City across the entire distribution of firms, from the least to the most productive. The productivity premium of Dhaka City over peri-urban areas is evident for the average firm but does not hold at the bottom or top of the distribution. The productivity premium makes Dhaka City the most sought-after urban location in Bangladesh for garment firms.

Access to labor, in particular skilled labor, and access to markets are Dhaka City's main comparative advantages. Excluding Chittagong EPZ, Dhaka City has the best access to skilled labor, the factor that garment firms value the most. It also has good access to buyers and is the best-performing city location for proximity to suppliers, subcontractors, machine repair technicians, and support businesses (EPZ locations excluded).

Outside of the EPZs, Dhaka City has the best access to power supply among the surveyed locations. Garment firms rate access to power as the second-most important factor determining where they locate (just after access to skilled labor). Although the surveyed firms consider the quality of the power supply inadequate in all city locations, the duration of power outages in Dhaka City (4.2 hours a

Figure 5.2 Productivity Distribution of Garment Firms in Dhaka City

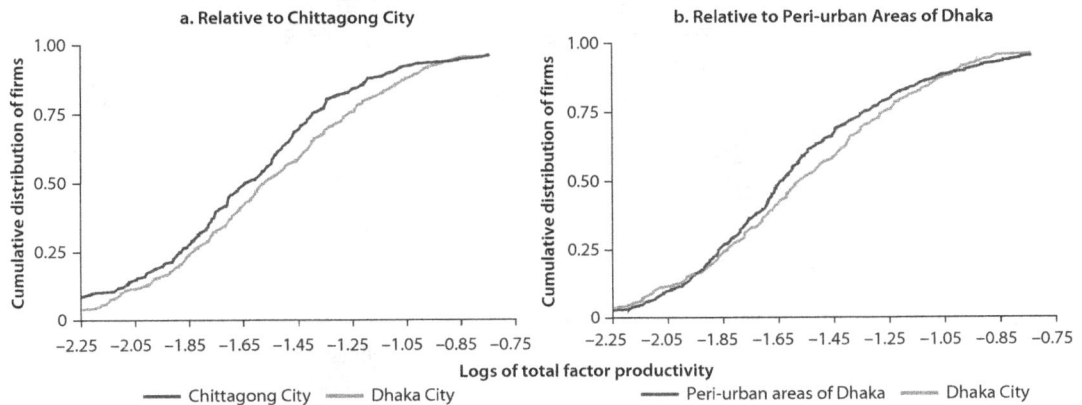

Source: Garment Firm Survey 2011.
Note: Dhaka City refers to the Dhaka City Corporation. Dhaka refers to the Dhaka metropolitan area. Chittagong City refers to the Chittagong City Corporation.

Bangladesh • http://dx.doi.org/10.1596/978-0-8213-9859-3

day) is shorter than in Chittagong City (4.9 hours a day) and peri-urban areas of metropolitan Dhaka (4.5–4.8 hours a day) (see figure 5.18 on page 82).

Firms perceive access to infrastructure other than power supply as mixed. Access to public water and sewerage and social services in Dhaka City is considered broadly satisfactory, although the city is outperformed by Chittagong City. These results are in contrast with the latest available statistics, which indicate that Dhaka City has the best access to infrastructure (except drainage) in Bangladesh (USAID and others 2008). The discrepancy between perceived and actual level of services could be explained by differences in firms' standards across locations or by high intra-urban variation in access to services that is not captured by the survey findings.

The competitiveness of Dhaka City matters regardless of firms' locations. About 57 percent of firms in peri-urban areas of metropolitan Dhaka and 55 percent of firms in Chittagong City travel to Dhaka regularly. Firms in peri-urban areas of metropolitan Dhaka travel to Dhaka City at least 13 times a month; firms in Chittagong City do so 3 times a month. About 25 percent of firms not based in Dhaka have an office in Dhaka City, and another 25 percent would be willing to open one. Firms in peri-urban areas of metropolitan Dhaka cite the need to deal with government paperwork as the main reason for traveling to Dhaka City; firms in Chittagong cite the need to meet with buyers (about 13 percent of Chittagong firms meet regularly with their main buyer in Dhaka City) (figure 5.3).

Despite its advantages, Dhaka City has started falling behind other city locations in accessibility, and costs are beginning to outweigh opportunities. Dhaka

Figure 5.3 Reasons Why Garment Firm Managers Go to Dhaka City

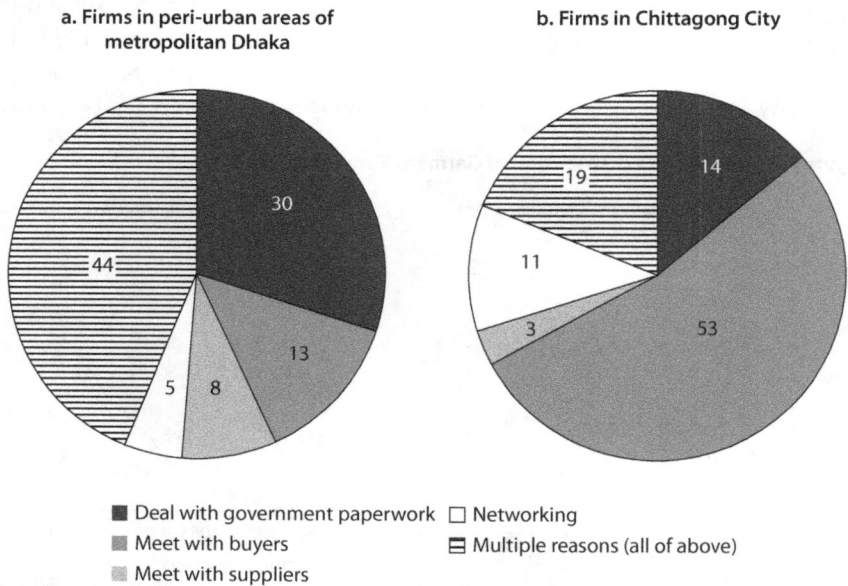

a. Firms in peri-urban areas of metropolitan Dhaka

b. Firms in Chittagong City

■ Deal with government paperwork □ Networking
▨ Meet with buyers   ▤ Multiple reasons (all of above)
▨ Meet with suppliers

Source: Garment Firm Survey 2011.
Note: Figures show percentage of firms. Dhaka City refers to the Dhaka City Corporation. Chittagong City refers to the Chittagong City Corporation.

Bangladesh • http://dx.doi.org/10.1596/978-0-8213-9859-3

City performs worst in terms of urban mobility and access to the highway. Traffic congestion, the limited availability and high prices of land and housing, and a deteriorating urban environment characterized by overcrowding and lack of amenities are also adding to firms' costs.

Dhaka City is crippled by the high costs of congestion, despite being one of the least motorized megacities in Asia. About 90 percent of daily travel trips in Dhaka City are by bus, foot, or nonmotorized vehicle, and almost 60 percent are zero-emissions trips (walking or cycle rickshaw). However, Dhaka City is unable to capitalize on these strengths. Although its vehicle fleet is not large, Dhaka City has the highest congestion index and one of the highest commuting times in South Asia, with an average commute time of 50 minutes that can reach two hours at peak time (CSE and FEJB 2011).[4] Long travel times impose major costs on both individuals and the economy, including poor air quality, which has now reached alarming levels (MCCI and CMILT 2010). The Dhaka Metropolitan Chamber of Commerce and Industry estimates that traffic congestion in Dhaka City costs about $3 billion a year, equivalent to almost 5 percent of national gross domestic product (GDP) (MCCI and CMILT 2010). Wasted time on the streets accounts for nearly 60 percent of total costs (3.2 million business hours are lost every day to congestion), followed by environmental cost (11 percent) and business loss of passenger transport and freight industries (10 percent).

Firm managers based in Dhaka City spend an average of 2.5 hours a day traveling to and from business meetings, compared with 0.9 hours for managers based in Chittagong City. Travel time accounts for 35 percent of their total visiting time (figures 5.4 and 5.5).

Congestion has led to a ban on commercial trucks during the daytime in Dhaka City, raising shipping costs for firms located there. Almost two-thirds of garment firms report being affected by the ban, 43 percent of firms report an increase in delivery time (and therefore lead time), and 25 percent report an increase in delivery costs (figure 5.6). The limited accessibility to the highway in Dhaka City may also be related to the ban on commercial trucks and traffic congestion.

The scarcity and high costs of land and real estate development are constraints for firms in Dhaka City. Monthly rent per square foot (Bangladesh taka [Tk] 11) is higher than in Chittagong City (Tk 8) (controlling for the age of the building) (figure 5.7). Factories in peri-urban areas of metropolitan Dhaka are on average more land intensive (defined as factory square footage per production worker) than factories in Dhaka City. Production by firms in peripheral municipalities is 43 percent more land intensive than production by firms in Dhaka City; production by firms in rural peri-urban areas is 28 percent more land intensive (figure 5.8).[5]

The high productivity of the garment workforce in Dhaka City has not led to better living conditions for workers. Garment workers in Dhaka City have significantly lower access to housing and services than the average urban dweller in the metropolitan area. For example, only 41 percent of garment workers in Dhaka City have access to piped water supply, significantly below the average for the Dhaka metropolitan area of 74 percent (USAID and others

Figure 5.4 Average Number of Hours Spent Traveling by Garment Firm Managers to and from Business Meetings, by Location

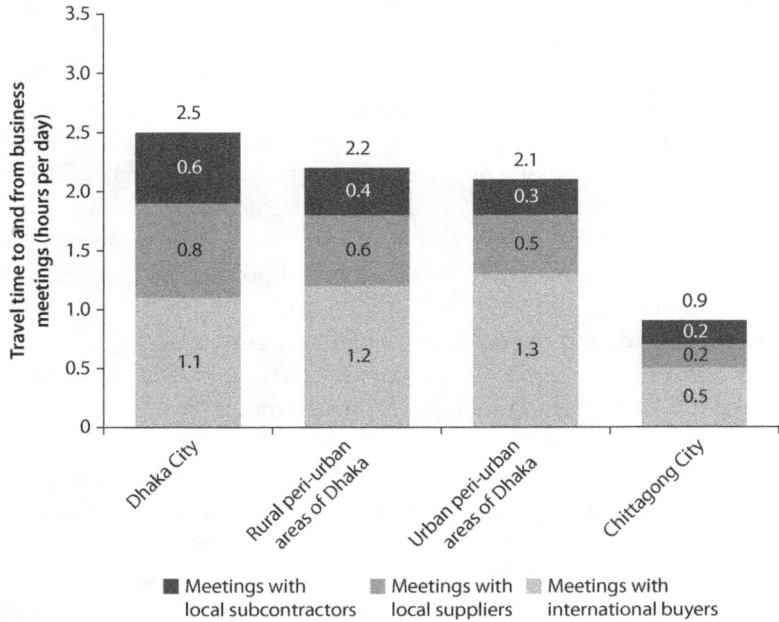

Source: Garment Firm Survey 2011.
Note: Dhaka City refers to the Dhaka City Corporation. Dhaka refers to the Dhaka metropolitan area. Chittagong City refers to the Chittagong City Corporation.

Figure 5.5 Share of Visiting Time Spent Traveling by Garment Firm Managers, by Location

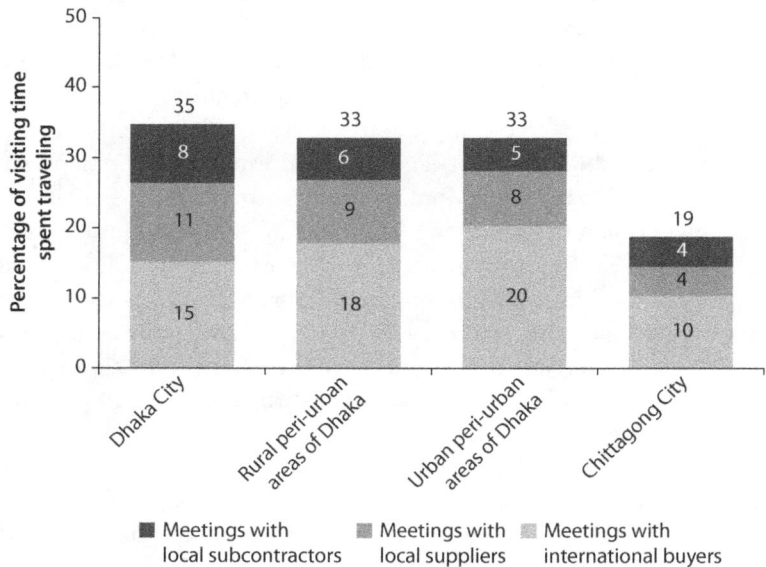

Source: Garment Firm Survey 2011.
Note: Dhaka City refers to the Dhaka City Corporation. Dhaka refers to the Dhaka metropolitan area. Chittagong City refers to the Chittagong City Corporation.

Figure 5.6 Impact of Daytime Ban on Commercial Trucks in Dhaka City on Garment Firms' Delivery Costs and Time, by Location

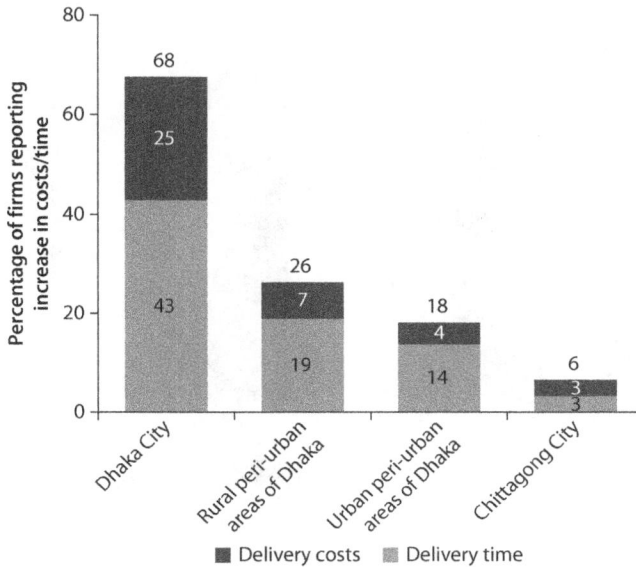

Source: Garment Firm Survey 2011.
Note: Dhaka City refers to the Dhaka City Corporation. Dhaka refers to the Dhaka metropolitan area. Chittagong City refers to the Chittagong City Corporation.

Figure 5.7 Garment Firms' Rent by Location

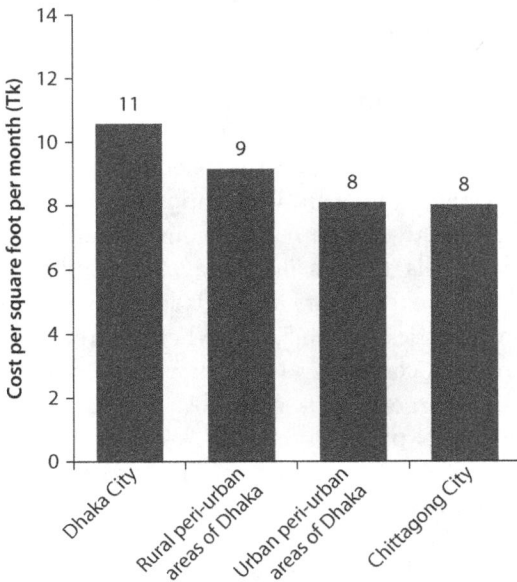

Figure 5.8 Land Intensity of Garment Production, by Location

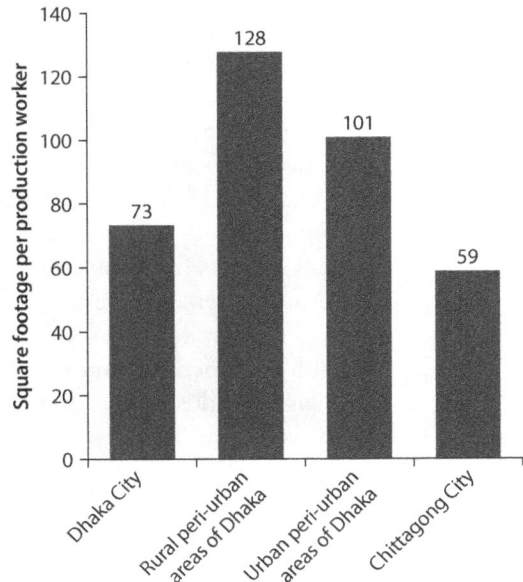

Source: Garment Firm Survey 2011.
Note: Tk = Bangladesh taka. Dhaka City refers to the Dhaka City Corporation. Dhaka refers to the Dhaka metropolitan area. Chittagong City refers to the Chittagong City Corporation.

Figure 5.9 Percentage of Garment Workers with Regular Access to Power Supply, by Location

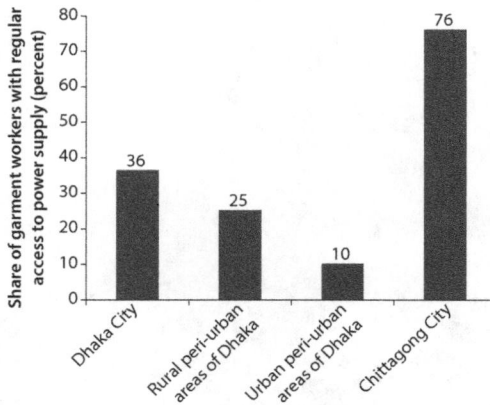

Figure 5.10 Percentage of Garment Workers with Regular Access to Piped Water, by Location

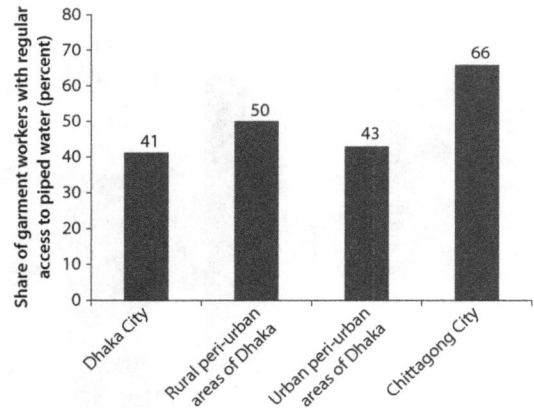

Source: Garment Firm Survey 2011.
Note: Dhaka City refers to the Dhaka City Corporation. Dhaka refers to the Dhaka metropolitan area. Chittagong City refers to the Chittagong City Corporation.

2008). Relative to garment workers in Chittagong City, garment workers in Dhaka City live in a deteriorating urban environment, characterized by crime and violence, overcrowding, and significantly lower access to housing and services. About 36 percent of garment workers have regular access to power supply in Dhaka City, compared with 76 percent in Chittagong City. Only 41 percent of garment workers have regular access to piped water supply, compared with 66 percent in Chittagong City. The overcrowding index for garment workers in Dhaka City is 3.1 people per room, compared with 2.6 in Chittagong (figures 5.9–5.11). Dhaka City is also perceived as the least safe of the surveyed locations—a perception that is consistent with recent statistics (World Bank 2007). The high level of crime and violence in Dhaka City imposes considerable economic costs, including loss of productivity as a result of injuries and direct financial costs from the collection of "tolls" (that is, illegal payments, bribes).

Annual employee turnover in the garment industry in Bangladesh (18 percent) is higher than in many other Asian countries (figure 5.12). When it is related to healthy competition among employers, a certain level of turnover is considered a sign of industry dynamism. High turnover can raise costs, however. The surveyed firms indicate their willingness to pay an additional Tk 20,000 a year to workers with one year of experience. The incremental salary is a proxy for the costs of training newly recruited workers and can be considered a lower-bound estimate of the cost of worker separation.

Dhaka City has the highest level of urban-related inefficient turnover (defined as separations caused by an inefficient urban environment rather than by more competitive job offers), primarily because of the shortage of affordable housing and the high cost of living (figures 5.13 and 5.14). The overall cost of

urban-related inefficient turnover to firms in Dhaka City is conservatively
estimated at about 1 percent of the wage bill, or 0.2 percent of annual sales.[6]
These results are consistent with the Economic Intelligence Unit (EIU)'s livability ranking, which places Dhaka among the bottom 10 cities among 140 cities
worldwide (figure 5.15).

Figure 5.11 People per Room in Garment Workers' Housing, by Location

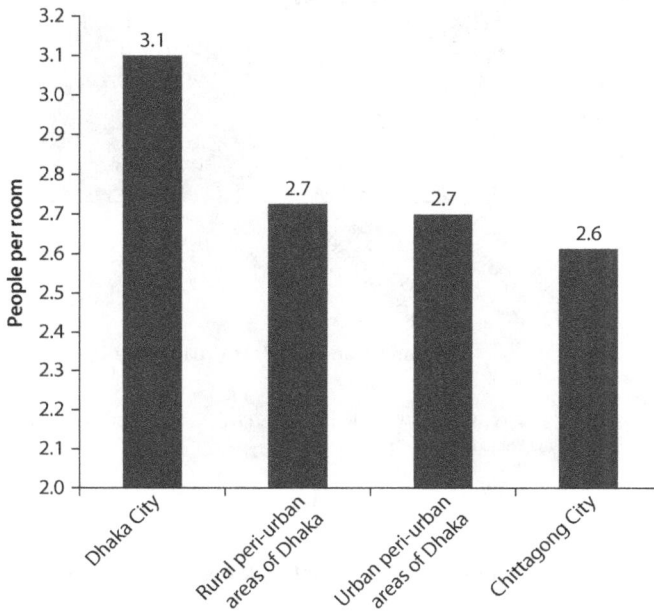

Source: Garment Firm Survey 2011.
Note: Dhaka City refers to the Dhaka City Corporation. Dhaka refers to the Dhaka metropolitan area. Chittagong City refers to
the Chittagong City Corporation.

Figure 5.12 Turnover of Manufacturing Workers in Selected Asian Countries, 2005

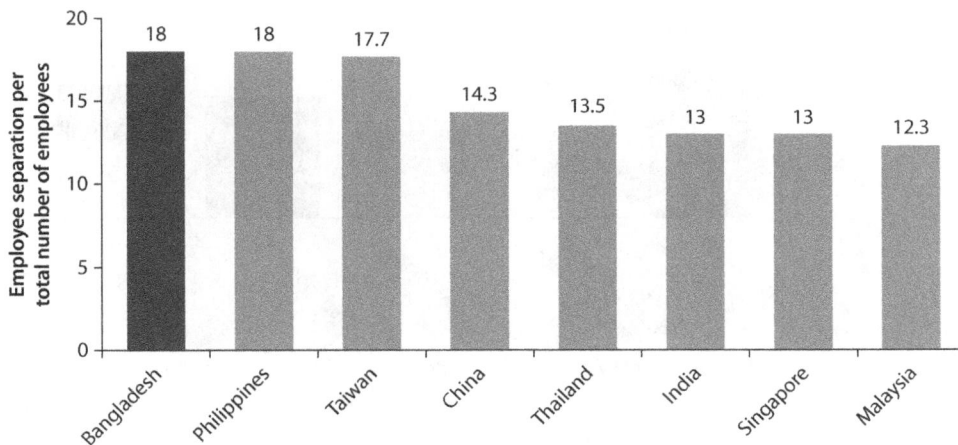

Source: Yang and Jiang 2007.

Bangladesh • http://dx.doi.org/10.1596/978-0-8213-9859-3

Figure 5.13 Urban-Related Inefficient Employee Turnover in Garment Firms, by Location

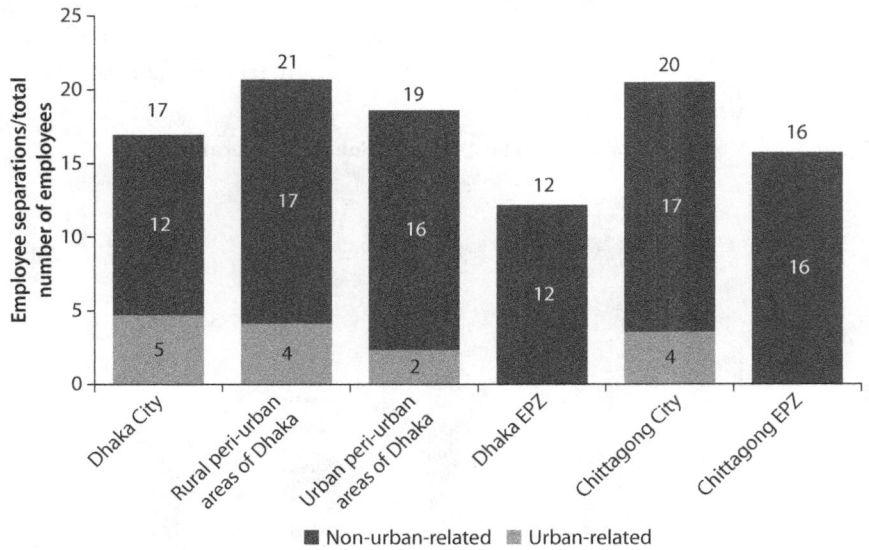

Source: Garment Firm Survey 2011.
Note: EPZ = export processing zone. Dhaka City refers to the Dhaka City Corporation. Dhaka refers to the Dhaka metropolitan area. Chittagong City refers to the Chittagong City Corporation.

Figure 5.14 Causes of Urban-Related Inefficient Employee Turnover in Garment Firms, by Location

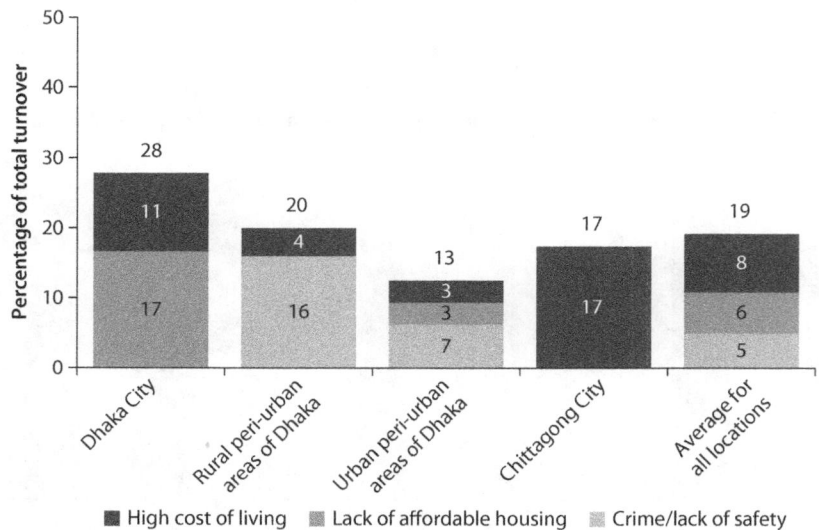

Source: Garment Firm Survey 2011.
Note: No cases of urban-related inefficient turnover are reported in the Dhaka or Chittagong export processing zones. Dhaka City refers to the Dhaka City Corporation. Dhaka refers to the Dhaka metropolitan area. Chittagong City refers to the Chittagong City Corporation.

Bangladesh • http://dx.doi.org/10.1596/978-0-8213-9859-3

Figure 5.15 International Benchmarking of Living Conditions in Dhaka City, 2010

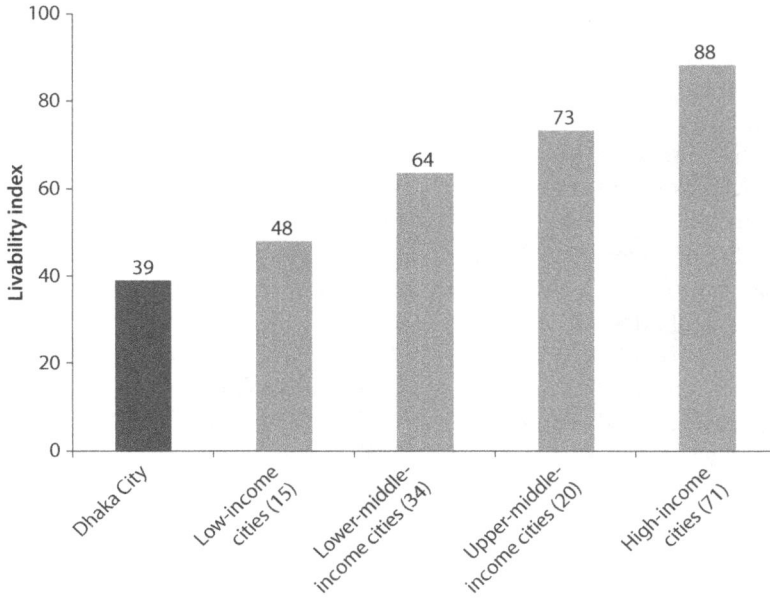

Source: EIU 2010.
Note: 80–100 = there are a few challenges to living standards; 70–80 = day-to-day living is fine, but some aspects of life may entail problems; 60–70 = negative factors have an impact on day-to-day living; 50–60 = livability is substantially constrained; 50 or less = most aspects of living are severely restricted. Dhaka City refers to the Dhaka City Corporation. Number of cities shown in parentheses.

Lack of affordable housing, land, and building is a major constraint for firms and workers.

Bangladesh • http://dx.doi.org/10.1596/978-0-8213-9859-3

Peri-Urban Areas of Metropolitan Dhaka

The birth of new garment firms, rather than the relocation of existing firms, is driving the peri-urbanization of garment production. The bulk of deconcentration from Dhaka City is accounted for not by relocations but by higher levels of net firm birth in the peri-urban areas of metropolitan Dhaka relative to Dhaka City.

Peri-urban firms are younger than firms in Dhaka City. On average, firms located in Dhaka City have been in operation for 11.2 years, compared with 8.6 years in urban and 8.0 years in rural peri-urban areas of metropolitan Dhaka (see table B.1 in appendix B). Relocations account for a small part of the deconcentration story: only 10 percent of surveyed firms report having relocated; 88 percent of all relocations took place within the same area.

Peri-urbanization is associated with the growth of a vertically integrated business model in the garment sector. Peri-urban garment firms are more likely to be vertically integrated (that is, derive 100 percent of raw materials from internal production) and to be more land intensive than garment firms in Dhaka City. In Dhaka City, 37 percent of garment firms are vertically integrated, compared with 46 percent of firms in peri-urban areas of metropolitan Dhaka.[7] The finding suggests that younger firms are opting for a consolidated, vertically integrated business model, which has advantages for international competitiveness. Lead time measures the number of days required to deliver an order from the time the order is received; together with price, it is the most important measure of international competitiveness in the garment industry. Vertically integrated firms have statistically significantly lower lead times than the average garment firm (with a time savings of four days) and are therefore better equipped to compete internationally, given the critical importance of lead time in the garment sector. These findings are consistent with the stronger employment growth performance of the knitwear subsector (where 77 percent of firms are vertically integrated), which grew at an average annual rate of 9.1 percent between 2001 and 2009. The woven garment subsector (in which virtually no firm is vertically integrated) grew at a slower annual pace of 7.1 percent. The vertically integrated business model is also developing in response to international buyers' preference for larger, "one-stop-shop" factories, which are easier to monitor for corporate social responsibility and compliance with environmental standards (such as treatment of effluents).

Peri-urban areas have a comparative advantage in accessibility and a cost advantage in land and housing. They perform better than Dhaka City in urban mobility and access to the highway—a critical advantage positioning them as competitive locations for the garment sector. Both urban and rural peripheral areas are perceived as safer than Dhaka City. They also have an advantage over Dhaka City in access to housing for workers.

Transport and access to land are the two major forces driving relocation to peri-urban areas. Although relocation is not the main driver of peri-urbanization, understanding the reasons why some firms relocated from Dhaka City to peri-urban areas can shed light on the comparative advantages of peri-urban areas. About half the firms that relocated to peri-urban areas from Dhaka City

Figure 5.16 Reasons Why Garment Firms Relocate from Dhaka City to Peri-Urban Areas

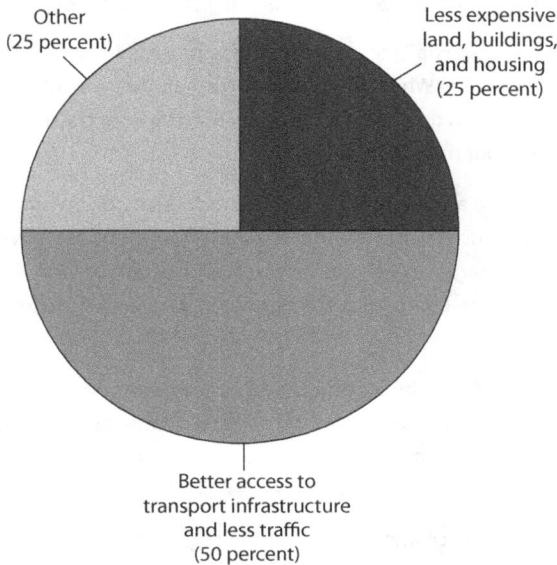

Other
(25 percent)

Less expensive
land, buildings,
and housing
(25 percent)

Better access to
transport infrastructure
and less traffic
(50 percent)

Source: Garment Firm Survey 2011.
Note: Other includes access to markets and labor. Dhaka City refers to the Dhaka City Corporation.

cite a desire to gain better access to transport infrastructure and avoid Dhaka's congestion as the primary reason. Another 25 percent cite the cost or availability of land, buildings, and housing as the main driver of deconcentration (figure 5.16). These results confirm that although Dhaka City is still the most productive location for the garment sector, the costs associated with congestion and the availability of land and real estate have started outweighing the advantages of being located in Dhaka City for a number of firms.

This trend is in line with experience of peri-urbanization in the manufacturing sector in other countries (box 5.1). The relatively small number of respondents citing land and buildings as relocation drivers can be partially explained by the variation of land and real estate costs within Dhaka City: firms wishing to relocate primarily to save on land and building costs can do so without leaving the city limits. Of the 38 firms that relocated within Dhaka City, about half cite land-related factors as their main reason for doing so.

Peri-urban areas indirectly suffer from congestion in Dhaka City, and they experience longer power outages. Access to public water and sewerage is considered inadequate, and the difference in performance relative to Dhaka City is statistically significantly. Garment workers in the peri-urban areas of metropolitan Dhaka report significantly less regular garbage collection than workers in the other surveyed locations (figure 5.17). Access to social services is also considered inadequate. Relative to Dhaka City, peri-urban areas are at a disadvantage in informal networking and proximity to government.

Box 5.1 Agglomeration Forces and Peri-Urbanization in the Manufacturing Sector

From firms' perspectives, location decisions are the outcome of a process involving two opposing forces promoting agglomeration and dispersion. When dispersion forces prevail, manufacturing suburbanizes. Although the drivers of peri-urbanization in the manufacturing sector vary from country to country, and from city to city, they can be classified into four main categories.

- *Urban vibrancy.* In highly competitive and vibrant cities, the productivity premium bids up costs, pushing less productive or maturing industries to peri-urban areas. The city of Tel Aviv-Jaffa, for example, attracts start-ups in their nascent stages (seed and research and development [R&D]) because of its highly competitive environment. Once companies start growing, they are more likely to leave the city (figure B5.1.1).

- *Urban inefficiency.* Peri-urbanization driven by inefficiency occurs when institutional and policy failures, rather than a productivity premium, bid up the cost of land and create diseconomies, such as road congestion. In the early stages of economic development, inefficiencies in land and housing markets are the main factors pushing firms out of core urban areas—as they have in Dhaka City.

- *Urban decline.* Peri-urbanization is often accompanied by a shrinking of the urban population, as both economic activities and population relocate out of the city center. This pattern is common in cities highly dependent on a single industry such as mono-cities in the Russian Federation and Detroit.

- *Connectivity.* As a country urbanizes and develops, rapid progress in transportation and communication technology tends to significantly reduce trade and transport costs, facilitating the dispersion of economic activities. This trend is typical of middle- and high-income countries, such as Brazil and the Republic of Korea.

Figure B5.1.1 Life Cycle and Location Choice of High-Tech Firms in Tel Aviv-Jaffa

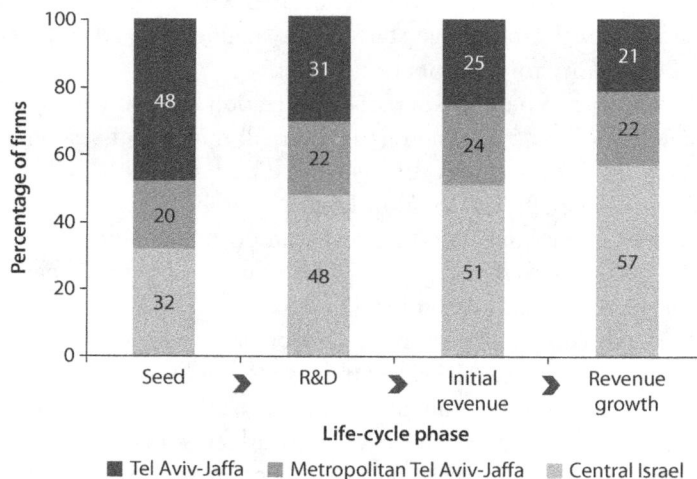

Source: Tel Aviv-Jaffa Municipality 2011.
Note: R&D = research and development.

Figure 5.17 Percentage of Garment Workers with Regular Garbage Collection, by Location

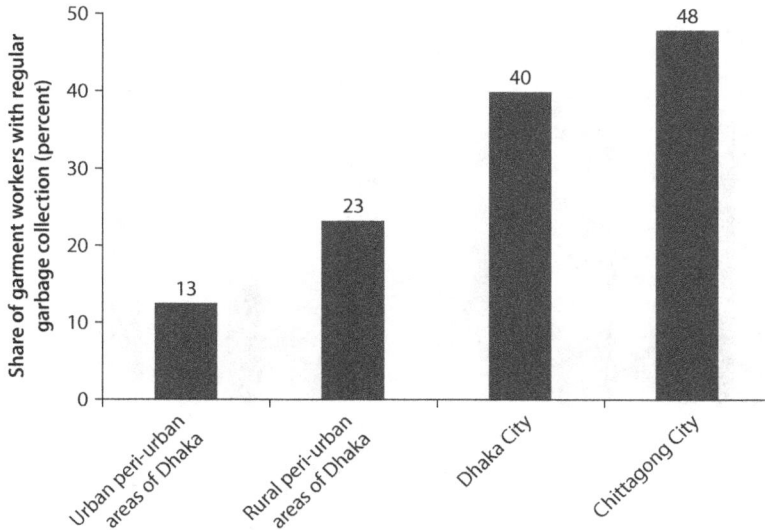

Source: Garment Firm Survey 2011.
Note: Dhaka City refers to the Dhaka City Corporation. Dhaka refers to the Dhaka metropolitan area. Chittagong City refers to the Chittagong City Corporation.

Although garment firm managers rate peri-urban areas of metropolitan Dhaka as safer than Dhaka City, worker turnover associated with crime and violence is highest in Dhaka's peri-urban areas, in particular in peripheral municipalities, where 18 percent of worker turnover is associated with crime and violence. Evidence from the survey indicates that crime and violence increase worker turnover. Unsafe locations have statistically significantly higher levels of turnover, controlling for firm and location characteristics. In locations workers consider unsafe, turnover is 25 percent, compared with 15 percent in locations that are perceived as very safe. This finding suggests that firm managers' perceptions may not be in line with garment workers' perception of safety.

Chittagong City

Chittagong City has lower garment productivity than Dhaka. It is a less competitive location than Dhaka City in access to markets. It has less access to skilled labor—the most important factor determining location for garment firms—and is farther from suppliers and support businesses. Chittagong City has adequate access to water, sewerage, telecommunications, and social services, according to surveyed firms, but access to power supply—a critical input for garment firms—is considered highly inadequate, less reliable than in Dhaka City and the peri-urban areas of metropolitan Dhaka (figure 5.18).

Figure 5.18 Power and Water Outages Reported by Garment Firms, by Location

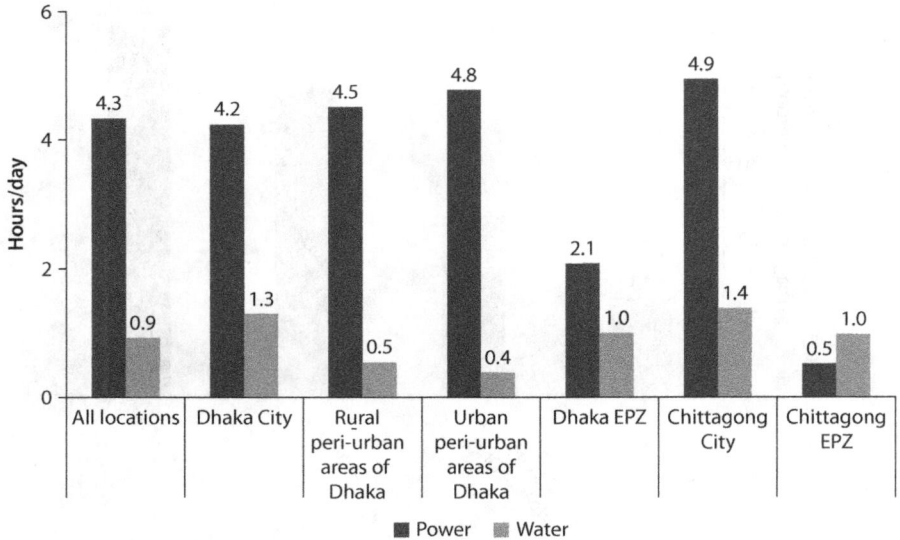

Source: Garment Firm Survey 2011.
Note: EPZ = export processing zone. Dhaka City refers to the Dhaka City Corporation. Dhaka refers to the Dhaka metropolitan area. Chittagong City refers to the Chittagong City Corporation.

As the largest seaport in Bangladesh, Chittagong City has a marked comparative advantage in accessibility to the port, airport, and highway as well as urban mobility. Chittagong handles 80–85 percent of the country's foreign trade, including the bulk of its main export, garments. Port cities like Chittagong can play an important role in rapidly urbanizing economies (box 5.2). Chittagong has not been able to leverage its natural comparative advantage as a port, however, because the port is inefficient. A ship that takes 8–12 hours to turn around in Singapore takes 4.5 days to do so in Chittagong; discharge of freight times for Calcutta are about 10 hours, compared with at least 18 hours in Chittagong (Haider 2007).

Lower costs compensate for lower productivity in Chittagong City. Garment firms rank Chittagong City as the best location for availability and cost of land, buildings, and housing for workers. Garment workers in Chittagong have significantly better working conditions than garment workers in Dhaka City, including better access to piped water supply, power supply, and garbage collection (see figures 5.9–5.11).

Dhaka and Chittagong perform equally well on regulation and governance (both broadly satisfactory). Chittagong City performs better than Dhaka City on ease of obtaining permits (see figure B.4 in appendix B).

The Chittagong port is a major bottleneck for the international competitiveness of the garment sector. Lead time among the surveyed firms is 88 days—far higher than China's 40–60 days or India's 50–70 days (Haider 2007). Ninety percent of surveyed garment firms cite the port as the main factor negatively affecting lead time in the industry. Half the firms cite the time it takes to unload at port as the main bottleneck, 30 percent cite regulatory constraints (the time required to obtain port clearance) as the main obstacle, and 10 percent cite the lack of a deep-sea port (figure 5.19).

Box 5.2 The Competitive Advantages of Coastal Cities

Port cities played a key role in shaping the first stages of the urban transition in Europe and the United States. Because roads and rail were costly, during the 19th and 20th centuries, every large city in the United States was located on a waterway.

The prominence of port cities declined with the reduction in transportation costs for manufacturing goods. A few coastal cities, like New York, managed to transform themselves and remained competitive. Others, like Liverpool, lost their competitive edge.

In many developing countries, port cities still have strong competitive advantages. Urbanization in China is concentrated in coastal areas. Its dynamic coastal cities are growing much more rapidly than its inland cities, thanks to their access to overseas markets. The government has proactively supported the development of coastal cities, amplifying their comparative advantages by investing in urban infrastructure ahead of demand and proactively seeking foreign investment by designating areas as "special economic zones." In India, proximity to international seaports and highways connecting large domestic markets is the most important factor affecting a city's competitiveness and attractiveness for private investment.

Source: Lall and others 2010.

Chittagong's port—the largest in Bangladesh—gives the city a major comparative advantage.
© Safia Azim. Used with permission. Permission required for further re-use.

Figure 5.19 Factors Affecting Order Lead Time in the Garment Industry

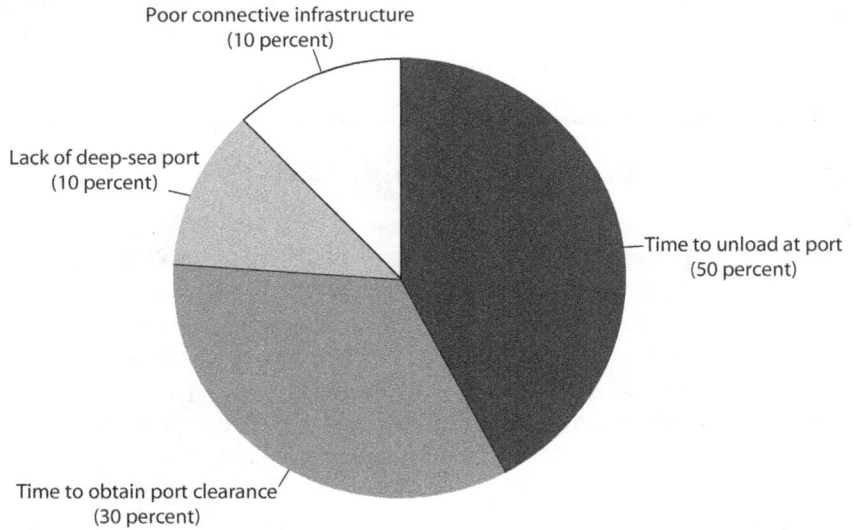

Poor connective infrastructure
(10 percent)

Lack of deep-sea port
(10 percent)

Time to unload at port
(50 percent)

Time to obtain port clearance
(30 percent)

Source: Garment Firm Survey 2011.

Export Processing Zones

An EPZ is a type of free trade zone established to promote exports. EPZs are higher-productivity, higher-cost garment production centers than non–EPZ locations. Firms located in the Dhaka and Chittagong EPZs are characterized by significantly higher foreign ownership than firms outside the EPZs: about 65 percent of the surveyed EPZ firms are fully foreign owned, compared with just 1 percent of non–EPZ firms located in metropolitan Dhaka and Chittagong City.

Garment firms in Dhaka and Chittagong EPZs are more productive than non–EPZ firms, even after controlling for firm characteristics such as foreign ownership (see table B.9 in appendix B). The higher productivity suggests that EPZ firms are partially shielded from urban inefficiencies. No cases of urban-related inefficient turnover are reported by firms located in the Chittagong EPZ (see figure 5.14). Firms located in EPZs in both areas also benefit from more reliable access to power supply: the duration of daily power outages is 2.1 hours in the Dhaka EPZ and 0.5 hours in the Chittagong EPZ, compared with more than 4 hours outside EPZs (see figure 5.18). Chittagong's EPZ is the best-performing among the surveyed locations and the only one with satisfactory performance across all factors rated as important by garment firms, including access to power supply. In the Dhaka EPZ, the main bottlenecks are inadequate access to the port, distance from support businesses, and difficulty obtaining permits (see figures B.3 and B.4 in appendix B).

Wages and building rents are also higher in EPZs (see table B.7 in appendix B). For example, the average monthly cost per square foot is Tk 15 in Dhaka EPZ, Tk 11 in Dhaka City, and Tk 9 in the Chittagong EPZ. The cost differential suggests that from a productivity viewpoint, the attractiveness of the EPZs is interacting with constraints on the supply-side to bid up wages and rents. The quality of factory premises may also be playing a role in increasing costs. The results are consistent with the fact that both Dhaka and Chittagong EPZs are sought-after locations for garment firms, and they have higher export density and employment density than all other EPZs in Bangladesh.

The EPZ program has failed to make lagging regions competitive and attractive for garment firms. In contrast to the very successful Dhaka and Chittagong EPZs, the Ishwardi, Mongla, and Uttara EPZs—all located in the lagging western region of Bangladesh—have not succeeded in attracting firms, as indicated by low export and worker densities (figure 5.20 and box 5.3).

Figure 5.20 Export and Employment Performance of Bangladesh's Export Processing Zones, 2011–12

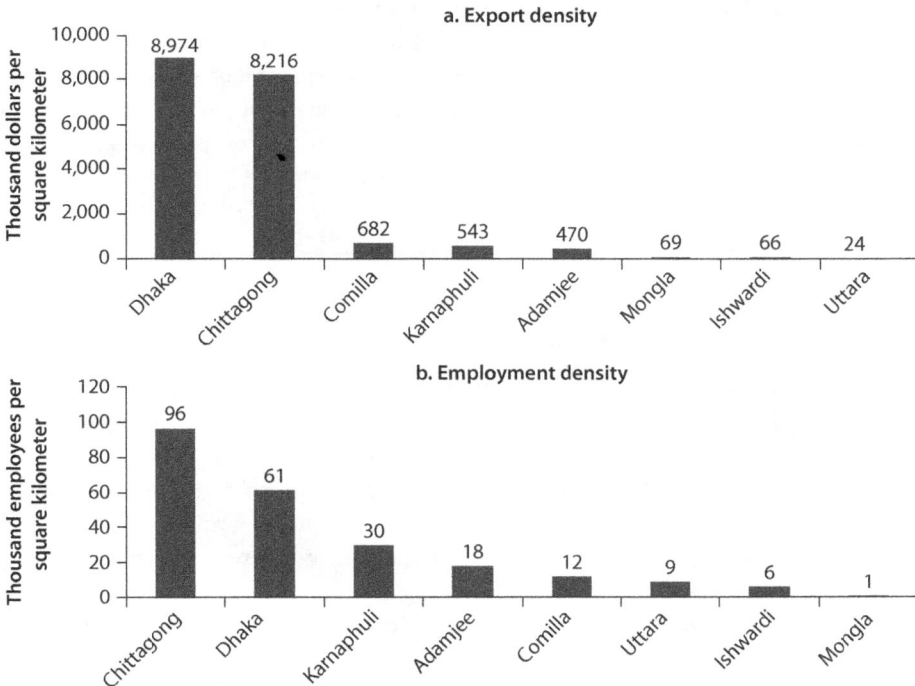

Source: Bangladesh Export Processing Zones Authority 2012 (www.epzbangladesh.org.bd).

Bangladesh • http://dx.doi.org/10.1596/978-0-8213-9859-3

Box 5.3 Policy Objectives and Achievements of Bangladesh's Export Processing Zones

Bangladesh's EPZ program was established in the early 1980s, before the extraordinary growth of garment exports, as a policy tool to catalyze industrial development, attract foreign private investment, and generate employment. The program was also conceived as a spatially targeted policy to direct investments to lagging regions and reduce regional inequalities—an attempt to "move jobs to people." Although the EPZ program has been relatively successful in attracting investment, the strategy of using EPZs to deconcentrate economic production outside the Dhaka and Chittagong metropolitan areas has not worked.

The first EPZ, in Chittagong, was completed in 1983–84 (Farole 2010). The second, in Dhaka, was established in 1993 and expanded in 1997. Eight EPZs currently operate under the Bangladesh Export Processing Zones Authority (BEPZA), with two new zones in the planning stage.

The first privately managed zone, operated by the Youngone Corporation of Korea, is under construction in Chittagong. After more than 10 years of negotiations, however, the privately owned EPZ has yet to take off. Youngone Corporation, the private investor, which acquired the land in 1999, received its operating license only in 2007; as of 2012, the EPZ remained in limbo, because of poor access to gas and electricity.

The success of EPZs in Dhaka and Chittagong was driven almost entirely by the growth of the garment sector, with almost two thirds of companies in EPZs operating in it. (Farole 2010; Farole and Akinci 2011).

Bangladesh's EPZ program has not succeeded in "moving jobs to people." Although the zones are spread across the country, economic activity is highly concentrated, with the Chittagong and Dhaka EPZs accounting for 90 percent of all exports and 67 percent of all jobs in EPZs in 2012. The Adamjee EPZ—located in Narayan-ganj, within the Dhaka metropolitan area, and opened in 2005—and the Karnaphuli EPZ—located near Chittagong and opened in 2006—have been attracting investments at a fairly rapid pace since they opened. Both were created from the conversion of two closed loss-making state-owned enterprises (Adamjee Jute Mills and Chittagong Steel Mills). The Comilla zone—located on the Dhaka-Chittagong corridor—has grown gradually but steadily mostly due to its strategic location and its relatively good connectivity. In contrast, the Ishwardi, Mongla, and Uttara EPZs, located in the western region, have performed poorly. These zones, located far from the Chittagong port and Dhaka, have generated only 1 percent of total exports in EPZs.

Sources: Farole 2010; Farole and Akinci 2011.

Small and Medium-Size Cities

Small and medium-size cities are uncompetitive "distant places" from the perspective of the private sector. The overwhelming majority of firms report inadequate access to skilled labor as the main constraint, followed by distance to other garment firms and inadequate access to transport infrastructure, including the port (table 5.1). These results confirm that proximity to Dhaka is an important locational advantage for garment firms because it provides access to markets and labor.

Small and medium-size cities need to develop a competitive advantage by relying on local entrepreneurship rather than attempting to attract firms from elsewhere through relocation incentives. Garment firms' location choices are characterized by path dependency. Only 10 percent of the sampled firms relocated, and another 10 percent report that they would like to relocate. Of firms

Table 5.1 Garment Firms' Assessment of Disadvantages of Selected Small and Medium-Size Cities

| Location | Disadvantage | | |
	Most important	Second-most important	Third-most important
Barisal	Lack of skilled labor	Limited accessibility	Distance from garment firms
Bogra	Distance from the port	Distance from garment firms	Limited access to government
Comilla	Lack of skilled labor	Distance from garment firms	Distance from the port
Khulna	Lack of skilled labor	Distance from garment firms	Limited access to suppliers
Jessore	Lack of skilled labor	Distance from the port	Distance from garment firms
Rajshahi	Lack of skilled labor	Difficulty of loading and unloading final product and raw materials	Distance from garment firms
Sylhet	Lack of skilled labor	Distance from garment firms	Distance from the port

Source: Garment Firm Survey 2011.
Note: Barisal, Comilla, Khulna, Rajshahi, and Sylhet are City Corporations; all other small and medium-size cities are municipalities (*pourashava*).

Figure 5.21 Relocation of Garment Firms

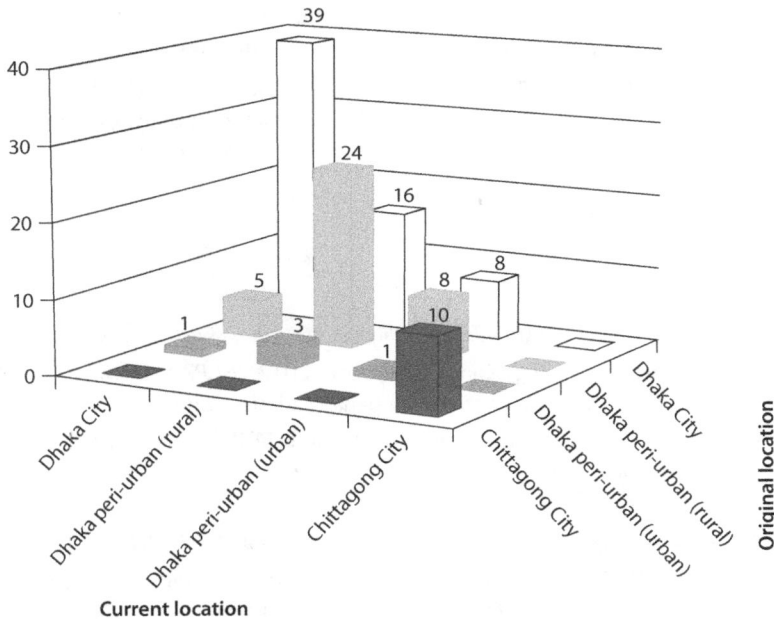

Source: Garment Firm Survey 2011.
Note: Figures show number of firms. Dhaka City refers to the Dhaka City Corporation. Dhaka refers to the Dhaka metropolitan areas. Chittagong City refers to the Chittagong City Corporation.

that relocated, no firm moved to another city (figure 5.21). This path dependency reflects a tendency for firms to move to nearby locations, a finding that is in line with evidence from other countries, such as Brazil (Hamer 2005). The path dependency in firms' location choices suggests that cities far from Dhaka and Chittagong will have limited success in attracting garment firms and that small and medium-size cities need to rely on local entrepreneurship to reap the benefits of private sector investments.

Notes

1. The analysis is not a full competitiveness assessment of the garment sector, as industry-specific factors affecting competitiveness are outside the scope of the study. Although the analysis looks at the urban agenda through the lens of the garment sector, it recognizes the important role played by other private sectors and public administration as drivers of job creation.

2. Unless otherwise stated, Dhaka refers to the Dhaka metropolitan area, including Dhaka City and the peri-urban areas. Dhaka City refers to the Dhaka City Corporation, the core urban center of the Dhaka metropolitan area. Chittagong refers to the Chittagong metropolitan area, including Chittagong City and the peri-urban areas. Chittagong City refers to the Chittagong City Corporation, the core urban center of the Chittagong metropolitan area. See box 4.1 in chapter 4 for an overview of Bangladesh's urban structure.

3. Total factor productivity is the portion of output not explained by the volume of inputs used in production.

4. The congestion index is composed of travel time, residential density, and city population (Asian Development Bank 2001). It provides a measure of crowding.

5. These findings are based on ordinary least squares regression analysis.

6. The cost of turnover is estimated as the difference between the wage for experienced workers and the wage for new workers, multiplied by turnover caused by urban inefficiency.

7. The difference is statistically significant.

References

Asian Development Bank. 2001. *Urban Indicators for Managing Cities*. Manila.

Bangladesh Export Processing Zones Authority. 2012. *BEPZA Information—Yearwise Employment and Yearwise Export*. www.epzbangladesh.org.bd.

CSE (Centre for Science and Environment) and FEJB (Forum of Environmental Journalists of Bangladesh). 2011. *Challenge of Urban Air Quality and Mobility Management*. New Delhi.

EIU (Economic Intelligence Unit). 2010. *Liveability Ranking Report*. London.

Farole, Thomas. 2010. *Special Economic Zones in Africa: Comparing Performance and Learning from Global Experience*. Directions in Development. Washington, DC: World Bank.

Farole, Thomas, and Gokhan Akinci, eds. 2011. *Special Economic Zones: Progress, Emerging Challenges, and Future Directions*. Washington, DC: World Bank.

Haider, Mohammed. 2007. "Competitiveness of the Bangladesh Ready-Made Garment Industry in Major International Markets." *Asia-Pacific Trade and Investment Review* 3 (1): 3–27.

Hamer, Andrew. 2005. "Decentralized Urban Development and Industrial Location Behavior in São Paulo, Brazil: A Synthesis of Research Issues and Conclusions." World Bank Staff Working Paper, World Bank, Washington, DC.

Lall, Somik, Hyoung Wang, and Uwe Deichmann. 2010. "Infrastructure and City Competitiveness in India." UNU-WIDER Working Paper 2010/22, United Nations University–World Institute for Development Economics Research, Helsinki.

MCCI (Metropolitan Chamber of Commerce and Industry) and CMILT (Chartered Institute of Logistics and Transport). 2010. *Traffic Congestion in Dhaka City: Its Impact on Business and Some Remedial Measures*. Dhaka.

Tel Aviv-Jaffa Municipality. 2011. *Tel Aviv Tech Center: Work Plan 2012*. Global City Administration, Tel Aviv-Jaffa.

USAID (U.S. Agency for International Development), NIPORT (National Institute of Population Research and Training), MEASURE Evaluation, ICCDR, B (International Centre for Diarrhoeal Disease Research, Bangladesh), and ACPR (Associates for Community and Population Research). 2008. *2006 Bangladesh Urban Health Survey*. Dhaka and Chapel Hill, NC.

Yang, Qin, and Crystal X. Jiang. 2007. "'Location Advantages and Subsidiaries' R&D Activities in Emerging Economies: Exploring the Effect of Employee Mobility." *Asia Pacific Journal of Management* 24 (3): 341–58.

World Bank. 2007. "Dhaka: Improving Living Conditions for the Urban Poor." Bangladesh Development Series Paper 17, Dhaka.

CHAPTER 6

Strategic Directions for Building a Competitive Urban Space in a Global Economy

Bangladesh needs to build a competitive urban space to accelerate growth in order to attain middle-income status by 2021. The country's urban areas have to take proactive measures to improve and sustain all three drivers of competitiveness: innovation, connectivity, and livability. Strengthening competitiveness across Bangladesh's cities calls for coordinated and multipronged interventions to transform Dhaka into a globally competitive metropolitan area; leverage Chittagong City's natural comparative advantage as a port city; promote strategically located export processing zones (EPZs) to foster industry competitiveness and spearhead urban reforms; and create the enabling environment for local economic development in small and medium-size cities.

Introduction

A competitive urban space in a global economy is innovative, connected, and livable (OECD 2006; World Bank 2010). Promotion of local entrepreneurship and innovation, a high-quality urban environment with an effective supply of land and properties, and efficient infrastructure with good internal and external connectivity are critical for urban competitiveness.

Bangladesh's urban space is falling behind in all three drivers of urban competitiveness. To improve city competitiveness and support the transition to middle-income country status, Bangladesh needs to transform its urban areas in the following ways:

- *Enhance the capacity to innovate within a productive and diversified urban economy.* Bangladesh cannot accelerate growth without a fundamental transformation in the economy of the Dhaka metropolitan area, which needs to move away from the production of low-value manufacturing products toward a high-value industrial and service mix. The formation of new firms around high-value products or technologies is a positive-sum game, not just for the metropolitan area but for the country as a whole. Moving to high-value products and services requires highly skilled human resources and an innovation capacity fueled by the cross-fertilization of ideas that is characteristic of large metropolitan areas. For example, well-performing metropolitan areas such as Stockholm and Helsinki have developed high-value clusters in telecommunications, biopharmaceuticals, and to a lesser extent financial and business services and transport and logistics, supported by a network of universities, by making use of the economic diversity that a metropolitan area can provide (OECD 2006).

- *Improve connectivity, both internally and with the global economy.* The most successful cities have the infrastructure to move goods, services, and people quickly and efficiently. Dhaka City's traffic congestion imposes high economic costs; Chittagong City's port is a major bottleneck to the competitiveness of Bangladesh's industries. The main competitiveness constraint on small and medium-size cities is their "distance" to markets. The Dhaka metropolitan area needs to be better connected internally and with its peri-urban areas, and both Dhaka and Chittagong have to strengthen their connectivity to the global economy. Improved connectivity within Bangladesh's system of cities—particularly within the Dhaka-Chittagong corridor—is important for productivity and export competitiveness.

- *Increase livability and attractiveness for firms and workers alike.* The development of an economically dynamic urban space in the Dhaka metropolitan area has occurred at the expenses of livability. Dhaka is one of the world's 10 worst cities to live in, according to the Economic Intelligence Unit (EIU) global livability index (EIU 2010). Improving Dhaka's livability and amenities is a priority to support Bangladesh's transformation to middle-income status. Dhaka City's inadequate living conditions have already started eroding its comparative advantage in low-value-added labor-intensive manufacturing, by increasing firms' operational costs as a result of high worker turnover and high levels of crime and violence. The livability of the urban space will become an even more binding constraint to economic growth as Bangladesh transitions to a new economic model based on higher-value-added industries and services, which require a highly skilled and internationally mobile workforce.

Although market forces contribute to shaping the development of the urban landscape, urban policies and actions are increasingly important for competitiveness as large cities compete globally to attract mobile labor and capital. Increasing the competitiveness of the urban space requires a shift from reactive and remedial measures to proactive urban policies. It also requires bringing local

Table 6.1 Policies and Actions to Improve the Competitiveness of Bangladesh's Urban Space

Objective	Infrastructure	Institutions	Incentives
	Policy tool		
Enhance capacity to innovate	• Improve infrastructure (power supply and telecommunications) to leverage Dhaka City's productivity advantage and improve Chittagong City's competitiveness. • Upgrade infrastructure in order to transform peri-urban areas of Dhaka into globally competitive manufacturing centers. • Provide basic services in small and medium-size cities to create the enabling environment for local entrepreneurship.	• Strengthen the coordinating role and convening power of local authorities to foster a business environment that rewards entrepreneurship and innovation in the Dhaka metropolitan area.	• Develop EPZs near markets and in line with the comparative advantages of localities in order to enhance the international competitiveness of Bangladesh's industries. • Build support for urban change through EPZ demonstration effects.
Increase connectivity, internally and globally	• Improve urban mobility, in order to manage the growing diseconomies of agglomeration in Dhaka City. • Leverage the natural comparative advantage of Chittagong as a port city, as part of a modern logistic chain within the Dhaka-Chittagong corridor. • Invest in spatially connective infrastructure to link small and medium-size cities to markets.	• Develop appropriate institutional mechanisms for core-periphery coordination in the Dhaka metropolitan area.	
Improve livability for firms and workers alike	• Make growth in Dhaka City and Chittagong City more environmentally and socially sustainable. • Create a level playing field in the provision of basic services across and within urban areas.	• Strengthen institutions for a more efficient and integrated land and housing market in the Dhaka metropolitan area and in Chittagong City. • Strengthen municipal management and capacity for service delivery and local economic development in small and medium-size cities.	

Bangladesh • http://dx.doi.org/10.1596/978-0-8213-9859-3

governments to the forefront of the local competitiveness agenda, in partnership with central government agencies, the private sector, and research institutions, as it is the quality and the competitiveness of local assets—a city's capacity to innovate and connect and its livability—that ultimately determine the competitiveness of the urban space.

This study identifies four strategic policy directions to improve innovation, connectivity, and livability across the spectrum of Bangladesh's cities:

A: Transforming Dhaka into a globally competitive metropolitan area;
B: Leveraging Chittagong's natural comparative advantage as a port city;
C: Promoting strategically located EPZs to strengthen industry competitiveness and spearhead urban reforms;
D: Developing the enabling environment for local economic development in small and medium-size cities.

Implementing these strategic directions requires three complementary policy tools: infrastructure, institutions, and incentives. Empirical evidence reinforces the policy imperative for improving infrastructure and services in Bangladesh's cities for enhanced livability and productivity and connective infrastructure for improved access to markets. It also points to the need to pay more attention to building institutions to manage rapid urbanization and providing incentives for innovation. Most important, it suggests that all three policy tools need to be pursued in a coordinated fashion.

The rest of the chapter identifies policies and actions to achieve the four broad strategic directions. Table 6.1 classifies the main policies and actions by policy tool (infrastructure, institutions, and incentives).

A. Transform Dhaka into a Globally Competitive Metropolitan Area

A.1: Develop appropriate institutional mechanisms for core-periphery coordination in the Dhaka metropolitan area. Concern over the size of Dhaka is misplaced: even the largest megacities in the world can be successful if they are well managed. Primate cities pose special management and planning challenges, however. Planning and provision of services have not kept up with the growth of the Dhaka metropolitan area, whose economic boundaries are rapidly expanding. Despite their important economic function as industrial centers, peri-urban areas are growing under the radar.

Managing an expanding urban agglomeration the size of Dhaka requires institutional mechanisms to support coordination between the core and the periphery. Such mechanisms are particularly important today, because of the emergence of peri-urban areas as prime manufacturing centers. But the metropolitan area does not have political-jurisdictional powers. As a result, there is currently no institutional mechanism to ensure integrated economic and physical planning or the provision of infrastructure and services at the metropolitan level. The priority is to define the boundaries of the Dhaka metropolitan area based on economic criteria, such as self-contained labor markets, and to develop coordination mechanisms to integrate peri-urban areas into spatial planning and economic development at the appropriate administrative level. International experience suggests that there is no one-size-fits-all model for metropolitan coordination and management; solutions need to be tailored to the local context (box 6.1).

Box 6.1   One-Tier, Two-Tier, and Voluntary Cooperation Models of Metropolitan Governance

The efficient delivery of urban services in a metropolitan area requires an appropriate governance structure. As economically dynamic regions outgrow their local political boundaries, municipalities often deliver services within their own jurisdictions, even though most urban services (including transportation, water, solid waste management, and housing) spill over municipal boundaries. Improving the quality of urban services is therefore not only a question of resources but also a question of governance. How metropolitan areas are governed affects local governments' ability to coordinate service delivery across municipal boundaries, deliver and pay for services, and share costs throughout the region in an equitable and efficient way. The governance structure of a metropolitan area also has an impact on citizen access to government and government accountability to citizens.

A variety of metropolitan governance models exists. They can be broadly classified as one-tier consolidated government models, two-tier government models, and voluntary cooperation. A review of the literature suggests that no one model stands above the rest. The type of model that is appropriate in a city is always context specific—and may change over time. The optimal design also depends on the objectives driving the establishment of a metropolitan governance structure. Achieving economies of scale, externalities, and equity generally calls for large government units governing an entire metropolitan area; improving local responsiveness and accountability is best achieved by smaller government units.

One-Tier Consolidated Metropolitan Governments
Under the one-tier consolidated government model of urban governance, a single local government is responsible for providing the full range of services within the entire metropolitan area. Large single-tier governments are generally formed by amalgamating lower-tier local governments. The main advantages of this model are better service coordination, clearer accountability, more streamlined decision making, and greater efficiency. International experience shows, however, that consolidation does not necessarily reduce costs. Shanghai and Toronto are examples of the one-tier consolidated government model.

Two-Tier Metropolitan Governments
The two-tier government model consists of an upper-tier governing body encompassing the metropolitan geographic area and lower-tier local government units. The upper tier provides regionwide services characterized by economies of scale and externalities (such as

box continues next page

Box 6.1 One-Tier, Two-Tier, and Voluntary Cooperation Models of Metropolitan Governance (continued)

transportation, land use planning, and solid waste management); the lower tiers are responsible for services of a local nature (such as local roads and solid waste collection).

Two-tier systems have potentially important advantages in terms of accountability, efficiency, and local responsiveness. If not well implemented, however, this model can lead to uncertainty and higher costs as a result of duplication of service provision. The Comunidad Autonoma de Madrid is an example of a two-tier system with 179 lower-tier municipalities.

Voluntary Cooperation

Voluntary cooperation between existing units of local governments with no permanent, independent institutional status requires a minimal metropolitan government. Examples include intermunicipal cooperation and special purpose districts for the provision of infrastructure and services such as environmental protection, cultural facilities, and transit. Although it may not be the optimal model in terms of efficiency or accountability, voluntary cooperation has the advantage of preserving local autonomy and flexibility. The São Paolo ABC Region is an example of a successful bottom-up approach to metropolitan governance in which pilot projects have incrementally built trust among the main actors. Voluntary cooperation is common in France and the United States.

Sources: OECD 2006; Slack 2007.

A.2: Improve infrastructure to leverage Dhaka City's productivity advantage. Garment firms identify power supply and telecommunications as among the most important factors they value in choosing a location. Although Dhaka City has an advantage over peri-urban areas and Chittagong City in the reliability of power supply, its power supply is inadequate to support the growth of globally competitive and high-value-added industries and services. Strengthening the quality of and access to telecommunication services is an important step in transforming Dhaka into a globally competitive metropolitan area that will support the growth of emerging sectors. The priority is to prepare a plan for integrated infrastructure investment and capital development for the entire metropolitan level, with strong stakeholder coordination to identify investment priorities and financing options.

A.3: Enhance urban mobility in order to manage the growing diseconomies of agglomeration in Dhaka City. Lack of mobility is the main obstacle to competitiveness in Dhaka City, and the costs of traffic congestion are quickly spreading to the entire metropolitan area. Large-scale, coordinated, and sustainable road and public transportation investments, including a mass rapid transport system, and incentives to discourage the use of private cars (such as economic road pricing) are needed. Particular attention should be paid to linking Dhaka City with peripheral rural areas, which are playing an important economic function but have a connectivity disadvantage relative to peripheral municipalities.

Bangladesh • http://dx.doi.org/10.1596/978-0-8213-9859-3

A.4: Upgrade infrastructure in order to transform peri-urban areas of metropolitan Dhaka into globally competitive manufacturing centers. A globally competitive garment sector needs competitive peri-urban areas. Because their infrastructure requirements have gone largely unmet, the peri-urban areas of metropolitan Dhaka have not been able to develop to their full potential. The peri-urbanization of the garment industry is expected to accelerate with the emergence of a new business model for garment production characterized by high land intensity. Although peri-urban areas benefit from proximity to Dhaka City and have a comparative advantage in accessibility and a cost advantage in land and housing, their infrastructure is not on par with Dhaka City's or adequate to support a globally competitive industry. Policy interventions should focus on improving productive infrastructure, in particular power supply and telecommunications, and basic services, such as water and sewerage, to support the newer garment clusters at the periphery of Dhaka City. Doing so requires understanding the business model of peri-urban garment clusters—which differ from the old, consolidated garment clusters in Dhaka City—and the challenges they face to remain competitive in a global economy and developing an action plan to strengthen their competitiveness.

A.5: Strengthen institutions for a more efficient and integrated land and housing market in the Dhaka metropolitan area. Land and housing shortages in Dhaka City are a manifestation of inefficient management of the city's agglomeration economies. If not addressed, they will stifle the long-standing tradition of local entrepreneurship and private sector dynamism that characterizes Dhaka City. The main reason garment workers in Dhaka City cite for "urban-related" separations is lack of housing, followed by the high cost of living (see figure 5.14). Functioning land and real estate markets in the Dhaka metropolitan area are particularly important in the short run because they would release land to the market and provide efficient price signals for firms locating in Dhaka's peri-urban areas; in the longer term, such markets would facilitate the reuse of land and real estate in Dhaka City's central business district. Developing a fully functioning housing market requires building accountable and service-oriented institutions for efficient land and housing markets, in partnership with the private sector. A priority is to assess the land and housing sector at the metropolitan level in order to identify the institutional and policy changes required to address demand and supply bottlenecks in the market.

A.6: Strengthen the coordinating role of local authorities to foster a business environment that rewards entrepreneurship and innovation in the Dhaka metropolitan area. To reach middle-income country status, Bangladesh needs a vibrant and economically diverse Dhaka City. Dhaka City currently lacks the economic diversity that is expected in a metropolitan area of its size. As garment production peri-urbanizes, there is limited evidence of high-value-added replacement industries and services emerging to ensure continued urban vitality in Dhaka City (see figure 4.1, panel a). The city needs to find its competitive edge in new sectors.[1] Dhaka City's main comparative advantages—its large pool of skilled labor and its tradition of local entrepreneurship—are the main assets it can harness to reinvent itself. In addition, the entire value chain in the garment cluster—from production of raw material to marketing and innovation—in both Dhaka City and peri-urban areas needs to be upgraded to enable the transition toward higher-value-added production.

Local governments, in close partnership with the private sector, have an important role to play as coordinators, conveners, and facilitators of a business environment that rewards entrepreneurship and innovation (World Bank 2010). In partnership with industry associations and universities, for example, government officials in Dhaka City and peripheral local authorities could coordinate skill upgrading and training initiatives at the metropolitan level to meet local skill shortages. They could facilitate the implementation of a cluster strategy for upgrading the garment sector's value chain, with a focus on capacity building and innovation initiatives (for example, establishment of design banks). They could support research and development (R&D) and innovation through business incubators and the creation of a knowledge network linking firms with universities and research centers. Box 6.2 provides examples of some local policies and actions that foster entrepreneurship and innovation.

Box 6.2 Local Entrepreneurship and Innovation in Urban Areas

Successful cities foster innovation and entrepreneurship. New York is an example of a city that reinvented itself after its manufacturing industries died. Other cities, like Detroit, that failed to do so fell into irreversible decline.

New York

New York City developed as a result of advances in water commerce in the 19th century, when cities sprang up around water-based highways, creating trading networks. New York became a manufacturing hub thanks to its strategic location as a port and an entry way for immigration. Industries took advantage of large pools of cheap immigrant labor. Garments became the nation's largest manufacturing cluster, with 50 percent more workers than Detroit's auto industry. New York's garment industry started shrinking in the 1950s, as location advantages diminished. As inland transport costs dropped, manufacturing firms relocated to cheaper places, including peri-urban areas, the southern United States, and China.

New York reinvented itself thanks to its resilience, tradition of entrepreneurship, and favorable city government environment. The explosion of entrepreneurship in financial services transformed New York from a manufacturing hub to a global financial sector. The city government established a public-private partnership to provide support to business incubators. Through its coordinating and convening power, it created an enabling environment in which entrepreneurship flourished.

Detroit

Like New York, Detroit developed as a hub of water commerce. The Detroit River was part of the path from Iowa's farmland to New York's kitchens. The volume of goods traveling along the Detroit River was once more than three times the volume passing through the ports of New

box continues next page

Box 6.2 Local Entrepreneurship and Innovation in Urban Areas *(continued)*

York or London. Detroit thrived as a hot-bed of small innovators (automobiles combined two industries that had long existed in Detroit, the carriage and the ship engine industries). In the 20th century, Detroit was dominated by a single industry—automobiles—which employed unskilled workers in a small number of vertically integrated firms.

By the 1950s, Detroit had begun to shrink. The assembly line increased the efficiency of Detroit's factories but reduced the need for human ingenuity. Automobiles allowed factories to locate far from rail lines and river nodes. As a result, manufacturing in Detroit underwent a process of suburbanization. Strong unions contributed to industrial stagnation and urban decline.

Unlike New York, Detroit failed to reinvent itself. The scale of Detroit's decline has been dramatic: a city of 1.85 million residents in 1950 had a population of less than 720,000 in 2010 (Glaeser 2011).

What Can Local Governments Do to Support Local Entrepreneurship and Innovation? A citywide entrepreneurial culture develops through extended formal and informal knowledge linkages between firms, universities, business support systems, and city institutions, all of which foster new firm formation, new product development, and retention of existing businesses. Governments play an important role in facilitating the development of clusters and local incubation centers, creating informal venture capital and developing specialist skills in education and technology based on priorities determined in partnership with local clusters. They also facilitate linkages between universities and businesses, in the form of academic spin-offs, science and technology parks, university incubators, mentoring, and sector-specific skill training.

Sources: OECD 2006; Glaeser 2011.

A.7: Improve livability and the quality of urban amenities in Dhaka City, and make growth there more environmentally and socially sustainable. Dhaka City's urban environment is less attractive than that of comparable cities at the same level of economic development. About 37 percent of the population lives in slums (USAID and others 2008). The city's highly productive workforce lives in an unsafe urban environment, characterized by limited access to services, and overcrowding (see figures 5.9–5.11). The EIU rates congestion in Dhaka as intolerable (EIU 2010).

The garment sector thrived on Dhaka City's abundant and cheap workforce. To attract the highly skilled internationally mobile workforce and capital required to make the leap to middle-income country status, however, Dhaka needs to improve living conditions.

Transport infrastructure bottlenecks and the lack of a fully functioning housing market are the factors contributing the most to Dhaka City's low livability ranking. Both challenges need to be addressed. Measures are also needed to make the urban transition more environmentally and socially sustainable—by upgrading environmental infrastructure; improving the quality of urban amenities (by creating open spaces and offering cultural events, for example); and extending basic services to underserved settlements. All of these measures would help make Dhaka City a more attractive location for workers and firms alike.

B. Leverage Chittagong's Natural Comparative Advantage as a Port City

B.1: Improve the competitiveness of Chittagong City's port as part of a modern logistic chain within the Dhaka-Chittagong corridor. Although agglomeration forces in Chittagong are not as strong as in Dhaka, the Chittagong metropolitan area has the potential to expand as a second industrial hub, given its comparative advantage in accessibility. As Bangladesh's largest port, Chittagong has a resource-based comparative advantage for expanding export-oriented manufacturing. This advantage is not being exploited: the inefficiency of the port is eroding Bangladesh's cost advantage in the garment sector (see figure 5.19). Leveraging the city's natural comparative advantage requires expanding port capacity, improving port infrastructure, and streamlining regulations to enhance trade competitiveness and improve access to markets—the city's main location disadvantage from the perspective of garment firms. To enhance connectivity in Bangladesh, planners should combine port development with investments in improved logistic services and intermodal connectivity to integrate the three modes of transportation (road, rail, and inland waterways systems) within the Dhaka-Chittagong corridor.

B.2: Invest in institutions and infrastructure to leverage Chittagong City's cost advantage and improve productivity and livability as the city expands. Chittagong

The capacity of the Bhairab Railway Bridge over the Meghna River connecting Dhaka to Chittagong needs to be expanded.

City has a growing and diversifying manufacturing base, and its peri-urban areas have strong potential to develop as industrial centers (see figure 4.1, panels c and d). Chittagong City should tap into its comparative advantage as a lower-cost location (relative to Dhaka City) and take steps to sustain its advantages as the city expands by investing in productive infrastructure (power and telecommunications) and developing institutions to address land and housing bottlenecks before they become binding constraints for private sector development. As in Dhaka City, the city needs to ensure that economic dynamism does not come at the expense of livability by investing in environmental infrastructure (sewerage and solid waste management) and improving the quality of and access to basic services.

C. Develop Strategically Located Export Processing Zones to Strengthen Competitiveness and Spearhead Urban Reforms

C.1: Develop EPZs near markets and in line with locations' comparative advantages to enhance the international competitiveness of Bangladesh's industries. International evidence indicates that, when strategically located near markets, EPZs are highly attractive locations for businesses (see figure 5.20). Investing in developing zones in "distant" locations is not an effective way to develop lagging regions; to be successful, EPZs need to be aligned with the comparative advantages of the country and locations in which they are established. Rather than fighting agglomeration forces, Bangladesh's growth strategy should include the development of a coherent EPZ policy based on a transparent set of criteria for determining locations.

C.2: Build support for urban change through EPZ demonstration effects. EPZs should not be developed in lieu of avoiding or delaying critical reforms to reduce the costs of doing business in urban areas. Instead, Bangladesh should use them to create the conditions and build support for urban change by testing the impact of reforms as well as reducing opposition through demonstration effects (see, for example, Farole 2010).

D. Develop an Enabling Environment for Local Economic Development in Small and Medium-Size Cities

D.1: Connect small and medium-size cities to markets. Small and medium-size cities—not only cities in the lagging western region but also cities closer to the Dhaka metropolitan area and Chittagong City, such as Comilla—are unattractive "distant" locations from the perspective of the garment firms interviewed. Policies aiming to move jobs to people based on firms' relocation incentives, such as the EPZ program, have not succeeded in overcoming the powerful agglomeration forces that move people to jobs in the western region. Connecting small and medium-size cities to markets requires spatially connective infrastructure.

Investing in connective infrastructure can help expand opportunities in lagging regions and reduce disparities in living standards. Whether enhanced connectivity will lead to industrialization of the south-western region and a reduction in regional disparities in welfare, however, will depend on local socioeconomic

---

Box 6.3 Regional Development Policies: What Works and What Does Not

Countries often resort to spatially targeted policies to encourage firms to move to lagging regions. Fiscal incentives, transfers, and direct expenditures in the form of serviced land and infrastructure are among the most widely adopted interventions to accelerate industrialization in lagging regions. Special economic zones are often located in such regions to promote regional development policy. Interventions that attempt to "move jobs to people" are seldom successful in overriding the powerful agglomeration forces that "move people to jobs" and promote concentration of economic production. Bangladesh's EPZ program is a case in point (see box 5.3).

Governments can deploy a variety of policy tools to improve welfare in lagging regions. They can raise living standards without distorting market forces by investing in people—in particular in portable assets such as health and education—and creating a level playing field for development. They can improve the local investment climate, by providing adequate access to services and infrastructure. Governments can also expand opportunities in backward areas located near agglomerations by improving connectivity. When there is evidence of unrealized economic potential, governments can play a more active role by coordinating private and public actors around emerging clusters and helping lagging regions capitalize on natural competitive advantages.

Evidence suggests that when combined with adequate investments in human capital and innovation, expanding market access through spatially connective policies can increase the returns to education and unlock the natural competitive advantage of a lagging region (OECD 2009). When improvements in connectivity are not supported by adequate human capital, however, improving market access can deindustrialize lagging regions. In Italy, for example, regional interventions in the 1950s focused on increasing connectivity between the north and south of the country to stimulate economic activities in the south. Rather than achieve the desired objectives, these policies deprived southern firms of the protection they had received, accelerating their deindustrialization (Faini 1983).

Expanding opportunities in the lagging south-western part of Bangladesh will require investments in both connectivity and human capital. Despite being the poorest regions in Bangladesh (based on 2005 poverty estimates), Khulna and Barisal have higher primary enrollment rates for both boys and girls than do Dhaka, Chittagong, and Sylhet. Khulna has the highest enrollment rates in the country at both the primary and secondary level. Barriers to connectivity may partly explain why these important education achievements have not translated into poverty reduction. By opening up market access, enhanced connectivity between the south-western and the eastern parts of Bangladesh can go a long way toward increasing the returns to education and expanding opportunities in the south-west.

Sources: Faini 1983; OECD 2006; World Bank 2008.

---

conditions. Global experience suggests that improved market access contributes the most to regional economic development when it is accompanied by investments in human capital and innovation (box 6.3). With higher than average primary and secondary enrollment rates, the south-western region is well placed to capitalize on the economic benefits of enhanced connectivity.

D.2: Create a level playing field in the provision of basic services across urban areas, and strengthen municipal management to improve livability and foster local entrepreneurship. Small and medium-size cities need to find their comparative advantages. Local entrepreneurship, not the relocation of existing industries, will drive urban vibrancy and growth in these cities. Traditional sectors such as ceramics, for example, can be turned into a lever for opening up new paths of innovation (see box 4.2). Policy interventions should focus on providing the enabling environment for building economic density by creating a level playing field for private sector development. The priority is to provide adequate access to basic services (water and sanitation, solid waste management, and power supply) to redress the current bias in favor of the largest cities. In a highly centralized country like Bangladesh, devolution of responsibilities and fiscal powers to local governments could help create a level playing field across cities by strengthening municipal management and capacity for service delivery and local economic development.

Note

1. The shift-share analysis, based on data from the Bangladesh Bureau of Statistics (2001, 2009), indicates that industrial growth, rather than local competitiveness, is the main driver of employment growth in the emerging telecommunications and information technology sectors in Dhaka City.

References

Bangladesh Bureau of Statistics. 2001. *Economic Census*. Dhaka.

———. 2009. *Economic Census*. Dhaka.

EIU (Economic Intelligence Unit). 2010. *Liveability Ranking Report*. London.

Faini, Riccardo. 1983. "Cumulative Process of Deindustrialization in an Open Economy: The Case of Southern Italy." *Journal of Development Economics* 12 (3): 277–301.

Farole, Thomas. 2010. *Special Economic Zones in Africa: Comparing Performance and Learning from Global Experience*. Directions in Development. Washington, DC: World Bank.

Glaeser, Edward. 2011. *The Triumph of the City*. New York: Penguin Press.

OECD (Organisation for Economic Co-operation and Development). 2006. *Competitive Cities in the Global Economy*. OECD Territorial Review. Paris: OECD.

———. 2009. *How Regions Grow: Trends and Analysis*. Paris: OECD.

Slack, Enid. 2007. "Managing the Coordination of Service Delivery in Metropolitan Cities: The Role of Metropolitan Governance." Policy Research Working Paper 4317, World Bank, Washington, DC.

USAID (U.S. Agency for International Development), NIPORT (National Institute of Population Research and Training), MEASURE Evaluation, ICCDR, B (International Centre for Diarrhoeal Disease Research, Bangladesh), and ACPR (Associates for Community and Population Research). 2008. *2006 Bangladesh Urban Health Survey.* Dhaka and Chapel Hill, NC.

World Bank. 2008. "Poverty Assessment for Bangladesh: Creating Opportunities and Bridging the East-West Divide." Bangladesh Development Series Paper 26, Washington, DC.

———. 2010. *Competitiveness and Growth in Brazilian Cities: Local Policies and Actions for Innovation.* Washington, DC: World Bank.

APPENDIX A

The Location Quotient and Shift-Share Analysis of Urban Areas

Introduction

This appendix presents the results of the diagnostic assessment of the economic base and cluster composition of Bangladesh's urban areas based on location quotient (LQ) and shift-share analysis techniques. These widely used techniques are used to identify the main clusters of economic activities and growth drivers of local economies.

A measure of the concentration of economic activity within urban areas is the LQ analysis. LQs are useful as primary tools for identifying clusters and highly concentrated sectors. The LQ compares the share of local employment with the share of national employment in a given sector. An LQ below 1 indicates that the area is less specialized in a particular sector than the country as a whole; an LQ above 1 indicates that the sector is more concentrated in the area than in the country as a whole. The interaction between LQ and (below- and above-average) employment growth is used to determine the importance of a particular sector in the local economy (figure A.1).

The upper-right-hand quadrant includes the most important sectors to the economy—sectors with both high LQs and above-average employment growth. Local development strategies may focus on these sectors to create or maintain adequate economic dynamism. The upper-left-hand quadrant includes sectors with LQs above 1 and declining employment growth. These sectors provide opportunities to strengthen important areas of the local economy. The lower-left-hand quadrant presents sectors with low LQs and below-average employment growth. They represent the least promising sectors for local economies. The lower-right-hand quadrant shows sectors with LQs below 1 but with rapidly growing employment. These sectors represent possibilities as growth generators in the local economies and as potential emerging clusters. Table A.1 presents the results of the LQ analysis for Dhaka City; peri-urban areas of metropolitan Dhaka; Chittagong City; peri-urban areas of metropolitan Chittagong; secondary cities (Khulna and Rajshahi metropolitan areas and the Sylhet and Barisal City Corporations); and nonmetropolitan

Figure A.1 Location Quotient Analysis

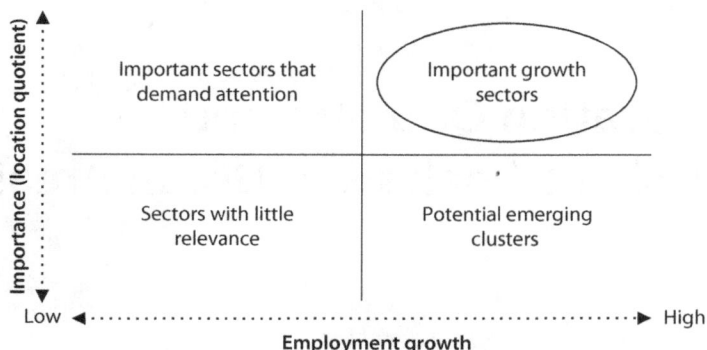

Source: World Bank 2010.

Table A.1 Sector Analysis for Urban Areas of Bangladesh, Based on Location Quotient and Employment Growth, 2001–09

a. Dhaka City

| | Employment growth | |
Low		High

Important sectors that demand attention (high importance, low growth)	**Important growth sectors (high importance, high growth)**
Manufacturing Woven garments; embroidery; luggage and handbags; publishing; rubber and plastics; fabricated metals; machinery and equipment; communication equipment; motor vehicles; furniture. *Services* Sale of motor vehicles; wholesale and retail (other than motor vehicles); hotels and restaurants; auxiliary transport; insurance and pension funds; financial services; real estate; renting of machinery and equipment; legal and accounting services; management and consultancies; architecture and engineering; advertising; landscaping.	*Manufacturing* Leather. *Services* Telecommunications; information technology; research and development (R&D).
Sectors with little relevance (low importance, low growth)	**Potential emerging clusters (low importance, high growth)**
Manufacturing Agro-processing (food and beverages); cotton; silk and synthetic textiles; jute textiles, pressing and bailing; handloom; rope; knitwear; footwear; chemical products; basic metals; electrical machinery; transport equipment. *Services* Transport.	*Manufacturing* Dyeing and bleaching of textiles; paper; nonmetallic minerals. *Services* None.

table continues next page

Bangladesh • http://dx.doi.org/10.1596/978-0-8213-9859-3

Table A.1 Sector Analysis for Urban Areas of Bangladesh, Based on Location Quotient and Employment Growth, 2001–09 *(continued)*

b. Peri-urban areas of metropolitan Dhaka

Low   *Employment growth*   High

Importance (location quotient) — High / Low

Important sectors that demand attention (high importance, low growth)
Manufacturing
Silk and synthetic textiles; embroidery; footwear; chemical products; rubber and plastics; fabricated metals; machinery and equipment; communication equipment.
Services
R&D.

Important growth sectors (high importance, high growth)
Manufacturing
Cotton; dyeing and bleaching of textiles; knitwear; woven garments; wearing apparel; paper; furniture; electrical machinery; transport equipment.
Services
None.

Sectors with little relevance (low importance, low growth)
Manufacturing
Tobacco; handloom; rope; luggage and handbags; printing; basic metals.
Services
Sale of motor vehicles; wholesale and retail (other than motor vehicles); hotels and restaurants; auxiliary transport; financial services; machinery and equipment.

Potential emerging clusters (low importance, high growth)
Manufacturing
Agro-processing (food and beverages); jute textiles, pressing and bailing; nonmetallic minerals.
Services
Insurance and pension funds.

c. Chittagong City

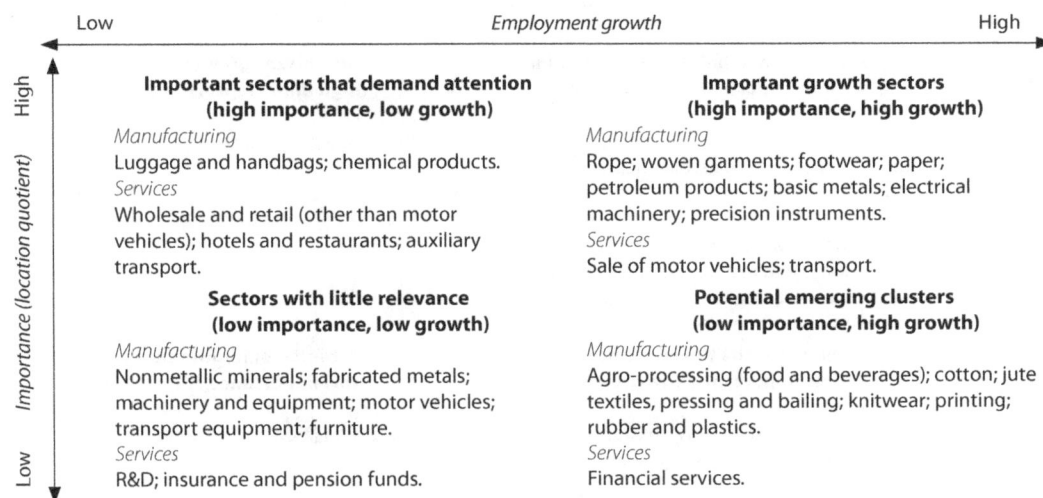

Low   *Employment growth*   High

Importance (location quotient) — High / Low

Important sectors that demand attention (high importance, low growth)
Manufacturing
Luggage and handbags; chemical products.
Services
Wholesale and retail (other than motor vehicles); hotels and restaurants; auxiliary transport.

Important growth sectors (high importance, high growth)
Manufacturing
Rope; woven garments; footwear; paper; petroleum products; basic metals; electrical machinery; precision instruments.
Services
Sale of motor vehicles; transport.

Sectors with little relevance (low importance, low growth)
Manufacturing
Nonmetallic minerals; fabricated metals; machinery and equipment; motor vehicles; transport equipment; furniture.
Services
R&D; insurance and pension funds.

Potential emerging clusters (low importance, high growth)
Manufacturing
Agro-processing (food and beverages); cotton; jute textiles, pressing and bailing; knitwear; printing; rubber and plastics.
Services
Financial services.

table continues next page

Table A.1 Sector Analysis for Urban Areas of Bangladesh, Based on Location Quotient and Employment Growth, 2001–09 (continued)

d. Peri-urban areas of metropolitan Chittagong

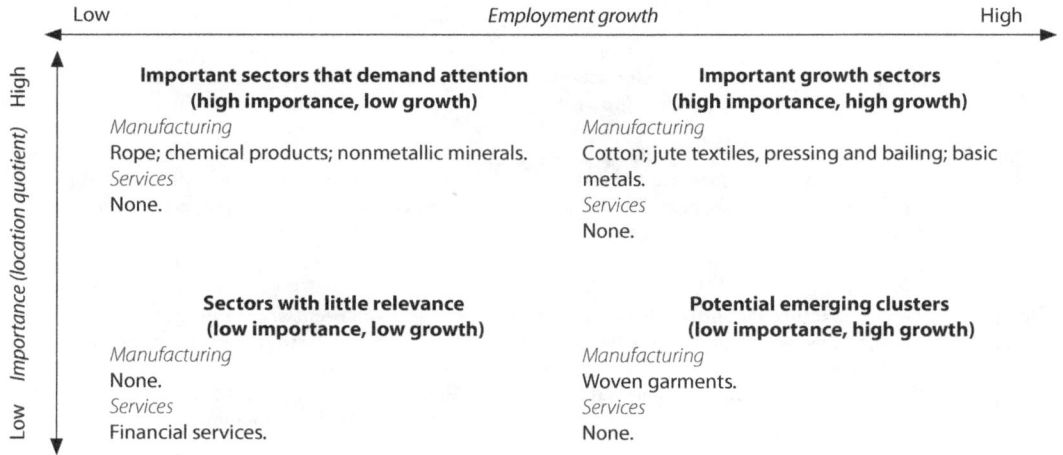

Low ←——————————————— *Employment growth* ———————————————→ High

Importance (location quotient) High ↑ ... Low ↓

**Important sectors that demand attention
(high importance, low growth)**
Manufacturing
Rope; chemical products; nonmetallic minerals.
Services
None.

**Important growth sectors
(high importance, high growth)**
Manufacturing
Cotton; jute textiles, pressing and bailing; basic metals.
Services
None.

**Sectors with little relevance
(low importance, low growth)**
Manufacturing
None.
Services
Financial services.

**Potential emerging clusters
(low importance, high growth)**
Manufacturing
Woven garments.
Services
None.

e. Secondary cities

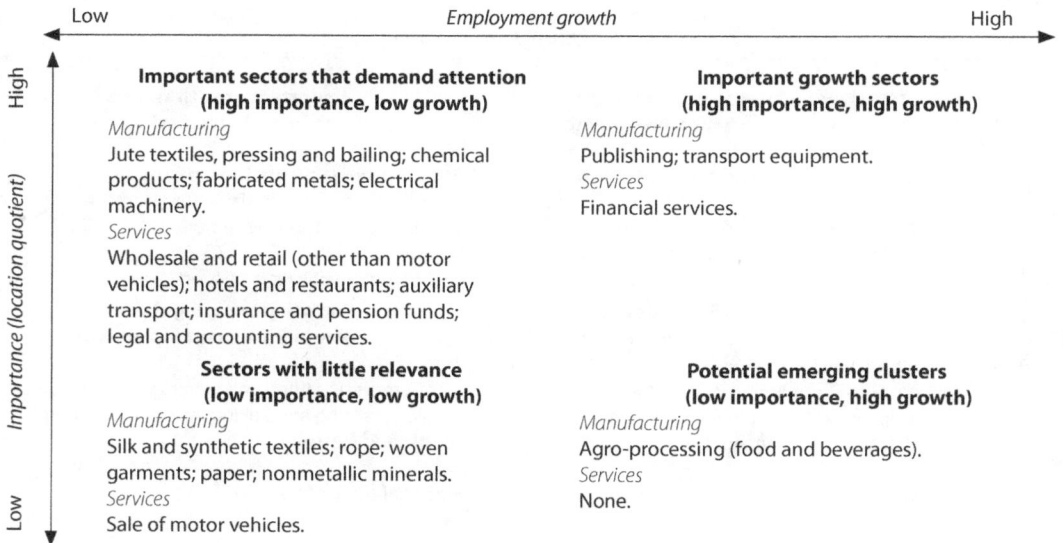

Low ←——————————————— *Employment growth* ———————————————→ High

Importance (location quotient) High ↑ ... Low ↓

**Important sectors that demand attention
(high importance, low growth)**
Manufacturing
Jute textiles, pressing and bailing; chemical products; fabricated metals; electrical machinery.
Services
Wholesale and retail (other than motor vehicles); hotels and restaurants; auxiliary transport; insurance and pension funds; legal and accounting services.

**Important growth sectors
(high importance, high growth)**
Manufacturing
Publishing; transport equipment.
Services
Financial services.

**Sectors with little relevance
(low importance, low growth)**
Manufacturing
Silk and synthetic textiles; rope; woven garments; paper; nonmetallic minerals.
Services
Sale of motor vehicles.

**Potential emerging clusters
(low importance, high growth)**
Manufacturing
Agro-processing (food and beverages).
Services
None.

table continues next page

Table A.1 Sector Analysis for Urban Areas of Bangladesh, Based on Location Quotient and Employment Growth, 2001–09 *(continued)*

f. Nonmetropolitan municipalities

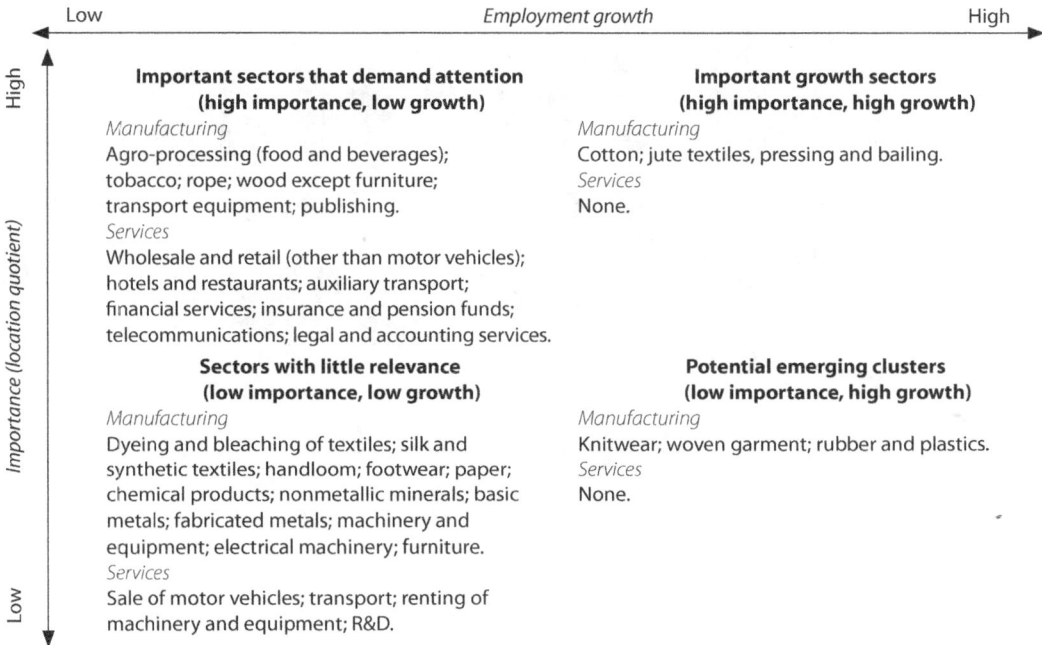

	Low ←——————————— *Employment growth* ——————————→ High

High ↑

Importance (location quotient)

Important sectors that demand attention
(high importance, low growth)
Manufacturing
Agro-processing (food and beverages); tobacco; rope; wood except furniture; transport equipment; publishing.
Services
Wholesale and retail (other than motor vehicles); hotels and restaurants; auxiliary transport; financial services; insurance and pension funds; telecommunications; legal and accounting services.

Important growth sectors
(high importance, high growth)
Manufacturing
Cotton; jute textiles, pressing and bailing.
Services
None.

Sectors with little relevance
(low importance, low growth)
Manufacturing
Dyeing and bleaching of textiles; silk and synthetic textiles; handloom; footwear; paper; chemical products; nonmetallic minerals; basic metals; fabricated metals; machinery and equipment; electrical machinery; furniture.
Services
Sale of motor vehicles; transport; renting of machinery and equipment; R&D.

Potential emerging clusters
(low importance, high growth)
Manufacturing
Knitwear; woven garment; rubber and plastics.
Services
None.

Low ↓

Source: Based on data from Bangladesh Bureau of Statistics 2001, 2009.
Note: Analysis is based on a 2001 classification of secondary cities and nonmetropolitan municipalities (pourashava) to ensure comparability over the 2001–09 period. Secondary cities are the Khulna and Rajshahi metropolitan areas and the Sylhet and Barisal City Corporations. Newly established city corporations are excluded from the analysis.

municipalities (*pourashava*) for the period 2001–09. The analysis is based on economic census data from the Bangladesh Bureau of Statistics. The classification of secondary cities and nonmetropolitan municipalities in the base year (2001) is used for the analysis, in order to ensure comparability over the period.

Shift-share analysis is an alternative method for identifying leading and lagging economic sectors in a location. It disaggregates local employment growth into three components:

- The national shift measures the part of local employment growth that can be attributed to growth of the national economy. If the country as a whole is experiencing employment growth, the local area is expected to grow as well.
- The industrial mix shift measures the effect of industry performance and competitiveness on the local economy. This component represents the effect of the performance of a particular industry on local employment. It isolates the fact that nationwide, some industries grow more rapidly or less rapidly than others.
- The local shift measures local factors or local city/municipality competitiveness effects on local employment. This component is usually attributed to

Figure A.2 Drivers of Local Employment Growth Identified by Shift-Share Analysis, by Location, 2001–09

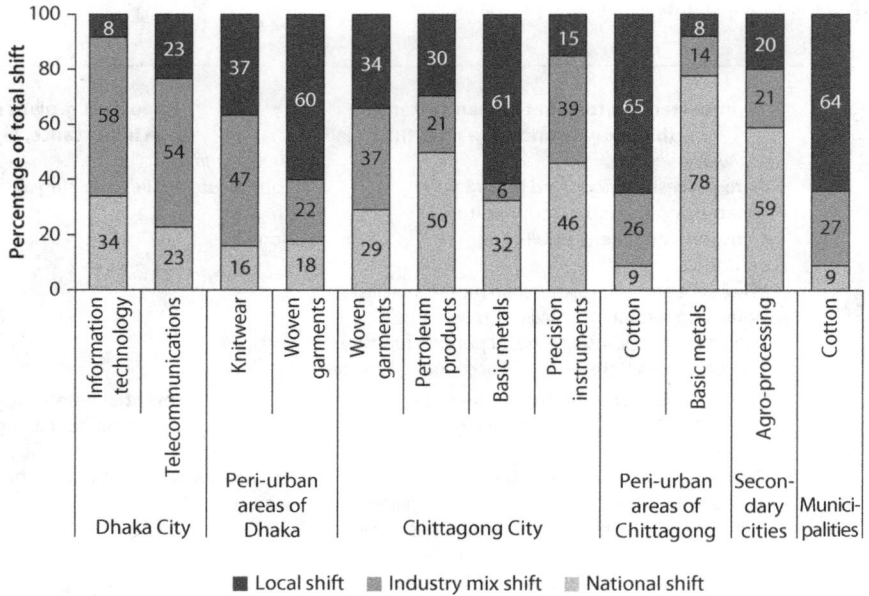

Source: Based on data from Bangladesh Bureau of Statistics 2001, 2009.
Note: Analysis includes growth and emerging sectors that are growing locally and nationally. Dhaka City refers to the Dhaka City Corporation. Chittagong City refers to the Chittagong City Corporation. Dhaka refers to the Dhaka metropolitan area. Chittagong refers to the Chittagong metropolitan area. Secondary cities are the Khulna and Rajshahi metropolitan areas and the Sylhet and Barisal City Corporations.

some local comparative advantage, such as natural resources, linked industries, or favorable labor conditions. The local component helps identify a local area's economic strengths. This element of the analysis measures how a region's competitive position can contribute to regional job growth.

Shift-share analysis, particularly the local share component, can identify industries that enjoy local comparative advantage (figure A.2). This local shift measures how a region's competitive position can contribute to regional job growth. It cannot, however, identify what the actual comparative advantage is, that is, what factors have contributed to the local area outperforming nationwide growth (World Bank 2010).

References

Bangladesh Bureau of Statistics. 2001. *Economic Census*. Dhaka.

——— . 2009 *Economic Census*. Dhaka.

World Bank. 2010. *Competitiveness and Growth in Brazilian Cities: Local Policies and Actions for Innovation*. Washington, DC: World Bank.

Sampling Methodology and Key Findings of the Garment Firm Survey

Introduction

This appendix describes the sampling methodology used for the garment firm survey. It then presents the regression results on location competitiveness and the analysis of productivity in the sampled locations.

Sampling Methodology

The 2009 update of Bangladesh's economic census was used to determine the sample for the survey, demarcate the research areas, and define the geographical and nongeographical strata. Individual garment and knitwear firms were randomly selected from the directories of the Bangladesh Garments Manufacturers and Exporters Association (BGMEA), the Bangladesh Knitwear Manufacturers and Exporters Association (BKMEA), and the Bangladesh Export Processing Zones Authority (BEPZA).

The Dhaka metropolitan area was divided into three strata: the City Corporation (hereafter, Dhaka City); urban peri-urban areas (the Gazipur, Tongi, Savar, Kadamrasul municipalities [*pourashava*] and the Naganyanj City Corporation); and rural peri-urban areas (map B.1). The Chittagong City Corporation (hereafter, Chittagong City) served as a single stratum. In addition, two strata were taken from the export processing zones (EPZs) in Dhaka and Chittagong. Within the six geographical strata, woven (or ready-made) garment and knitwear companies were independently sampled according to size classes. The cut-off point for size classes was the median size for producers with 100 or more employees. Representative samples of each size class were created based on the number of garment and knitwear companies registered in the 2009 update of the economic census.

Map B.1 Sampling Areas in the Dhaka Metropolitan Area

Source: Garment Firm Survey 2011.
Note: EPZ = export processing zone. P = *pourashava* (municipality). Dhaka City refers to the Dhaka City Corporation.
Naganyanj City refers to Naganyanj City Corporation.

The number of garment firms based on 2009 economic census data was 2,619. Stratification led to a required total sample size of 1,000 firms. The sizes of the samples were calculated using the following formulas:

$$n = \frac{Nx}{(N-1) + E^2 + x}$$

$$x = Z \left(\frac{c}{100} \right)^2 r(100 - r)$$

$$E = \sqrt{\frac{(N-n)x}{n(N-1)}}$$

where n is the sample size; N is the size of the population (number of firms within a stratum); r is the response distribution, set to 50 percent; $Z(c/100)$ is the critical value, set at 1.96 (95 percent confidence limits); and E is the error margin, set at 10 percent. Figures B.1 and B.2 show the distribution of sampled firms by location and product type.

Bangladesh • http://dx.doi.org/10.1596/978-0-8213-9859-3

Figure B.1 Distribution of Sampled Firms by Location

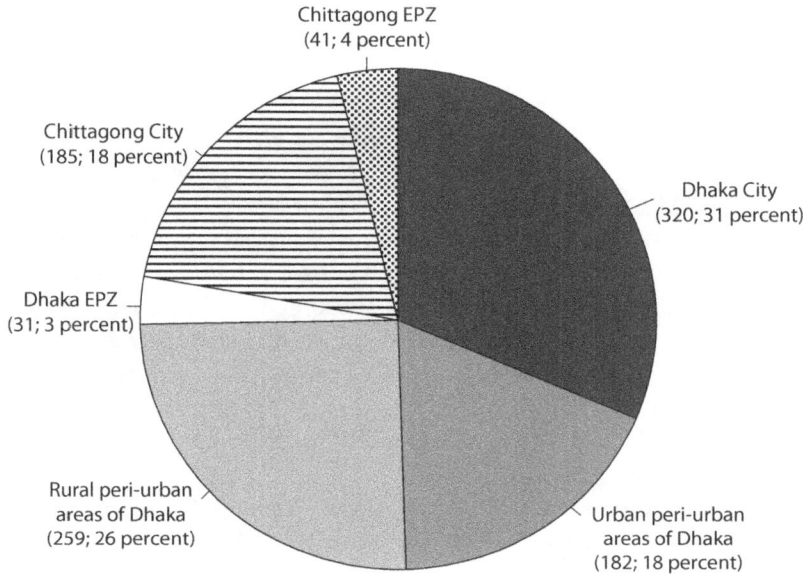

Chittagong EPZ
(41; 4 percent)

Chittagong City
(185; 18 percent)

Dhaka City
(320; 31 percent)

Dhaka EPZ
(31; 3 percent)

Rural peri-urban
areas of Dhaka
(259; 26 percent)

Urban peri-urban
areas of Dhaka
(182; 18 percent)

Source: Garment Firm Survey 2011.
Note: EPZ = export processing zone. Dhaka City refers to the Dhaka City Corporation. Dhaka refers to the Dhaka metropolitan area. Chittagong City refers to the Chittagong City Corporation. Number of firms and percentage of the whole are listed in parentheses.

Figure B.2 Distribution of Sampled Firms by Product

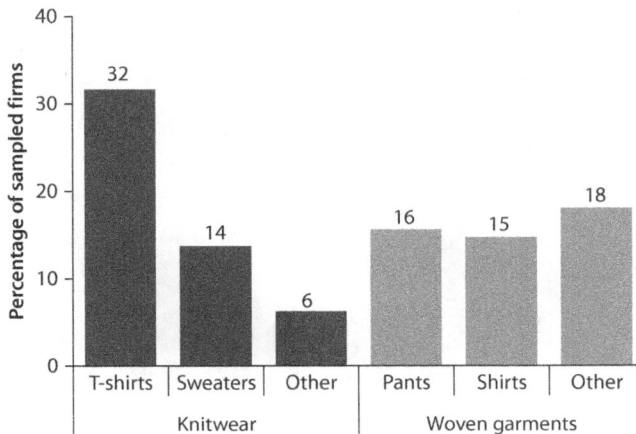

Source: Garment Firm Survey 2011.

Within each stratum the first firm was selected randomly; further selection was done systematically by taking every *N/n*th observation, where *N* is the number of firms within the stratum and *n* the number of firms sampled within the stratum.

For the 200 worker interviews, a subset of 40 firms from the firm sample was randomly selected. At each firm, five employees were interviewed. The sample was evenly spread across the strata.

As the BKMEA, BGMEA, and BEPZA directories include only export-oriented firms, a rapid market assessment was carried out to ascertain the size of the domestic market for garment production, based on interviews with members of garment associations. The assessment indicated that more than 90 percent of garment firms—and virtually all large garment firms—are export oriented. Four of the identified 14 largest non-export-oriented firms are included in the sample.

A total of 1,018 firms were interviewed. Table B.1 presents the characteristics of the surveyed firms.

Randomized firms were first contacted by telephone. Where it was not possible to establish contact (after several attempts), a substitute firm in the same stratum was randomly selected from the reserve list.

Questionnaires were designed and developed in collaboration with BGMEA and BKMEA. The instruments were extensively tested during pilot interviews and adjusted where necessary.

Table B.1 Characteristics of Surveyed Firms, by Location

Location	Percentage of sales to European Union	Percentage of sales to United States	Average annual sales (million Tk, fiscal 2008/09)	Age of plant (years)	Factory area (square feet)	Average number of full- and part-time production workers (fiscal 2008/09)
Dhaka						
Dhaka City	61.1	29.2	298.2	11.2	48,508	663
Urban peri-urban areas of metropolitan Dhaka	70.2	23.9	360.6	8.6	105,504	825
Rural peri-urban areas of metropolitan Dhaka	72.6	20.5	344.1	8	68,912	683
Dhaka EPZ	59.5	32.6	733.8	9.7	170,070	1,863
Chittagong						
Chittagong City	27.3	66.9	180.3	10.7	33,600	572
Chittagong EPZ	45.9	42.1	650.9	9.5	189,929	2,022
Average	58.9	33.5	327.1	9.7	70,577	772

Source: Garment Firm Survey 2011.
Note: EPZ = export processing zone; Tk = Bangladesh taka. Dhaka City refers to the Dhaka City Corporation. Chittagong City refers to the Chittagong City Corporation.

Bangladesh • http://dx.doi.org/10.1596/978-0-8213-9859-3

The survey questionnaire included a general module for firm managers and a financial module for firm accountants. Where it was not possible to obtain sufficiently complete information, a firm was removed from the sample and replaced with another. Supervisors performed random spot checks to ensure that interviews had been conducted and that the information collected was reliable.

After the information was collected, the data were entered into FoxPro, a Microsoft database. The internal integrity of the data was extensively checked using SPSS and SAS software. Inconsistencies were resolved through telephone conversations with respondents. In cases of major inconsistencies, revisits were conducted.

Location Competitiveness

A regression analysis was conducted to assess and compare the surveyed locations in terms of five factors affecting firms' location decisions: access to markets and labor, infrastructure, accessibility, land and housing, and governance and regulation. In each regression, the dependent variable is an indicator of location performance, as rated by the manager of each firm. The scale ranges from 1 (very poor) to 4 (excellent). The explanatory variables are dummies for each location of interest (urban peri-urban areas of metropolitan Dhaka, rural peri-urban areas of metropolitan Dhaka, the Dhaka EPZ, Chittagong City, and the Chittagong EPZ). As the excluded category is Dhaka City, the coefficient of the constant is interpreted as the mean performance in Dhaka City. The coefficient of each of the location dummies indicates the difference in performance between a location and Dhaka City. The model was estimated using ordinary least squares.

Figure B.3 displays garment firms' rating of the perceived performance of their location in the factors affecting their location decisions as well as the values they assign to these factors at each of the six locations studied. Figure B.4 and tables B.2–B.6 present the results of a regression analysis of the performance of the surveyed locations relative to Dhaka City. A benefit of a regression analysis over simple comparisons of mean performance across locations is that it indicates whether observed differences in performance are statistically significant.

Figure B.3 Perceptions of Location Performance and Rating of Importance of Factors Affecting Firms' Location Decisions, by Location

a. Dhaka City

Performance scale: Excellent (4), Adequate (3), Poor (2), Very poor (1)

Importance scale: Not important (1), Moderate (2), Important (3), Very important (4)

Category	Factor	Performance	Importance
Access to markets and labor	Proximity to competitors	3.4	2.3
	Proximity to support businesses	3.4	3.2
	Proximity to subcontractors	3.3	2.2
	Proximity to buyers	3.3	2.7
	Proximity to machine repair technicians	3.2	2.6
	Proximity to suppliers	3.2	3.0
	Access to skilled labor	3.1	3.7
	Access to unskilled labor	3.0	2.4
	Average	3.3	2.8
Governance and regulation	Proximity to government offices	3.0	2.4
	Ease of access to government	3.0	2.2
	Ability to operate at night	2.9	2.2
	Time to obtain permits	2.9	2.4
	Average	3.0	2.3
Infrastructure	Access to and quality of telecommunication services	3.0	3.2
	Availability and quality of public water and sewerage	2.9	2.9
	Access to and quality of social services	2.8	2.6
	Reliability of public power supply	1.9	3.7
	Average	2.6	3.1
Land and housing	Availability of adequate and affordable housing	2.8	2.8
	Safety/low crime in the vicinity of the factory	2.7	2.7
	Availability and price of buildings	2.4	2.7
	Availability and cost of land	2.4	2.7
	Average	2.6	2.7
Accessibility	Access to the airport	3.0	3.0
	Access to the highway	2.8	3.3
	Access to the port	2.3	3.2
	Low traffic congestion	2.0	3.5
	Average	2.5	3.2

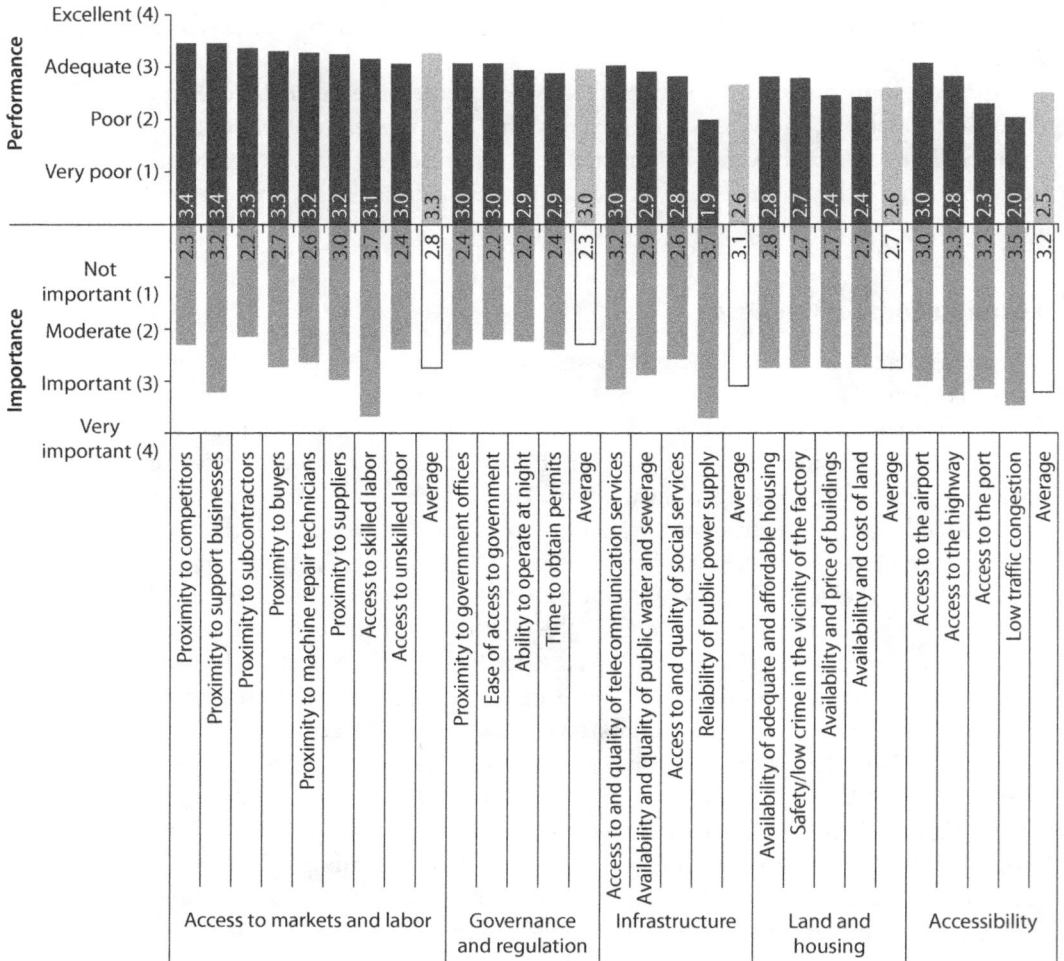

figure continues next page

Figure B.3 Perceptions of Location Performance and Rating of Importance of Factors Affecting Firms' Location Decisions, by Location *(continued)*

b. Urban peri-urban areas of metropolitan Dhaka

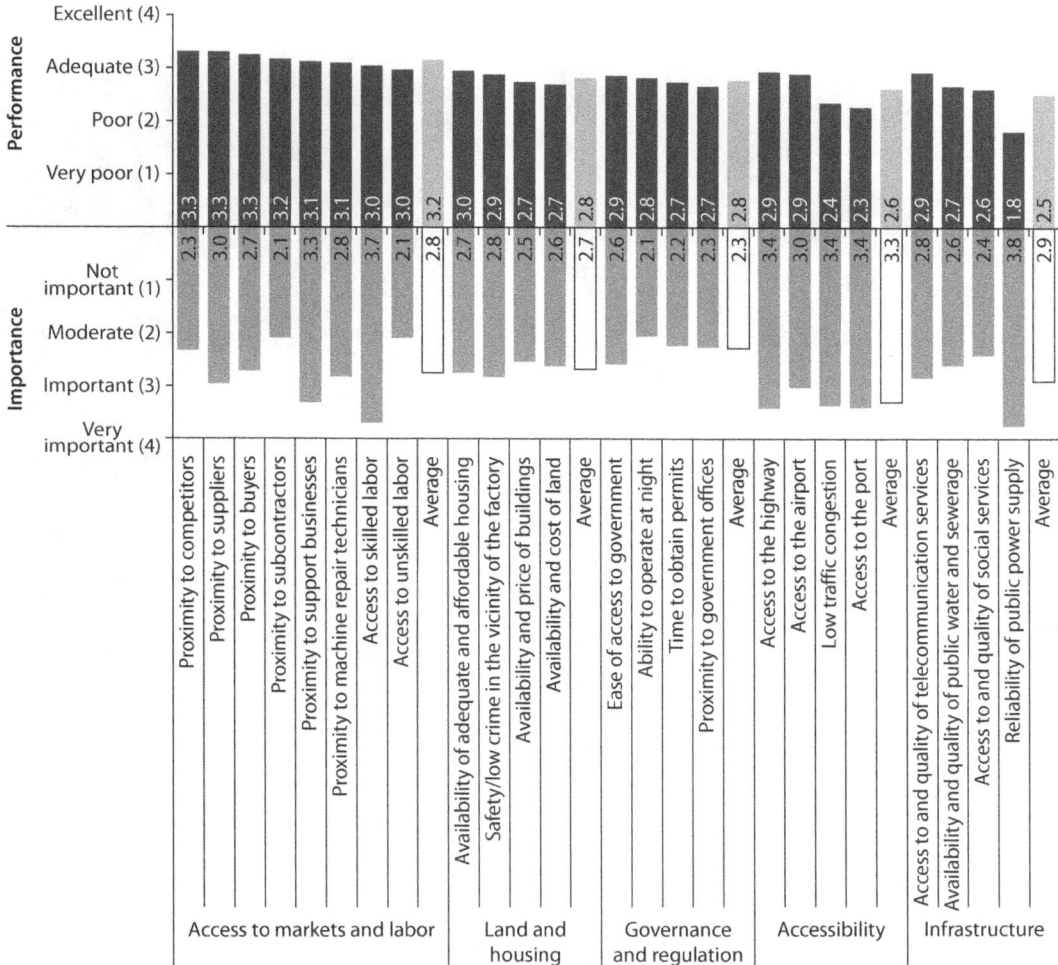

figure continues next page

Figure B.3 Perceptions of Location Performance and Rating of Importance of Factors Affecting Firms' Location Decisions, by Location (continued)

c. Rural peri-urban areas of metropolitan Dhaka

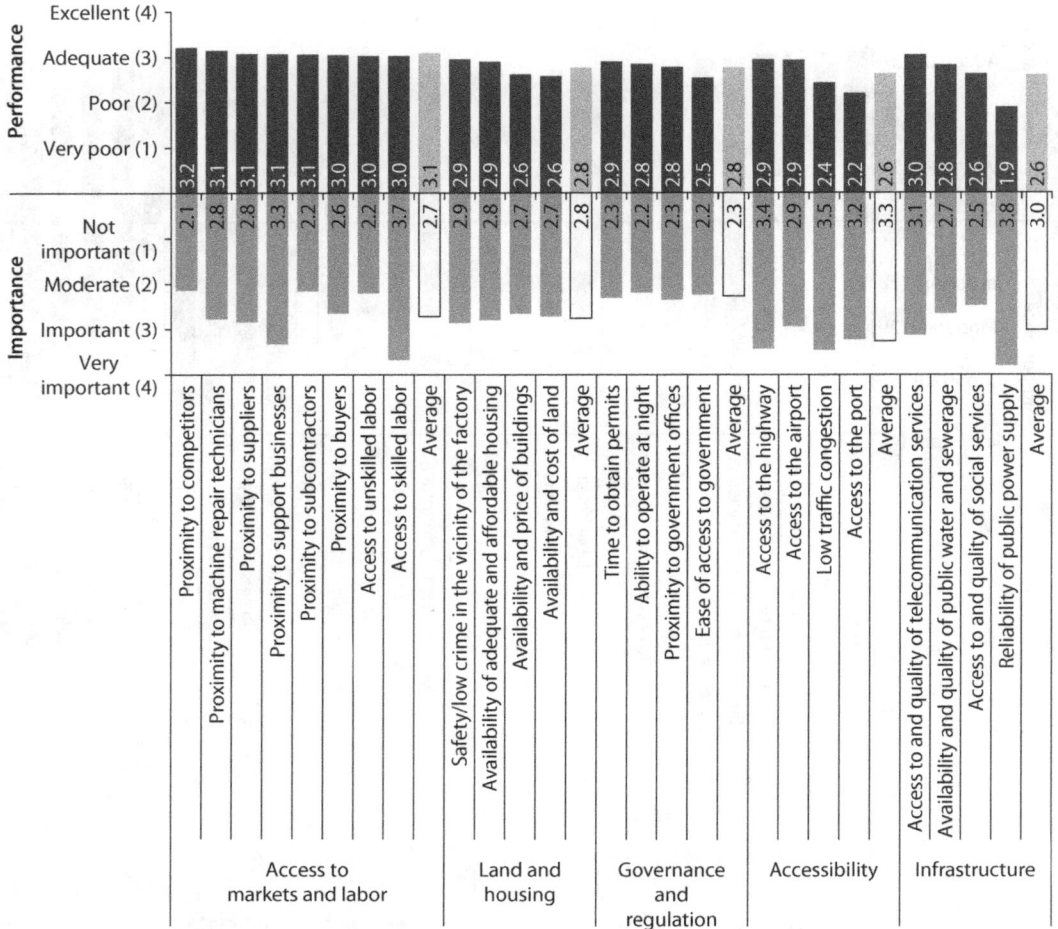

Performance (scale: Excellent (4), Adequate (3), Poor (2), Very poor (1))

Importance (scale: Not important (1), Moderate (2), Important (3), Very important (4))

Factor	Performance	Importance
Proximity to competitors	3.2	2.1
Proximity to machine repair technicians	3.1	2.8
Proximity to suppliers	3.1	2.8
Proximity to support businesses	3.1	3.3
Proximity to subcontractors	3.1	2.2
Proximity to buyers	3.0	2.6
Access to unskilled labor	3.0	2.2
Access to skilled labor	3.0	3.7
Average	3.1	2.7
Safety/low crime in the vicinity of the factory	2.9	2.9
Availability of adequate and affordable housing	2.9	2.8
Availability and price of buildings	2.6	2.7
Availability and cost of land	2.6	2.7
Average	2.8	2.8
Time to obtain permits	2.9	2.3
Ability to operate at night	2.8	2.2
Proximity to government offices	2.8	2.3
Ease of access to government	2.5	2.2
Average	2.8	2.3
Access to the highway	2.9	3.4
Access to the airport	2.9	2.9
Low traffic congestion	2.4	3.5
Access to the port	2.2	3.2
Average	2.6	3.3
Access to and quality of telecommunication services	3.1	3.1
Availability and quality of public water and sewerage	2.8	2.7
Access to and quality of social services	2.6	2.5
Reliability of public power supply	1.9	3.8
Average	2.6	3.0

Factor groupings: Access to markets and labor; Land and housing; Governance and regulation; Accessibility; Infrastructure.

figure continues next page

Figure B.3 Perceptions of Location Performance and Rating of Importance of Factors Affecting Firms' Location Decisions, by Location (continued)

d. Dhaka EPZ

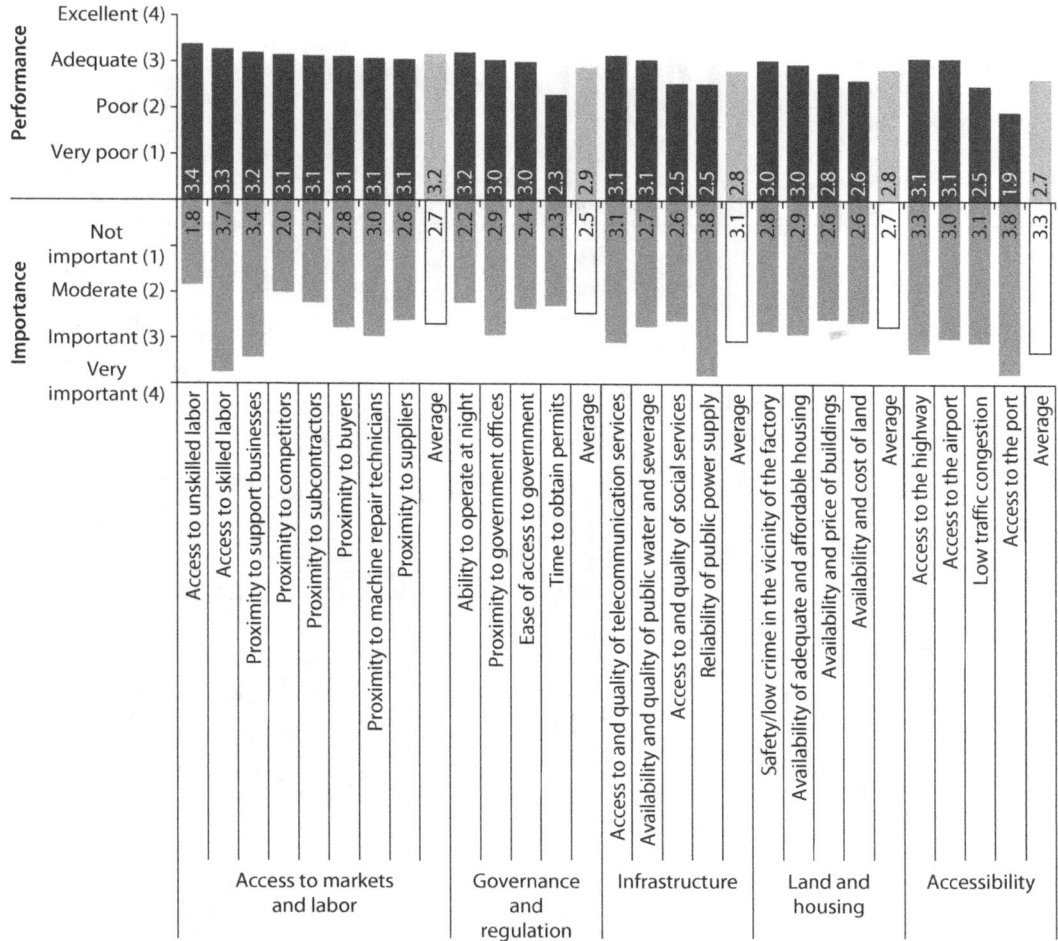

figure continues next page

Bangladesh • http://dx.doi.org/10.1596/978-0-8213-9859-3

Figure B.3 Perceptions of Location Performance and Rating of Importance of Factors Affecting Firms' Location Decisions, by Location (continued)

e. Chittagong City

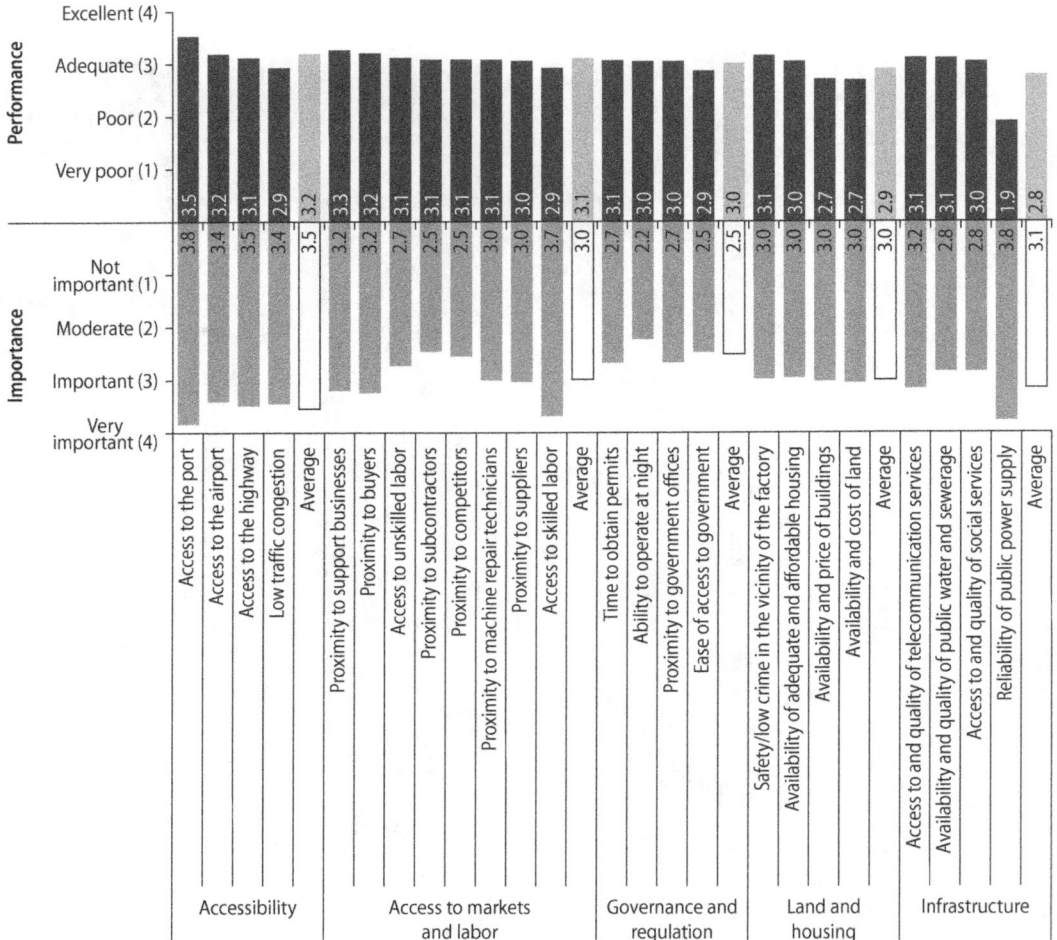

Performance scale: Excellent (4), Adequate (3), Poor (2), Very poor (1)

Importance scale: Not important (1), Moderate (2), Important (3), Very important (4)

Category	Factor	Performance	Importance
Accessibility	Access to the port	3.5	3.8
Accessibility	Access to the airport	3.2	3.4
Accessibility	Access to the highway	3.1	3.5
Accessibility	Low traffic congestion	2.9	3.4
Accessibility	Average	3.2	3.5
Access to markets and labor	Proximity to support businesses	3.3	3.2
Access to markets and labor	Proximity to buyers	3.2	3.2
Access to markets and labor	Access to unskilled labor	3.1	2.7
Access to markets and labor	Proximity to subcontractors	3.1	2.5
Access to markets and labor	Proximity to competitors	3.1	2.5
Access to markets and labor	Proximity to machine repair technicians	3.1	3.0
Access to markets and labor	Proximity to suppliers	3.0	3.0
Access to markets and labor	Access to skilled labor	2.9	3.7
Access to markets and labor	Average	3.1	3.0
Governance and regulation	Time to obtain permits	3.1	2.7
Governance and regulation	Ability to operate at night	3.0	2.2
Governance and regulation	Proximity to government offices	3.0	2.7
Governance and regulation	Ease of access to government	2.9	2.5
Governance and regulation	Average	3.0	2.5
Land and housing	Safety/low crime in the vicinity of the factory	3.1	3.0
Land and housing	Availability of adequate and affordable housing	3.0	3.0
Land and housing	Availability and price of buildings	2.7	3.0
Land and housing	Availability and cost of land	2.7	3.0
Land and housing	Average	2.9	3.0
Infrastructure	Access to and quality of telecommunication services	3.1	3.2
Infrastructure	Availability and quality of public water and sewerage	3.1	2.8
Infrastructure	Access to and quality of social services	3.0	2.8
Infrastructure	Reliability of public power supply	1.9	3.8
Infrastructure	Average	2.8	3.1

figure continues next page

Bangladesh • http://dx.doi.org/10.1596/978-0-8213-9859-3

Figure B.3 Perceptions of Location Performance and Rating of Importance of Factors Affecting Firms' Location Decisions, by Location *(continued)*

f. Chittagong EPZ

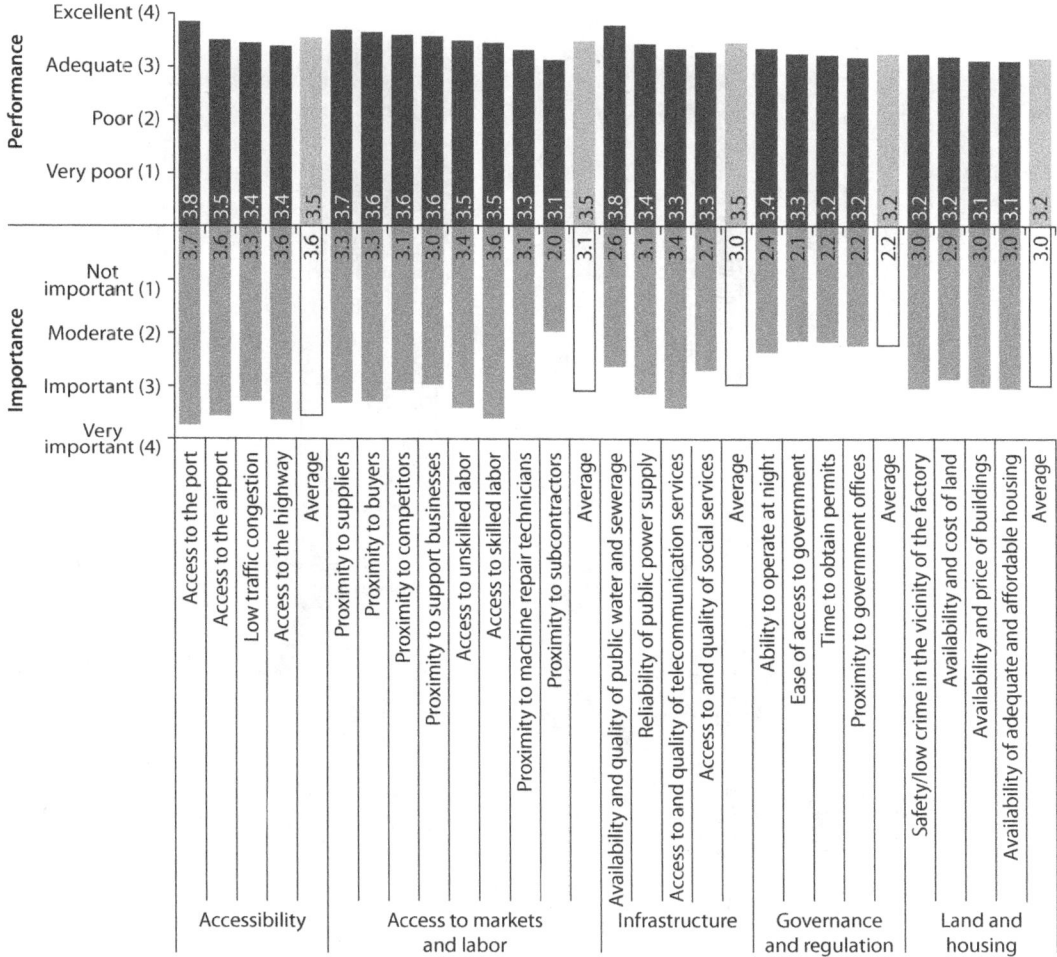

Performance scale: Excellent (4), Adequate (3), Poor (2), Very poor (1)

Importance scale: Not important (1), Moderate (2), Important (3), Very important (4)

Performance values: 3.8, 3.5, 3.4, 3.4, 3.5, 3.7, 3.6, 3.6, 3.6, 3.5, 3.5, 3.3, 3.1, 3.5, 3.8, 3.4, 3.3, 3.3, 3.5, 3.4, 3.3, 3.2, 3.2, 3.2, 3.2, 3.2, 3.1, 3.1, 3.2

Importance values: 3.7, 3.6, 3.3, 3.6, 3.6, 3.3, 3.3, 3.1, 3.0, 3.4, 3.6, 3.1, 2.0, 3.1, 2.6, 3.1, 3.4, 2.7, 3.0, 2.4, 2.1, 2.2, 2.2, 2.2, 3.0, 2.9, 3.0, 3.0, 3.0

Factors:
- Accessibility: Access to the port, Access to the airport, Low traffic congestion, Access to the highway, Average
- Access to markets and labor: Proximity to suppliers, Proximity to buyers, Proximity to competitors, Proximity to support businesses, Access to unskilled labor, Access to skilled labor, Proximity to machine repair technicians, Proximity to subcontractors, Average
- Infrastructure: Availability and quality of public water and sewerage, Reliability of public power supply, Access to and quality of telecommunication services, Access to and quality of social services, Average
- Governance and regulation: Ability to operate at night, Ease of access to government, Time to obtain permits, Proximity to government offices, Average
- Land and housing: Safety/low crime in the vicinity of the factory, Availability and cost of land, Availability and price of buildings, Availability of adequate and affordable housing, Average

Source: Garment Firm Survey 2011.
Note: EPZ = export processing zone. For each location, factors are ranked in order of perceived performance. Dhaka City refers to the Dhaka City Corporation. Dhaka refers to the Dhaka metropolitan area. Chittagong City refers to the Chittagong City Corporation.

Figure B.4 Comparison of Location Performance in the Factors Affecting Firms' Location Decisions

a. Access to markets and labor

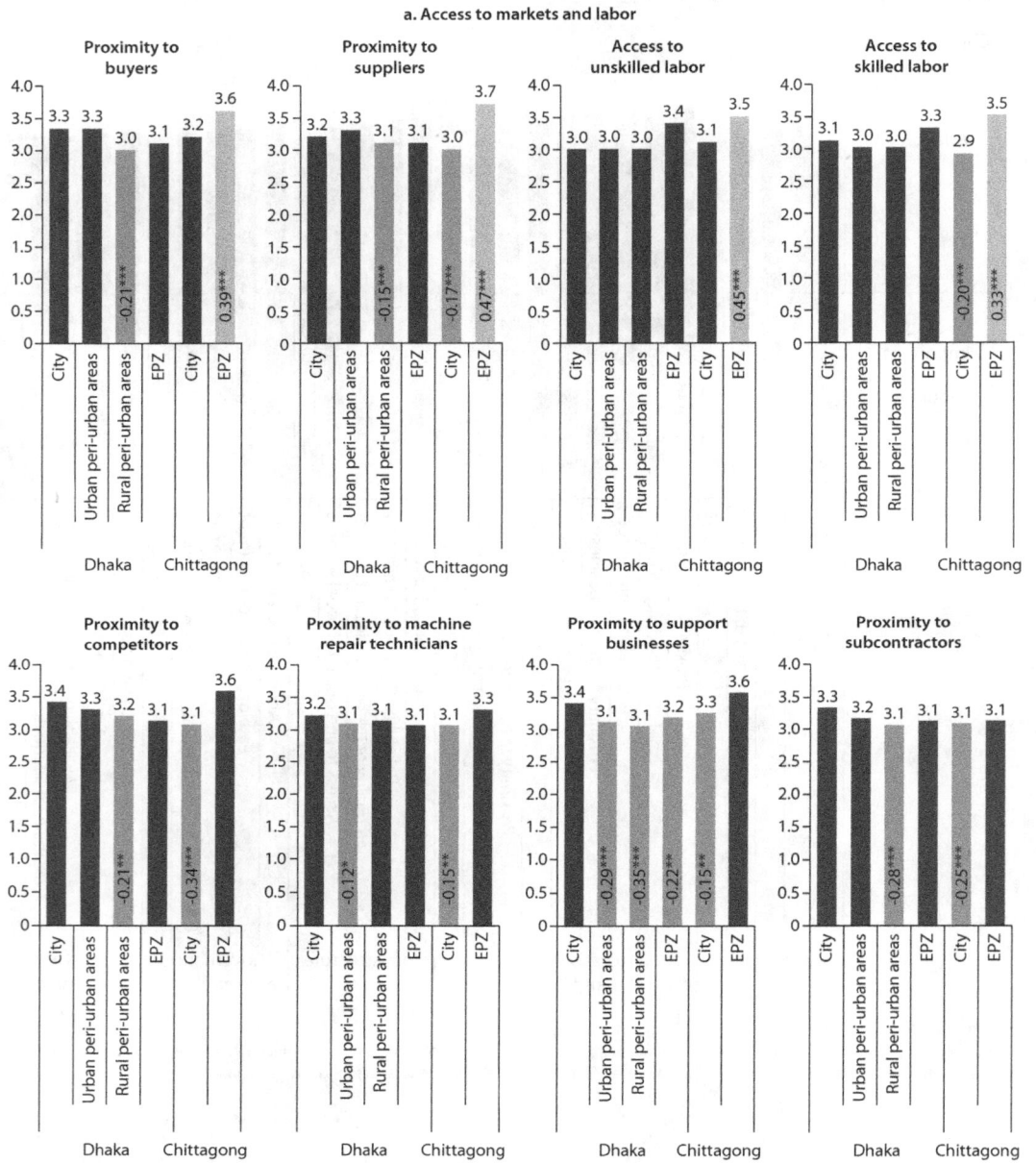

Figure B.4 Comparison of Location Performance in the Factors Affecting Firms' Location Decisions *(continued)*

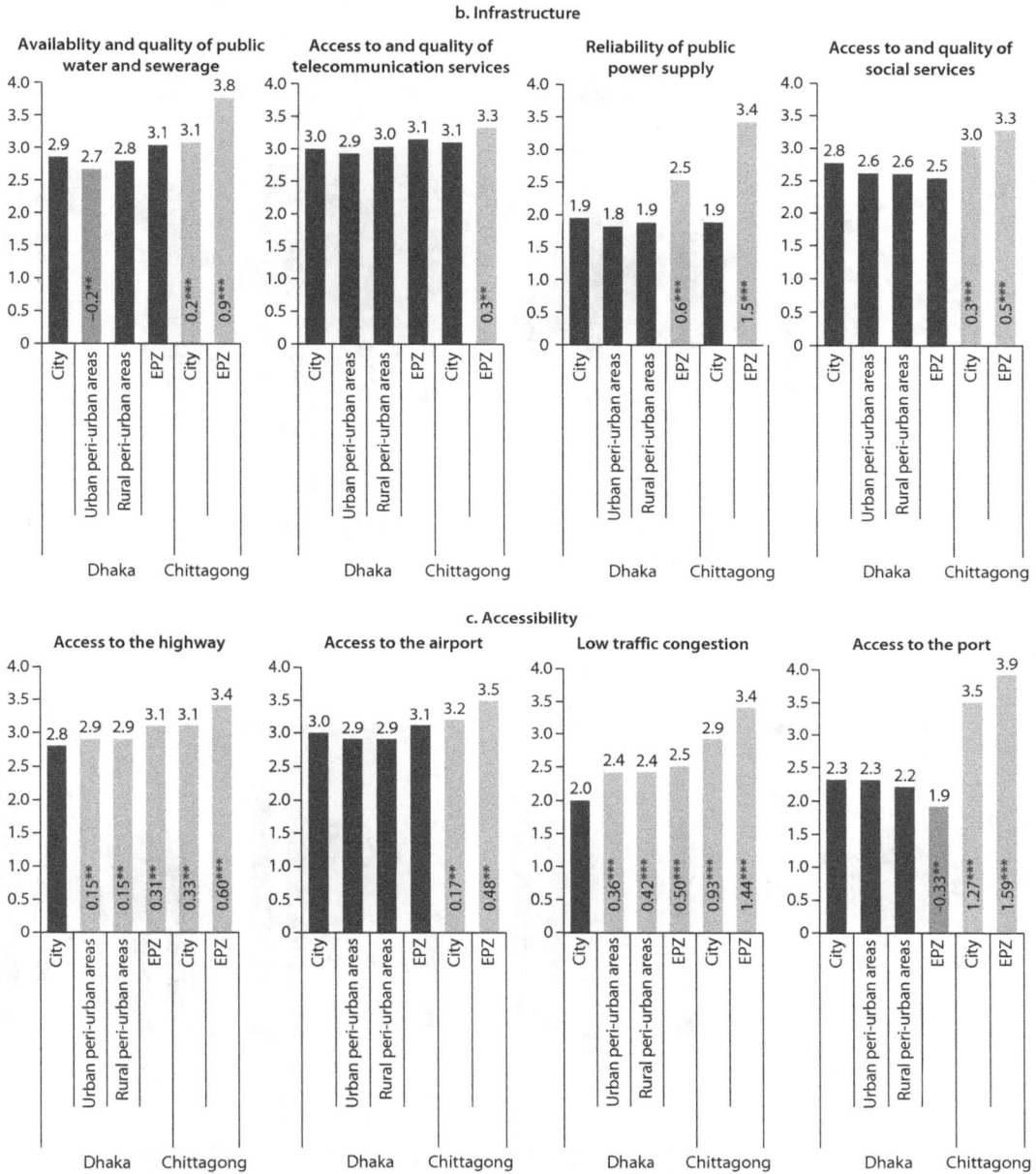

b. Infrastructure

c. Accessibility

figure continues next page

Figure B.4 Comparison of Location Performance in the Factors Affecting Firms' Location Decisions
(continued)

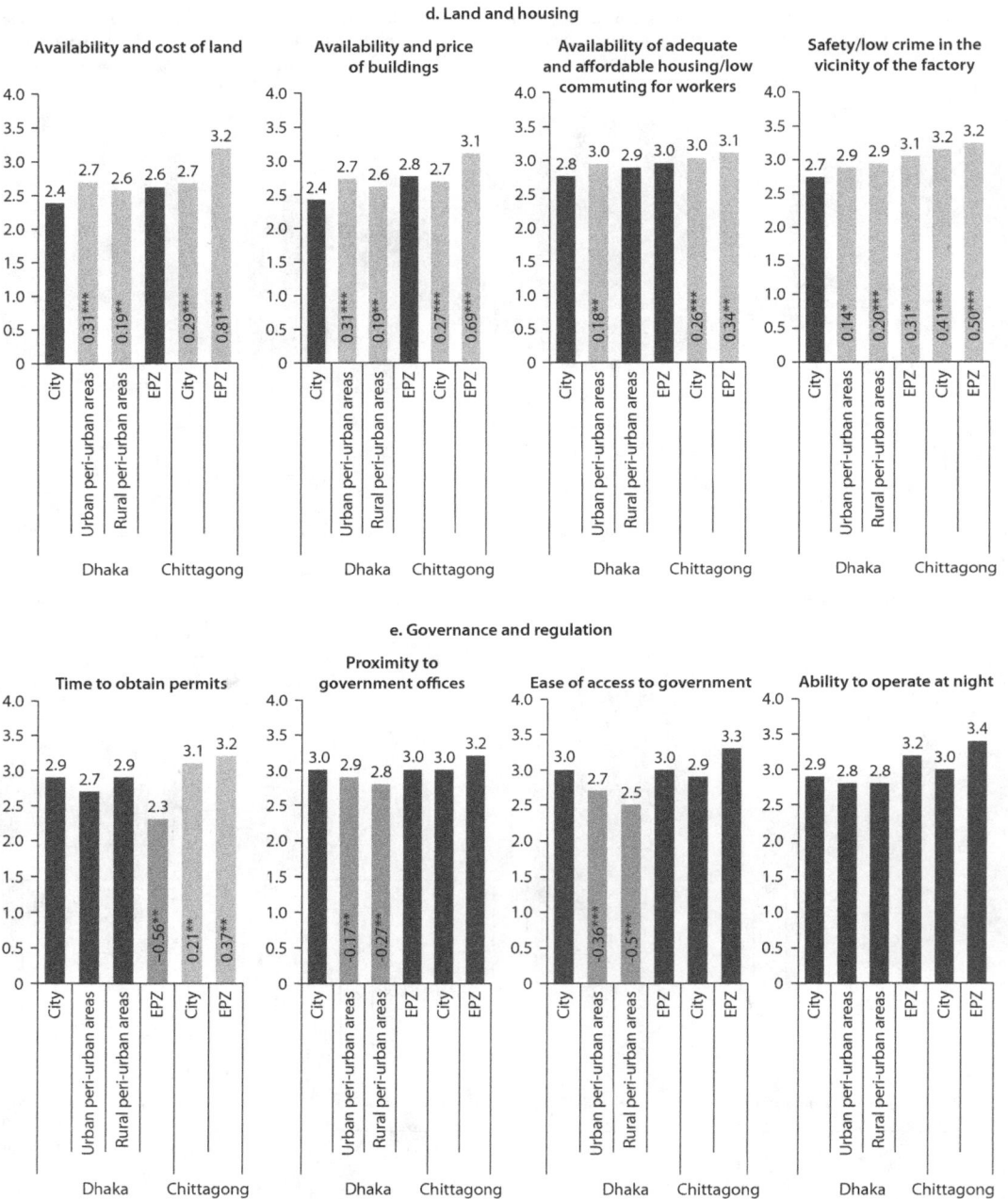

d. Land and housing

e. Governance and regulation

Source: Analysis based on data from Garment Firm Survey 2011.

Note: EPZ = export processing zone. The performance scale ranges from 1 = very poor, to 4 = excellent. Locations in green outperform Dhaka City and the difference is statistically significant; locations in orange underperform Dhaka City and the difference is statistically significant. Figures listed on the data bar indicate statistically significant differences. City refers to the city corporation. Urban and rural peri-urban areas refer to urban and rural peri-urban areas of metropolitan Dhaka.

Significance level: * = 10 percent, ** = 5 percent, *** = 1 percent.

Table B.2 Access to Markets and Labor: Location Performance Relative to Dhaka City

Location	Proximity to buyers	Proximity to suppliers	Proximity to subcontractors	Proximity to repair machine technicians	Proximity to competitors	Proximity to support businesses	Access to unskilled labor	Access to skilled labor
Dhaka								
Urban peri-urban areas of metropolitan Dhaka	-0.01 (0.076)	0.09 (0.062)	-0.17 (0.115)	-0.12* (0.068)	-0.11 (0.100)	-0.29*** (0.058)	-0.07 (0.098)	-0.07 (0.072)
Rural peri-urban areas of metropolitan Dhaka	-0.21*** (0.069)	-0.15*** (0.056)	-0.28*** (0.098)	-0.08 (0.064)	-0.21** (0.099)	-0.35*** (0.053)	-0.01 (0.085)	-0.10 (0.065)
EPZ	-0.15 (0.152)	-0.16 (0.140)	-0.21 (0.228)	-0.15 (0.119)	-0.28 (0.243)	-0.22** (0.109)	0.34 (0.234)	0.15 (0.146)
Chittagong								
City	-0.05 (0.068)	-0.17*** (0.060)	-0.25*** (0.092)	-0.15** (0.068)	-0.34*** (0.086)	-0.15** (0.060)	0.08 (0.080)	-0.20*** (0.072)
EPZ	0.39*** (0.115)	0.47*** (0.103)	-0.21 (0.167)	0.09 (0.107)	0.17 (0.125)	0.16 (0.115)	0.45*** (0.121)	0.33*** (0.128)
Constant	3.26*** (0.046)	3.21*** (0.037)	3.34*** (0.063)	3.22*** (0.044)	3.42*** (0.058)	3.42*** (0.036)	3.03*** (0.052)	3.12*** (0.043)
Number of observations	620	748	314	633	372	837	465	982
R-squared	0.046	0.063	0.034	0.014	0.064	0.069	0.040	0.021

Source: Analysis based on data from Garment Firm Survey 2011.

Note: EPZ = export processing zone. Figures in parentheses are standard deviations. City refers to the city corporation. Significance level: * = 10 percent, ** = 5 percent, *** = 1 percent.

Table B.3 Infrastructure: Location Performance Relative to Dhaka City

Location	Availability and quality of public water and sewerage	Access to and quality of telecommunication services	Reliability of public power supply	Access to and quality of social services
Dhaka				
Urban peri-urban areas of metropolitan Dhaka	−0.19** (0.091)	−0.07 (0.085)	−0.13 (0.079)	−0.16 (0.115)
Rural peri-urban areas of metropolitan Dhaka	−0.06 (0.080)	0.03 (0.074)	−0.07 (0.071)	−0.17 (0.101)
Dhaka EPZ	0.19 (0.171)	0.15 (0.155)	0.59*** (0.159)	−0.23 (0.227)
Chittagong				
City	0.23*** (0.086)	0.10 (0.082)	−0.06 (0.079)	0.26*** (0.099)
EPZ	0.92*** (0.160)	0.33** (0.137)	1.48*** (0.148)	0.51*** (0.160)
Constant	2.86*** (0.050)	3.00*** (0.050)	1.94*** (0.048)	2.77*** (0.066)
Number of observations	594	750	973	473
R-squared	0.084	0.013	0.121	0.065

Source: Analysis based on data from Garment Firm Survey 2011.
Note: EPZ = export processing zone. Figures in parentheses are standard deviations. City refers to the city corporation
Significance level: * = 10 percent, ** = 5 percent, *** = 1 percent.

Table B.4 Accessibility: Location Performance Relative to Dhaka City

Location	Access to the port	Access to the airport	Access to the highway	Low traffic congestion
Dhaka				
Urban peri-urban areas of metropolitan Dhaka	0.01 (0.084)	−0.12 (0.080)	0.15** (0.072)	0.36*** (0.085)
Rural peri-urban areas of metropolitan Dhaka	−0.08 (0.076)	−0.10 (0.073)	0.15** (0.065)	0.42*** (0.076)
EPZ	−0.33** (0.159)	0.07 (0.166)	0.31** (0.139)	0.50*** (0.184)
Chittagong				
City	1.27*** (0.079)	0.17** (0.076)	0.33*** (0.071)	0.93*** (0.087)
EPZ	1.59*** (0.140)	0.48*** (0.130)	0.60*** (0.124)	1.44*** (0.157)
Constant	2.26*** (0.051)	3.02*** (0.048)	2.79*** (0.044)	2.00*** (0.051)
Number of observations	853	781	888	899
R-squared	0.359	0.038	0.042	0.160

Source: Analysis based on data from Garment Firm Survey 2011.
Note: EPZ = export processing zone. Figures in parentheses are standard deviations. City refers to the city corporation
Significance level: * =10 percent, ** = 5 percent, *** = 1 percent.

Table B.5 Land and Housing: Location Performance Relative to Dhaka City

Location	Availability and cost of land	Availability and price of buildings	Availability of adequate and affordable housing/ low commuting for workers	Safety/low crime in the vicinity of the factory
Dhaka				
Urban peri-urban areas of metropolitan Dhaka	0.31*** (0.111)	0.31*** (0.105)	0.18** (0.089)	0.14* (0.083)
Rural peri-urban areas of metropolitan Dhaka	0.19** (0.094)	0.19** (0.091)	0.12 (0.078)	0.20*** (0.074)
EPZ	0.23 (0.236)	0.35 (0.229)	0.19 (0.159)	0.31* (0.165)
Chittagong				
City	0.29*** (0.092)	0.27*** (0.089)	0.26*** (0.085)	0.41*** (0.085)
EPZ	0.81*** (0.160)	0.69*** (0.149)	0.34** (0.135)	0.50*** (0.135)
Constant	2.38*** (0.060)	2.42*** (0.058)	2.77*** (0.053)	2.74*** (0.052)
Number of observations	579	590	636	667
R-squared	0.052	0.046	0.021	0.045

Source: Analysis based on data from Garment Firm Survey 2011.
Note: EPZ = export processing zone. Figures in parentheses are standard deviations. City refers to the city corporation
Significance level: * = 10 percent, ** = 5 percent, *** = 1 percent.

Table B.6 Governance and Regulation: Location Performance Relative to Dhaka City

Location	Time to obtain permits	Proximity to government offices	Ease of access to government	Ability to operate at night
Dhaka				
Urban peri-urban areas of metropolitan Dhaka	-0.11 (0.118)	-0.17** (0.089)	-0.36*** (0.13)	-0.08 (0.132)
Rural peri-urban areas of metropolitan Dhaka	0.05 (0.096)	-0.27*** (0.086)	-0.5*** (0.118)	-0.06 (0.101)
EPZ	-0.56** (0.264)	0 (0.143)	-0.03 (0.27)	0.3 (0.307)
Chittagong				
City	0.21** (0.09)	0 (0.087)	-0.18 (0.108)	0.14 (0.1)
EPZ	0.37** (0.172)	0.14 (0.172)	0.22 (0.198)	0.45*** (0.163)
Constant	2.85*** (0.062)	3.04*** (0.058)	3.03*** (0.075)	2.9*** (0.064)
Number of observations	384	491	322	319
R-squared	0.047	0.033	0.076	0.040

Source: Analysis based on data from Garment Firm Survey 2011.
Note: EPZ = export processing zone. Figures in parentheses are standard deviations. City refers to the city corporation
Significance level: * = 10 percent, ** = 5 percent, *** = 1 percent.

Productivity, Wage, and Rent Levels across Locations

Regression analysis was conducted to analyze the effect of location and firms' characteristics on total factor productivity (TFP), labor productivity, average monthly wage, and rent.

TFP is the portion of output not explained by inputs. Ten closely related methods were used to estimate TFP, all of them based on the assumption that the underlying technology firms employed can be characterized by a Cobb-Douglas production function. The methods differ regarding the assumptions about the degree of disaggregation of the inputs to the production function and whether or not constant returns to scale were imposed on the production function (at the factory level).

The estimates of TFP were highly correlated across methods. In the analysis below, the focus is on two methods. The relatively simple method (method 1) uses more aggregated measures of inputs. The more complex method (method 2) uses more disaggregated methods.

In method 1, TFP was computed for each firm by first estimating a log-linearized Cobb-Douglas production function using the ordinary least squares method:

$$\ln(VA) = \alpha_0 + \alpha_1 \ln(K) + \alpha_2 \ln(E) + \alpha_3 \ln(L) + \varepsilon$$

where VA denotes the surveyed firm's total value added (sales minus direct material costs); K denotes the firm's capital stock, as proxied by the net book value of property, plant, and equipment; E the level of energy inputs, as measured by aggregate energy costs; and L the level of employment, as proxied by the estimated total number of months worked by all full-time permanent and temporary production workers. The results of this regression were then used to estimate firm-specific TFP:

$$TFP = \exp(a_0 + \varepsilon).$$

In method 2, capital was divided into the value of machinery/equipment (K^{equip}) and the value of the remaining elements of the capital stock (K^{other}). Energy was divided into the value of electricity (E^{elec}) and the value of other energy inputs (E^{other}). The following log-linearized Cobb-Douglas production function was then estimated:

$$\ln(VA) = \alpha_0 + \alpha_1 \ln(K^{equip}) + \alpha_2 \ln(K^{other}) + \alpha_3 \ln(E^{elec})$$
$$+ \alpha_4 \ln(E^{other}) + \alpha_5 \ln(L) + \varepsilon.$$

Labor productivity was then computed as follows:

$$LP = \frac{VA}{(n^{perm} \times months_{op}) + (n^{temp} \times months_{temp})}$$

where VA denotes the surveyed firm's total value added (sales minus direct material costs); n^{perm} the total number of full-time permanent workers employed; n^{temp} the total number of temporary production workers; $months_{temp}$ the average number of months temporary production workers worked during the fiscal year; and $months_{op}$ the number of months during the fiscal year in which the factory was operational. Labor productivity was also calculated using the total number of full-time, permanent production workers, yielding similar results.

The average monthly wage (W) was computed as follows:

$$W = \frac{TOTWAGES}{(n^{perm} \times 12) + (n^{temp} \times months)}$$

where TOTWAGES denotes the surveyed firm's total wage bill (including benefits). The average monthly wage was also estimated including only new full-time production workers with no previous experience (including and excluding benefits). The results were similar.

Controls were added for a set of firm characteristics that might also influence productivity and wages, including the following:

- total number of full-time permanent workers employed in fiscal 2008/09;
- percentage of full-time permanent workers classified as managers;
- ownership structure of the firm (locally owned, joint venture with majority foreign ownership, joint venture with majority local ownership, 50 percent foreign owned, 100 percent foreign owned);
- whether the factory was part of a group;
- whether the firm exported to the United States or the European Union;
- whether all the firm's sales in fiscal 2008/09 came from knitwear;
- whether all the firm's sales in fiscal 2008/09 came from woven garments;
- whether the firm operated one or more separate office buildings;
- age of the factory.

Tables B.7–B.9 present the summary statistics and regression results.

Table B.7 Summary Statistics for Productivity, Wages, and Rent, fiscal 2008/09

| Variable | Total factor productivity | | Labor productivity | | Average monthly wage (Tk) | | | Rent (Tk) |
	Aggregated capital	Disaggregated capital	Production workers	All workers	All workers, including benefits	New workers, excluding benefits	New workers, including benefits	
All (n =1018)								
Mean	0.24	0.24	18,676	17,148	6,592	2,908	4,119	10
Median	0.20	0.20	14,973	13,709	5,720	3,000	4,000	8
Standard deviation	0.17	0.17	18,683	16,994	5,602	423	745	4
Coefficient of variation	0.71	0.73	1	1	1	0	0	0
Maximum	2.67	2.64	345,924	320,583	114,857	5,000	7,500	25
Minimum	0.04	0.04	3,163	2,830	51	1,600	2,000	3
Skew	6.96	6.89	10	10	12	0	1	1
Kurtosis	79.40	76.86	136	141	200	7	4	5

table continues next page

Bangladesh • http://dx.doi.org/10.1596/978-0-8213-9859-3

Table B.7 Summary Statistics for Productivity, Wages, and Rent, 2008/09 *(continued)*

Variable	Total factor productivity		Labor productivity		Average monthly wage (Tk)			Rent (Tk)
	Aggregated capital	Disaggregated capital	Production workers	All workers	All workers including benefits	New workers excluding benefits	New workers including benefits	
Mean for Dhaka								
All areas (*n* = 792)	0.24	0.24	19,136	17,620	6,607	2,862	4,116	10
City (*n* = 320)	0.25	0.24	20,265	18,672	6,894	2,889	4,137	11
Urban peri-urban area of metropolitan Dhaka (*n* = 182)	0.23	0.23	18,463	16,901	6,322	2,836	4,038	9
Rural peri-urban areas of metropolitan Dhaka (*n*=259)	0.23	0.23	18,612	17,178	6,637	2,854	4,094	8
EPZ (*n* = 31)	0.24	0.24	15,806	14,683	5,074	2,807	4,531	15
Mean for Chittagong								
All areas (*n* = 226)	0.23	0.23	17,062	15,491	6,539	3,069	4,130	9
City (*n* = 185)	0.22	0.23	17,171	15,541	6,570	3,016	4,000	8
EPZ (*n* = 41)	0.27	0.27	16,575	15,266	6,399	3,307	4,717	13
Median for Dhaka								
All areas (*n* = 792)	0.20	0.20	15,401	14,095	5,653	3,000	4,000	8
City (*n* = 320)	0.21	0.21	16,156	14,685	5,691	3,000	4,000	10
Urban peri-urban area of metropolitan Dhaka (*n* = 182)	0.19	0.19	14,858	12,870	5,545	3,000	4,000	8
Rural peri-urban areas of metropolitan Dhaka (*n* = 259)	0.20	0.20	14,924	13,860	5,786	3,000	4,000	7
EPZ (*n* = 31)	0.19	0.19	13,095	12,493	5,000	3,000	4,300	14
Median for Chittagong								
All areas (*n* = 226)	0.20	0.20	14,393	13,218	5,837	3,000	4,000	7
City (*n* = 185)	0.19	0.20	14,342	13,220	5,804	3,000	4,000	7
EPZ (*n* = 41)	0.23	0.23	14,633	12,680	6,195	3,350	4,500	16

Source: Analysis based on data from Garment Firm Survey 2011.

Note: EPZ = export processing zone; n = number of observations; Tk = Bangladesh taka. City refers to the city corporation.

Table B.8 Estimated Differences in Wage Bill and Rent, by Location
(percentage difference from base location)

	Average monthly wage (Tk)			
	All workers including benefits	New workers, excluding benefits	New workers, including benefits	Rent (Tk)
Dhaka metropolitan area (relative to Chittagong City)	4.1	−7.0***	−1.5	15.7***
Urban peri-urban areas of metropolitan Dhaka (relative to Dhaka City)	4.0	−1.7	−2.5	−13.5***
Rural peri-urban areas of metropolitan Dhaka (relative to Dhaka City)	4.7	−0.7	−0.9	−27.3***
Chittagong City (relative to Dhaka City)	−4.9	5.1***	−0.6	−28.9***
EPZ firms (relative to non-EPZ firms)	8.7	2.4	9.3*	26.5***
Woven garment firms (relative to knitwear firms)	−15.0***	−1.3	1.7	13.6***

Source: Analysis based on data from Garment Firm Survey 2011.
Note: EPZ = export processing zone; Tk = Bangladesh taka. City refers to the city corporation.
Significance level: *** = 1 percent, ** = 5 percent; * = 10 percent.

Table B.9 Estimated Total Factor Productivity Premiums, by Location

	Total factor productivity
Dhaka City's productivity premium over Chittagong City	
Without controls	8.8**
With controls	7.9*
Dhaka City's productivity premium over peri-urban areas of metropolitan Dhaka	
Without controls	6.7**
With controls	5.6*
EPZ's productivity premium over non-EPZ locations	
Without controls	12.8**
With controls	12.7*

Source: Analysis based on data from Garment Firm Survey 2011.
Note: EPZ = export processing zone. Controls are firm-specific variables affecting firms' productivity. City refers to the city corporation.
Significance level: *** = 1 percent, ** = 5 percent, * = 10 percent.